THE HEART of COMMITMENT

THE HEART of COMMITMENT

SCOTT STANLEY
PH.D.

THOMAS NELSON PUBLISHERS
Nashville

Published in Nashville, Tennessee, by Thomas Nelson, Inc.

Scripture quotations noted NKJV are from THE NEW KING JAMES VERSION.
Copyright © 1979, 1980, 1982, Thomas Nelson, Inc.

Scripture quotations noted NIV are from the HOLY BIBLE: NEW INTERNATIONAL
VERSION®. Copyright © 1973, 1978, 1984 by International Bible Society. Used by
permission of Zondervan Publishing House. All rights reserved.

Scripture quotations noted KJV are from THE KING JAMES VERSION of the Bible.

Scripture quotations noted *The Message* are from *The Message: The New Testament in
Contemporary English.* Copyright © 1993 by Eugene H. Peterson.

Library of Congress Cataloging-in-Publication Data

Stanley, Scott, 1955–
    The heart of commitment : Compelling research that reveals the secrets of a lifelong,
intimate marriage / Scott Stanley
        p.   cm.
    Includes bibliographical references.
    ISBN 0-7852-7087-6 (hardcover)
    1. Married people—Religious life. 2. Marriage—Religious aspects—Christianity.
3. Marriage. I. Title.
BV4596.M3S73   1998
248.8'44—dc21   98-13886
                                                                                CIP
Printed in the United States of America.

1 2 3 4 5 6 BVG 03 02 01 00 99 98

To Nancy for your love and support,
To Luke and Kyle for showing me how to play, and
To Mom and Dad for all your prayers.

CONTENTS

ACKNOWLEDGMENTS IX

FOREWORD XI

INTRODUCTION XIII

1. STICKING, STUCK, OR STOPPED? 1

PART 1: CHOICES AND THE PATH OF COMMITMENT

2. MAKING THE CHOICE TO GIVE UP CHOICES 25

3. THE THREAT OF ATTRACTIVE ALTERNATIVES 47

4. GRIEVING OVER THE LOSSES THAT COME WITH COMMITMENT 67

PART 2: DEVELOPING AND MAINTAINING THE LONG-TERM VIEW

5. SHORT- AND LONG-TERM VIEWS 93

6. INVESTING FOR THE LONG HAUL 115

7. A LASTING VISION, A VISION TO LAST 137

PART 3: FOSTERING WE-NESS AND CONTAINING ME-NESS

8. ONENESS AND TEAMWORK 161

9. SACRIFICE AND SERVICE 183

MOVING FORWARD

10. LIVING ON LOVE 207

NOTES 229

ABOUT THE AUTHOR 241

ACKNOWLEDGMENTS

I have been blessed in this endeavor by many people. While there is no way I could mention every one, several stand out. First and foremost, I thank my wife, Nancy, who has supported me and my work in all of our life together. She has made many contributions to my thoughts about commitment, and she has helped me put these thoughts on paper. While she has added to my thoughts and the flow of this book, she's really done far more. She shows, day in and day out, what real commitment looks like.

Next, I want to acknowledge a number of marital researchers whose work has been very influential in my own thought and research. First, there is my longtime friend and colleague, Howard Markman, who has been a great source of encouragement and support. He is one of the true pioneers in the study of how marriages thrive over time. In the specific study of commitment in marriage, I wish to note a few researchers who have impacted the field greatly—and whose work has influenced me: Caryl Rusbult, Michael Johnson, and George Levinger.

There are a few friends and colleagues who have helped me in the development of this book and thoughts on commitment. Natalie Jenkins stands out as one who was immensely helpful in bringing this book to life. She provided many insights and suggestions for both the presentation of ideas and the editing of the manuscript. In addition, Veronica Johnson provided wonderful feedback throughout. I also greatly appreciate the thoughts and suggestions of William Coffin, Janice Levine, Steve Smith, Seth and Cheryl Hewitt, Sharon Hilty, Sue Vander Kooy, Phyllis Lemons, Ken Glasier, Dan Trathen, Savanna McCain, Milt Bryan, Diane Sollee, Lisa Hoyer, and Elizabeth Collins. These are people whom I am privileged to know.

I cannot thank Gary Smalley enough. He's become a friend and a role model. Gary brought this material to the attention of Thomas Nelson, and he's provided wonderful feedback to me on my work for some time. Mostly, I appreciate Gary as an example of someone who loves God and people. He walks the path of honor that he so often speaks about.

I wish to also note the support and suggestions of the team at Thomas Nelson: Rolf Zettersten, Victor Oliver, and Brian Hampton. This book is simply better than it would have been because of them. Lastly, I thank all of the couples who have, in some way, allowed all of us to learn through their participation in research on marriage. (All of the couples mentioned in this book are fictitious, unless specifically noted otherwise.)

The Lord is good. He created marriage as a blessing to the beings He made. May we thank Him for His example of love and commitment to us all. Amen.

FOREWORD

I first met Scott Stanley in 1994. Since then I've become convinced that he is an answer to a prayer of mine. Why is it that married couples separate? What helps them stay together in a loving way? I've prayed for years that someone would find the answers to my questions using reliable research in light of Scripture. *The Heart of Commitment* brings together so much of what I've prayed for. I believe that this work will not only help you stay together, but more important, it will inspire you to enter into the full blessing of marriage. The book you are holding in your hands has already been elevated to one of my three favorite marriage books, and there are many I love from various authors. The principles, the stories, and the accountability contained here will make a difference in your marriage.

It is reassuring to me that the insights presented in *The Heart of Commitment* are based on sound marital research. It is awesome to me how Scott Stanley takes that research and finds new depth and insights with a topic where it is too easy to become dispassionate. And this is a book about living passionately, in fullness of life. I have been increasingly drawn to Scott's depth as a man of God. You, dear reader, are in for a real treat, for here you will find neither condemnation nor license, but grace, encouragement, and solid instruction founded on timeless biblical principles. I know that Scott delights in grappling with how to apply clear scriptural truths to marriage where the realities are often far more complex than simple prescriptions. Reflecting on the Creator's design for marriage and the results of much research, Scott offers you practical insights beyond what you've ever thought could come of the topic of commitment. You will visualize a richer, deeper path for your own marriage.

Many in our society have come to believe that commitment is merely fulfilling an obligation, in other words, staying when you'd rather leave. I know there are times when commitment is incredibly hard, and even painful, but deeper commitment is not about being stuck; it's about sticking. Though the constraints in marriage help to keep us stable, this kind of commitment does not make for a great marriage by itself. There is another side of commitment, and all that comes with it, that compels us to give and invest in our marriages in ways that lead to greater joy, togetherness, and confidence for the future. This book is about that life-giving, thriving kind of commitment.

Commitment is not about making one choice once and for all; it is about making many choices every day. There are so many ways to give in marriage, the kind of giving that propels a marriage beyond stability to dynamic vitality. The pages to follow can cultivate within you this habit of giving in ways that promote and protect your love. The common sense of *The Heart of Commitment* will grab you and shake you up so that you'll no longer settle for ho-hum commitment. It is delightful reading; Scott shares his wonderful sense of humor with us in every chapter. He also shares his compassion and deep understanding of the pain and disappointment that come when it feels as if love is lost and can never be found again. He tenderly teaches you how you can develop and nurture what really matters in marriage.

Now it is your turn to see why I have been so excited about this work. May the Lord bless you and keep you.

Gary Smalley

INTRODUCTION

I was sitting at the kitchen table eating breakfast with my wife, Nancy, and our two boys, Kyle and Luke. Actually, they were eating; I was just sitting. Before coming to the table, I had been thinking and praying and had an insight that left me completely stunned. So I was sitting at the table with a faraway look on my face, trying to fathom this new thought. Nancy doesn't miss much and asked me what was up. I replied, "I think I understand something that I've never understood before." With her dry sense of humor, she replied, "Well, you should have asked me sooner!"

I love asking questions and I love finding answers. As a researcher at the University of Denver, I have studied marriage from a scientific perspective. I have also been a long-term student of what Scripture teaches about marriages and relationships. One of the great delights in my life is grappling with how God's view of things is reflected in sound research on marriage. Since God made us and designed marriage, it should be no surprise that such research would be consistent with what Scripture reveals. By thinking about the deeper complexity of things revealed in various ways, we sometimes learn something or see it in a new way that catches us off guard and brings a fresh appreciation for a concept that had grown stale. That's what I hope to bring to your life with this book. I know many people tend to think, *Commitment. How boring! That's just about staying in a marriage until you die.* But it's not really so simple. When you delve into rich insights from Scripture and findings from marital research, the picture that emerges is one that is wider, deeper, and more practical than most people expect.

If you have lived long enough to have figured out that commitment is not always easy, then this book is for you. However, realize that this book is not for the faint of heart, for it goes to the deep places of the soul. We will not sidestep the difficult issues of real life in marriage. So bring along your willingness to work hard and your sense of humor, and roll up your sleeves. Commitment asks us to *do* something. Let's dig in.

Expedients are for the hour, but principles are for the ages.
Just because the rains descend, and the winds blow,
we cannot afford to build on shifting sands.

—Henry Ward Beecher

Chapter 1

STICKING, STUCK, OR STOPPED?

To have and to hold
from this day forward,
for better or for worse,
for richer, for poorer,
in sickness and in health,
to love and to cherish;
and I promise to be
faithful to you,
forsaking all others,
until death do us part.

As reflected in these beautiful vows, commitment is a deeply fulfilling path. Most of us dream of journeying through life with the one person who knows how to make us smile, believe in ourselves, hold us close, and treasure us always. However, while we hope the committed path will take us to the mountaintops, it can take us through deep valleys too. I feel it is only fair to warn you again that this book is not for the faint of heart. We will go to the inner regions of the soul as we look at how a lifelong commitment is lived out. This will not be one long "you've made your choice, now live with it" sermon. Real commitment is far more than permanence, not simply "until death do us part." That vow reflects the sanctity of marriage, but it doesn't guarantee sticking together in lasting love. There is much more. We'll be examining the commitment expressed in the phrase "to love and to cherish."

I want to help you go way beyond *staying together* and understand how two people can really *be together* in the full mystery of marriage. Before we explore the deeper ideas of this book, we need to lay a solid foundation about the concept of commitment. We'll do that by investigating key concepts from the Scriptures, theory, and research. We have a lot to cover in this "basic training" on commitment, so let's begin by meeting two couples on their wedding day.

DREAMS AND FEARS

The big day had finally arrived. It was a carefully planned wedding and all the plans were going smoothly, except that Lisa didn't feel so smooth inside. As her mother helped her straighten her veil, Lisa whispered, "What if I'm not making the right choice?" Although she could have been expressing wedding day jitters, Lisa really did have doubts. She and Steven had dated a long time—four years. It seemed reasonable to go ahead and get married. She countered to herself, "I mean, who else has come along that I like as well?"

Lisa's mother and father had divorced when Lisa was seven. She remembered the pain of their separation as if it were yesterday. That event, and the years of preceding turmoil and conflict, had left her truly skeptical about whether any marriage could really work—at least over many years.

While Lisa was wondering whether she was doing the right thing, her mother tried to comfort her: "Honey, you don't have to worry so much. Remember, you can always come back home if things don't work out with you and Steven." To her mother's surprise, Lisa burst into sad and anxious sobs. Lisa didn't really want to hear that there was a lifeboat. She knew that she could go home if she had to. She wanted to hear that it was possible to have a lifelong, happy marriage with Steven. She had grave doubts, but she wanted the doubts to go away.

Lisa said to her mother through her tears: "Mom, thank you for trying to reassure me. But I desperately want to know that it's really possible for this to work. That it's not a fairy tale. I am so afraid that we don't have what it takes. But I want to make it last all my life. That just doesn't seem realistic, does it?"

Well, does it? What do you think? Her mother went on to answer with the reassurances that Lisa was hoping for. Mom told her that things could be different for her and Steven. She didn't need to end up unhappy in her marriage. She didn't have to end up divorced. Lisa managed a smile, but she still agonized inside and out: "Do we know how to live out a commitment over many years?" She entered her marriage on that day with all her desires and doubts intact. She was worried that they would end up *stuck,* but not *sticking.* Lisa desperately hoped that she and Steven would remain faithful in their dedication to each other for the rest of their lives, but she knew that they could end up just stuck together for decades.

On the same day, Jeremy and Suzanne were getting married across town. It was a day of anticipation and rejoicing for both families. Jeremy's best man was his brother, Chris, who had gotten married only two months earlier. Suzanne was with her mother, her sister, and Jeremy's mother getting ready in another part of the church.

While Jeremy's father and brother were in the room chatting with him, he closed the door and said, "I have something I want to say that I want you both to hear." Jeremy stood before father and brother and said, "The commitment that I am making today is sacred. I am committing myself to Suzanne for life, for all that I am and can be in this marriage. From this day forward, I remove the word *divorce* from my vocabulary. I am asking both of you to hold me accountable to this commitment. I am asking you to push me to love her in the fullest measure for all of my life."

Jeremy's father hugged his son, and the three men knelt in prayer for the love, commitment, and life together of Jeremy and Suzanne. The power of that moment in time will not be forgotten by the three men.

This family's closeness and devotion are unique in this day and age. Jeremy's parents have lived their commitment before their sons by demonstrating their love in the ups and downs of life. Both boys have seen real commitment in action over many years, and that is the model they brought to their marriages. Their parents' model helped both boys to "inherit" a clear sense for the sanctity of the wedding commitment.

Later that day, Jeremy and Suzanne said their vows together—the traditional vows that opened this chapter. Jeremy and Suzanne had pondered the words and meant every one of them. They were not planning on being *stuck;* they were planning on *sticking.*

Sticking, Stuck, or Stopped?

STICKING, STUCK, OR STOPPED: WHAT WILL IT BE FOR YOU?

Who gets married with the hope that the love won't last? Hardly anyone, I would guess. Most couples are sure that their love is so special, so strong, so wonderful, it will always triumph. But in reality, couples like Jeremy and Suzanne or Lisa and Steven are going to end up on one of three paths (or a bit on each):

1. Those who *stick*.
2. Those who are mostly *stuck*.
3. Those who simply *stop*.

Here in the United States, projections are that 40 to 50 percent of the young couples who marry for the first time will eventually divorce.[1] Many will end their marriages within the first few years of the wedding day. In contrast, most older couples have a very low risk of divorce. These couples truly married for life and have made it through some of the toughest trials of life. The divorce rate for these older couples will be nowhere near 40 to 50 percent, but the number of divorces has gone up steeply for older couples as well. There is no specific projection for what the divorce rate will be for the older group, but it has surely gone up from what it used to be.

Where do the promises of a marriage go? Most couples start out wanting the "until death do us part" marriage. Just as important, all couples I have met want that "to love and to cherish" part over the years together. The same goes for "to have and to hold." Most of us get married because we believe we have found these things with one special person. I am convinced that most couples start out believing that the divorce casualties will be made up of other couples, not themselves—though couples may increasingly fear that it can happen to them. Likewise, it's hard to see how their love will not be cherished and deepened over time. Many seem to think, *Our commitment can't possibly erode like that of so many other couples.*

Jeremy was determined that his promise to love and cherish Suzanne would not evaporate. He expressed to his father and brother his intense desire to really stick in his marriage. He was committed to do all he could to make his marriage great. That included a view that divorce was not an option.

An old naval expression conveys such total commitment. When a captain was heading into battle where surrender was not to be contemplated, he would order that the "colors be nailed to the mast." Having the flags nailed up high, there was no possibility of lowering them in the heat of battle in order to raise a flag of surrender. With surrender no longer an option, crew members were motivated to fix their minds on how to best win the battle.

Jeremy and Suzanne have that type of commitment. When Jeremy made his announcement to his father and brother, he was nailing his colors to the mast, and he wanted them to know it. But more than that, Jeremy was determined to do whatever it took on his part. Suzanne was likewise committed and eager to give her marriage the best. Together they were starting out with a strong foundation of commitment.

Lisa, too, was serious about her promises. She wanted to stick with her marriage, but she had serious reservations about whether or not she and Steven had what it would take. She was deeply afraid she would marry and find herself just plain together, but unhappy and mostly feeling more stuck. While her mother reminded her of the support she would have if things did not go well, that was not really what Lisa wanted to know. She wanted to know how to keep her marriage strong and vibrant, not merely stuck together. Most of all, she didn't want to become miserable and end up stopping altogether by getting a divorce, as her parents did. She saw the agony her parents went through, and she didn't want to walk the same path.

PROMISES, PROMISES

Wedding vows, taken seriously, embody the essence of the commitment made on the wedding day. Sometimes I'll hear someone suggest that marriages break up because couples are not sincere in making their vows. I acknowledge that some people get married with such immature understandings of marriage and relationships that they have not reflected on anything more important than where the bridesmaids will stand. Nevertheless, I believe most people generally mean what they vow on the wedding day—at least in the measure of how they understand the vows.

However, the vows that couples are making are changing in our society.

David Blankenhorn, of the Institute for American Values, laments the ways in which couples have been increasingly watering down their vows. Further, they no longer have a sense that their vows reflect a promise to anyone other than themselves, not to the community and not to God.[2] He believes, rightly so I think, that these changes reflect more profound shifts in the idea of what marriage is all about. He notes, "As the idea of marriage gets weaker, so does the reality."

Look at the difference between the vows "as long as we both shall live" and "as long as we both shall love." This common change in wording reflects a profound change in the meaning of marital commitment. I think most people want the bond that is broken only by death. But couples may become so intimidated by the odds of failing that they decide not to promise too much in the first place. Does that initial weakening of the vow also weaken the chances that the marriage will make it? Probably so. Shooting lower makes it less likely that a couple will hit the target of the lifelong bond that they really wanted.

Perhaps your vows reflected a high level of commitment, or maybe what you vowed did not reflect much commitment to your marriage at the start. The most crucial consideration is how you are going to live now. So, what is your commitment right now to your mate and to your marriage? How does your commitment fit with God's plan for marriage?

WHAT DID GOD INTEND?

As we talk about building, nurturing, and maintaining commitment, we must consider the original plans for marriage as God revealed them in Scripture. Let's look carefully at the key teaching in Genesis and then note how Jesus amplified the teaching. The core account on the idea of marriage is in the two verses at the end of Genesis 2, which directly follows the creation of Adam and Eve: "Therefore a man shall leave his father and mother and be joined to his wife, and they shall become one flesh. And they were both naked, the man and his wife, and were not ashamed" (Gen. 2:24–25 NKJV).

This passage illustrates that commitment in marriage fundamentally involves *choices,* and some of them will be hard. Many of these choices are about major allegiances in life. For example, when you get married, commitment implies leaving some things behind. The passage says that a man should leave his father and mother. That's the specific intention of the passage, but it also strongly points to the more general aspect of choice that will come up repeatedly in your marriage. You are called to make choices that reflect your priorities, and marriage requires a priority that overshadows even the devotion to parents. The full force of this passage is easier to appreciate if you bear in mind that the Torah (the first five books of the Bible) promotes a very high level of respect to parents. Your commitment to your spouse is to exceed that level of devotion and respect. It is a high calling. It is a choice.

This passage also portrays the picture of *permanence* in marriage. The Hebrew word for "joined" is *dabaq,* which means "to adhere," "to cling," "to cleave," or "to stick." You get the idea. It means to be joined together in a lasting bond. When this passage is quoted in the New Testament, the Greek word used is *kollao,* which literally means "to be glued together." Unfortunately for too many, the image of commitment in marriage—of being joined—is more that of being stuck than sticking. But that falls far short of God's plan for marriage. What is reflected in the text, and in God's design, is a deep intertwining of the two lives together. This joining, or cleaving, is not for entrapping but for freeing the couple for intimacy. Note what follows choice and the emphasis on permanence:

> *"They shall become one flesh."*
> *"And they were both naked, the man and his wife, and were not ashamed."*

Random thoughts about marriage? Not likely. You could write a book on either statement. There is a particular way in which marriage is to bring the two together into one, and this oneness portrays open connection and intimacy. So we can add *oneness* to the concepts of *choice* and *permanence* as core themes in an understanding of commitment. These are the major themes of this book. They reflect the fullest expression of commitment in marriage. *The first part of this book focuses on choice, the second on permanence, and the third on oneness.* Now let's hear what Jesus taught on the matter.

Jesus spoke of commitment in marriage at a time when the religious teachers wished to trap Him with a question. They were hoping to trap Him in an argument between those who held more liberal teachings and those who held more conservative teachings on divorce. Jesus did not step into their trap but calmly went to God's original design, teaching from the same core passage in Genesis:

> *The Pharisees also came to Him, testing Him, and saying to Him, "Is it lawful for a man to divorce his wife for just any reason?" And He answered and said to them, "Have you not read that He who made them at the beginning 'made them male and female,' and said, 'For this reason a man shall leave his father and mother and be joined to his wife, and the two shall become one flesh'? So then, they are no longer two but one flesh. Therefore what God has joined together, let not man separate." (Matt. 19:3–6 NKJV)*

Jesus amplified the Genesis text in several ways. First, He clarified that this view of marriage is God's intention and design. Second, He emphasized the idea of two becoming one. It's not as if the two are to become one blob, wherein one or both identities are lost.[3] Rather, the two form a new, highly prized identity of "us" that is to be nurtured and protected. This concept is very important in Jesus' teaching and in the founding passage in Genesis. It's so important, we'll focus on it in the third part of this book. Third, Jesus stressed permanence. The religious leaders' concern about the rules of divorce was overshadowed by this view of commitment. In fact, this emphasis led the disciples to remark shortly thereafter that perhaps no one was really up to it! Jesus' disciples objected, "If those are the terms of marriage, we're stuck. Why get married?" (Matt. 19:10 *The Message*).

The calling reflected in Jesus' teaching is pretty high. It scared the disciples. Does it scare you? While the permanence is easily seen in these biblical passages, the benefits of a secure commitment are perhaps more obscure, but they are surely there. As touched on earlier, only in the *safety* of a secure commitment does it become reasonable to become naked and unashamed. This fact weaves together the various threads seen here:

choice, priority, permanence, intimacy, and freedom. Did I say "freedom"? Yes. You see, only in the context of a total commitment are you free to develop greater levels of intimacy and connection—the things that are perhaps the very essence of oneness. So what appears to be a lack of freedom implied by joining, or cleaving, leads to the greater freedom of oneness and openness. If you really want the one, you have to act out the other.

Near Colorado Springs is a very high bridge over a canyon called the Royal Gorge. I forget how high the bridge is above the riverbed, but it's a long way down. It's far enough down that you look carefully at the bridge and its moorings before you walk across it. The last time I walked across this bridge, I checked to be sure the ends were securely attached. My point is this: if you didn't think the bridge was very secure, you'd never start out on it. Just as in marriage, your sense that the thing is firm gives you the confidence to walk across. If it's not secure, or you're not sure, you will not relax to enjoy the view. You may not go at all.

HOW CAN SUCH A VIEW BE PRACTICAL TODAY?

It seems that this is the question of the disciples. You are not alone if you ask it now. Can one man and one woman be joined together for life? Is it really possible? Some have suggested that it is not.[4] Since we are living longer than ever, who could stay devoted to the same person for fifty years or more? If that's your view, please consider one point before you choose to side with the skepticism of the disciples or the outright disbelief of the religious leaders: Isn't it striking to you that the core themes reflected in these biblical passages are the very things that most people deeply hope for on the wedding day? I think God's design for marriage is what most people long for it to be. Couples want security and safety; they want to be naked and unashamed. Sometimes, people fault God for seeming to impose a harsh or unreasonable ideal on us, yet what we really want deep inside is the very thing that He designed. The problem is not with the vision; it's with the fact that it's hard to attain.

Even if you are a skeptic who believes that a lifelong commitment is not possible, you can still read on and learn many powerful strategies for making your marriage stronger—ways to act on commitment that do matter over time. If you live out the strategies described here, you will also enact a full, and fulfilling, level of commitment in your marriage. Nevertheless, the higher view of commitment over the long haul makes for the most blessed marriages.

That brings me to one of my most serious reservations about this book. While advancing the higher view of marriage, it could raise expectations that are too high. Many people have trouble in their marriages because their expectations are too unrealistic. For example, having an expectation that your mate will be able to meet *all* your deepest longings and needs is not realistic. Having such an expectation puts an undue burden on your marriage, and it increases the likelihood that you will be unhappy.

To be sure, lowering truly unrealistic expectations is a very good thing to do. However, when it comes to commitment, lowering the bar brings about two fundamental problems. First, a lower view is not consistent with God's hope for us. Second, a lower view is not consistent with what most people deeply want. As I hope to show, it *is* realistic to live "until death do us part," cherishing and nurturing your relationship together into the years to come. A perfect marriage will not result, but a better marriage will if you act on the principles presented in these chapters.

Research and Theory on Commitment

Much of what you'll find in this book is based on solid research. When I say "research," I mean studies where people provide details on how their relationship works or does not work so that researchers can learn more about how couples who are doing well differ from those who are struggling. In various research centers such as our Center for Marital and Family Studies at the University of Denver (where Dr. Howard Markman and I lead a team of excellent social scientists), researchers study a wide range of elements affecting marriage, including communication, happiness, family backgrounds, expectations, problems, commitment, and conflict styles. Many of the studies are in-depth, with the couples allowing us to videotape them as they talk about problem areas in their marriages. As you read, you will find various research-based insights woven together with the dominant themes of *choice, permanence,* and *oneness* that we have been exploring.

What are the ways in which commitment is expressed in the warp and woof of a life together? Consider these two statements and what is reflected in each:

"Mary sure is committed to that project."
"Bob committed to that project; he can't back out now."

The different kinds of commitment reflected in these two statements profoundly affect your marriage. Michael Johnson, a researcher at Penn State University, noted this distinction some years ago. Our theories have diverged a bit over the years, but we have both retained an emphasis on this most basic distinction.[5] In the terms I use in my work, the first statement reflects commitment as *dedication,* and the second reflects commitment as *constraint.*

Dedication implies an internal state of devotion to a person or project. Dedication conveys the sense of a forward-moving force, a motivation based in thoughtful decisions to follow a certain path and give it your best. *Constraint* brings out the sense of obligation. Constraints refer to the factors that would be costs if the present course is abandoned. If dedication is a force drawing you forward, constraint is a force pushing you from behind. Let's look at how these forces work.

I SIGNED UP FOR THE ADVENTURE!

I want to use a military example to flesh out the concepts, before we go back to marriage. Not that I think that marriage is like war, but this example highlights the feelings of many people in their marriages over time.

Jason was up late one night, surfing the channels on TV. He was fresh out of high school—an eighteen-year-old with his life ahead of him. However, he was not certain where he wanted his life to lead him. He soon found the answer in a U.S. Marine Corps commercial: "Be one of the few and the proud." He thought to himself, *Look at that uniform! Look at the pride of those men! I want to be a part of something like that.*

Jason thought about it for weeks, with the idea steadily growing inside him. It was honorable work with a fine tradition. He got up his nerve and went to talk to the recruiter. The recruiter might have painted a picture for Jason that was not entirely realistic about the Corps—exotic lands, important duties, choices, options and, most important, adventure. Jason signed up on the spot. You probably didn't talk to a recruiter before you got married; however, like Jason and the Corps, many of us start out in marriage with unrealistic expectations, or we pay attention only to the really wonderful-sounding stuff. Basic training was pretty tedious for Jason, but combat training was more exciting and more like what he envisioned.

After all his training, Jason got his orders and was shipped out to some island in the Indian Ocean he had never heard of before. *No big deal,* he thought. *This is an adventure.* Well, six weeks later, he was into his fifth week of guard duty on a wharf for navy supply ships. *These aren't even interesting boats to look at!* Jason thought. It was not exciting work. It was not an adventure. It was pure, hot drudgery. *I may be one of the few, but I ain't so proud at the moment. I did not sign up for this!*

So, back to dedication and constraint. Jason was filled with a sense of dedication when he signed up for the marines. I say a "sense" because it was not a very rich dedication at that time. It was really more like *potential* dedication. Just as in marriage, you may have started with one concept of your devotion, but the shifting sands of life changed your sense of what that means. For Jason, his initial dedication carried him happily through the commitment of signing up, the work of basic training, and the excitement of combat training.

What had been enough through those early steps was not enough to see Jason through hard duties that carried no particular prospects for glory and adventure. His dedication began to drain away. He was still committed, but he was no longer a free man. He could not go to the staff sergeant and say something like, "Sir, this has been an interesting time so far, but I don't think I'm really into being a marine anymore. I'd like to be excused." Luckily for Jason, he figured out that it might not be wise to have that chat with the sergeant. He had it with the chaplain instead.

Jason came to know the full force of constraint. He could not simply get up and walk away. Actually, he could, but the Marine Corps takes a rather dim view of that. He mostly felt aware of the costs of leaving; he was less aware of the benefits of being a marine. Jason moved into the commitment with the force of dedication. He did not have to do it. It was his choice. He might not have had enough dedication to last, but his decision originated from dedication. Despite that, when he was faced with unmet and unrealistic expectations, deep disappointment grew. While he was no less constrained before his dedication left him, he was not very aware of it until then. And becoming aware of the constraint, he realized, *I cannot leave, or else I go to federal prison.* He felt trapped. And trapped he was. What was he to do?

Jason made it through the three-year commitment to the marines. He decided that being a marine was not what he wanted to do for his life's work, but he also found ways to muster his dedication while in the Corps. His attitude and the assignments got better. The awareness of his constraint led him to make the wise choice to embrace dedication again. He wanted to be sticking, not stuck. The dedication that moved him was more informed and more mature. He decided that he had made this choice and that he would do his best in it. *After all,* he thought, *as long as I am in this boat, I might as well quit shooting holes in the bottom of it and learn to sail.* Good attitude. Sometimes all of life hinges on such a shift in perspective.

The Greek word used in the New Testament for "repent" is *metanoeo.* This word literally means to "rethink something and change your mind," with the changing of your mind usually leading you to go another direction. Jason could have chosen to be stuck, but he changed his mind and headed off in the other direction. *When you hit the beach, you can sit there and get shot up, or you can take the hill. Go for the hill. Go for the higher ground.*

After fulfilling his duties with honor, Jason left the Corps and went back to his hometown. You might be tempted to say something like this: "Well, Scott, notice that he only had to decide to reacquire dedication for a few years, not for the rest of his life! What do you have to say about that?" Whether or not you are saying this, it's a fair question to ask. *These matters are more difficult in marriage* because most people (as well as biblical teaching, traditions, and community practices) do not view a vocational choice as a lifelong commitment. Marriage is surely different in that respect. Nevertheless, you can feel in this example the forces that tug and pull and push on all of us through life, including in marriage.

ENROLLED

Kristin agonized her entire senior year in high school about where to go to college and what to study there. She finally settled on a state school not too near home, but not too far away. That allowed her just enough distance to feel she was away from home, but she could easily return home on weekends. From the start, she struggled with the decision regarding her major. She had no trouble being interested in subjects. She was interested in too many things: biology, chemistry, and history. She was also good at all the subjects she tried, which made choosing a major all the more difficult. She felt that if she settled into one choice, she had to say good-bye to the others. She had increasingly noted the tension between choices, and she wondered if that was going to be an unpleasant fact of life. *Am I going to be agonizing over choices all my life?* she wondered.

She chose the sciences, with a major in biology, a minor in chemistry. *After all,* she thought, *what kind of work is there for a history major?* Over the next several semesters, she gained confidence in her choice. She developed a wonderful relationship with a couple of faculty members who taught her more about research and the inner workings of biology and chemistry. She was fascinated by what she learned, which diminished some of the drudgery of lab classes. She even *liked* the lab classes. She excelled in her science classes and loved it all—until one day.

In the first semester of her senior year, her best friend, Amy, who was a history major, suggested she come to a guest lecture given in the history department. Professor Harrold J. Stevens, a brilliant historian, was visiting from Oxford University in England. He was speaking on a topic related to the Renaissance period in Europe. The lecture was one of the more stimulating that Kristin had heard at college. She whispered to Amy, "I am amazed by the links he's drawing between events." "Yes," Amy whispered back, "I never thought of these things he's bringing out." Kristin had a delightful night. She and Amy went out for coffee afterward, joining several more of Amy's history major friends. The conversation that night was electric. *We don't have great conversations like this about chemistry,* Kristin noted to herself. She went to sleep that night, but slept fitfully.

Kristin woke up that next morning with a crystalline thought: *I made the wrong decision! The sciences are interesting, but* that *thrilled me. What have I done? Have I chosen a life of boredom?* Although she had been very dedicated in her choice of science, she had lost track of her love of history. Now that this love was brought back into her awareness, the issues of choice became prominent again in her thoughts. She had made a choice but was having serious second thoughts about it. While she was still dedicated to the choice she made to study science, she became more aware of the constraints involved in the commitment, which led her to feel trapped in science whenever she thought about history. She had three years of science courses under her belt and was one semester away from graduating. How could she go back and change to history? Her parents would be furious. There was no way to do that now, too much had been invested on the other path. She realized that. Most important, *she* had made the *choice* and was really committed to it on a number of levels.

Kristin had chosen the sciences and would follow through on her commitment, but not without a sense of loss. *Either way,* she reflected, *history still doesn't seem a very practical major.* She finally decided that even if she could turn the clock back, she would not choose it as a major. But she grieved over a sense of what was lost on the path not chosen. *I could have gone into history, gotten a Ph.D., and become a faculty member at a college. That would have been so fantastic,* she mused. On the other hand, she honestly noted that she did not want to go to school the several more years needed to get a Ph.D. in history. The realization that helped her the most was that despite having chosen the one path, she could engage her interest in history in many other ways. On the whole, it was a bittersweet review of her choices and her options. She gained an awareness she would not forget and would live again—that committing to one path in life carries with it occasional grieving about what was not chosen. *This is part of life,* she thought to herself with a knowing smile.

DÉJÀ VU

After Jason got out of the marines at the tender age of twenty-one, he decided to go to college. Before entering the Corps, he had not known what he really wanted to do. While he was in, though, he found that he really liked to work with computers. He was very good at it. His superiors caught on to his skill and asked him to complete a variety of tasks using higher-tech equipment and computers. At college, Jason met Kristin. She was a year younger, but two years ahead of him in her course work. They met one day in an open computer lab on campus. He thought she was beautiful. Also, she was interested, and she was not attached to anyone else. She likewise thought he was great-looking, except she asked, "What's up with the short hair?" He explained it as a throwback to being a marine. There was something intriguing about Jason being an ex-marine, and she liked that. Better yet, no tattoos.

Okay, Jason thought. *This is very good.* They hit it off from the start, falling deeply in love. They learned many things about each other while they were dating. Both shared an interest in the way things worked, hers more in sciences and his more in technology. They had similar church backgrounds, both coming from families with strong faith in the basics. After dating for nine months, Jason asked Kristin *the* question. She said, "Yes." Seven months later, they were married in a traditional ceremony at the church near campus, with a wealth of approving friends and family in attendance. Both were ecstatic. It was a fine day and a fine year. Fast-forward.

Six years after their wedding day, Jason and Kristin were struggling. She was directing a scientific lab that tested water and other samples for heavy industry. She liked her work. He was likewise doing fine, working on computer networks at a local firm that took good care of its employees. He was in line for promotion, and everyone at work liked him. However, things were not so good at home. It was far harder to deal with their relationship than either had imagined it could be. Kristin thought, *No one told me about how hard this could be.* Going into the marriage, Kristin really didn't have the idea that it could be tough. She hadn't known anyone who struggled much in marriage, at least from what she could see. Her parents had a delightful marriage that, though not perfect, was what most people want.

Jason and Kristin had one child, a girl named Kristi. Kristi was now three, and she was no problem at all to them. Both of them loved being parents and found they could have positive times together when playing with Kristi. But otherwise, things were unpleasant. They argued frequently. Neither had very good skills for handling conflict, so many of the arguments ended up with her yelling and his pulling into himself. The arguments could be about anything, it seemed, but most were about money, which is typical of most couples. When they talked, as often as not it was an argument, and that is a major danger sign for a marriage over time.[6] They rarely went out and did anything fun, and their sexual relationship had cooled.

They drifted. They lost the sense of being friends—another sign that the relationship was seriously off track. Neither tried hard anymore to meet the needs of the other. Déjà vu struck both. Kristin remembered the day in college when it hit her that life was going to be a series of choices with occasional griefs attached. But now she realized she had come to feel that way about Jason. Similarly, it struck Jason one day: *I've been here before, and this is not what I signed up for!* It wasn't the Corps, but it was constraint without dedication. This commitment *was* for more than three years! Again, he noticed he felt deeply discouraged and cheated. Both felt stuck.

Jason was no longer devoted to Kristin the way he used to be, and he knew it. He was far more aware of the costs of leaving than the desire to stay. Kristin was likewise just hanging on. "This happens to other people, not to me," she said to herself. They were committed, but it was more in terms of constraint than dedication. Kristin had managed to maintain more dedication than Jason had. She was trying to reach out to him in some ways, such as talking about key issues. Unfortunately, he thought she wanted to fight, so he ignored her.

Constraint doesn't make for deep commitment; it keeps you going in the direction you are headed—stuck, not sticking. In the marines and now in his marriage, Jason felt trapped. Kristin didn't feel as trapped, but she did feel betrayed, betrayed by Jason for not being who she thought he was and betrayed by herself for believing *her* marriage would be different. Both wondered about divorce, but neither considered it much of an option. They have a crucial choice to make. Will they stick, be stuck, or stop altogether?

The choices are not complex, but that does not mean they are easy or painless. Where will they land? It all depends on what they choose to do, and choosing to do nothing is choosing to remain stuck, at best. How can they recapture and protect dedication? More important, how can you never lose hold of it? The rest of the book will be about how to do that. If you are sticking and want to stay that way, many principles and strategies here can help you. If you are no longer sticking, but just plain stuck, these same strategies can help you recapture a fuller, more rewarding level of commitment.

THE TIES THAT *BIND*

As a marital researcher, I—and others like me—conduct studies to better understand how marriage works or doesn't work out for couples.

Various researchers and I have been studying the factors that produce greater constraint in a marriage.[7] Here is a list of things that can add to constraint commitment. A way to understand each of these factors is that, all other things being equal, the person with a greater presence of any of them will be more constrained. These factors are also associated with the costs of ending a marriage, for that is an essential matter addressed by the concept of constraint commitment:

- *Social pressure.* It is the degree to which one's friends, family, and community would disapprove of one's ending the marriage.
- *Morality of divorce.* It is the degree to which one believes that divorce is morally wrong and under what conditions.
- *Concern for the welfare of the children.* It is the degree to which one believes the children would be harmed by divorce.
- *Concern for the spouse's welfare.* It may not be as potent as the concern for children, but the concern about the effects on one's mate of leaving does constrain many people. This is not really dedication, but more compassion. Perhaps it's somewhere between dedication and constraint.
- *Financial considerations.* These can be quite complex for many people. The essence of the constraint here would be one's perception that the lifestyle outside the marriage would be worse somehow financially.
- *Termination procedures.* This is Michael Johnson's term, and it refers to the degree of difficulty of the steps that would be required if one did decide to end the marriage.
- *Alternative quality.* This refers to the overall quality (or perceived quality) of life apart from one's mate. It can encompass many dimensions, but for most people contemplating divorce, the greatest concern is the degree to which other people might be interested in them as a future mate. Most people want to *be* married, even if they don't want to *stay* married.

These considerations keep people committed when they may not want to be. However, notice a curious thing. These factors are equally present for a happy, dedicated couple and a struggling couple. Research confirms the obvious: the forces making up constraints accumulate over the changes in life that come with marriage. The engaged couple is more constrained than the dating couple, and the married couple is more constrained than the engaged couple. The married couple with children is much more constrained than the married couple without children. That's because having children ups the ante on virtually all the other dimensions. You see how this works. Constraints increase over time, and especially over changes in marriage. Keep in mind that your sense of the constraints could be entirely different from reality. That is why so many people find divorce far more horrible than they anticipated. Of course, some do not.

So constraints are just a fact of marriage over time. If you are married, you will have constraints, and they will increase. Some constraints could be more directly changed by thinking about them. For example, what you believe about the morality of divorce could change based on your thinking or reading more about it—and what you read most may well determine the course of your views.

People don't generally think much about constraints when things are going well. For example, PFC Jason did not think much about the forces that would keep him in the marines until he thought more about maybe wanting out of the marines. Kristin did not think about the eventual inertia of having chosen a major when she picked the sciences. The same principle applies in marriage. If you have been married for some time, you have a lot of constraint commitment, but you may not have thought much about it. However, if you are struggling in your marriage, you are probably very aware of the costs of ending it.

Jason and Kristin were in the same troubled waters that too many couples have sailed. Their dedication, along with their joy and attachment, had seriously eroded. Each was aware of how much he or she hated the idea of divorce. Jason was also thinking about how mad his family would be if he left Kristin. Kristin was fearful about what it would mean to Kristi if their marriage failed. Both knew they could not make ends meet without each other. Basically, they were in deep trouble—stuck, but not necessarily sticking. Jason and Kristin have enough constraint that they *will* stay together. The really big question for them is whether they will reengage and act on dedication.

Sticking, Stuck, or Stopped?
_____

Constraints come with the territory when you make commitments. You cannot modify them very much unless it's about your basic values regarding divorce. Constraints tend to sound negative when defining them. That's because, theoretically, they come most into play when there is trouble, and they act as barriers to ending a marriage. But for most couples, most of the time, constraints play a very positive role in stabilizing marital commitment. Without constraint commitment, not too many marriages would last very long because they would have no rootedness when the foul winds blow.

There is one dimension that I initially thought would be more related to constraint, but it turns out to be more related to dedication. I call it metacommitment. In other words, it's commitment to commitment. It's the belief that you finish what you start. Many people strongly hold this value regardless of religious or philosophical background. It's a commitment to personal responsibility. The core of it is this attitude: "I made this choice. I'm going to make the best of it and do the best with it." You may have noted that in Jason's experience in the marines and Kristin's in college, the turning point for resolving the sense of being trapped was this recognition of personal choice. They owned their commitments and decided how to move forward in the best way from there.

Research shows that couples who maintain and act on dedication are happier, more connected, and more open with each other. Those who lose dedication are going to be together and miserable (hardly a pleasant situation for the couple or their children), or they will come apart. Stuck or stopped, not sticking. The loss of dedication represents the loss of a will to try, the loss of a sense of "us," and the loss of the actions that protect a marriage over time. Furthermore, a marriage without dedication is a marriage without passion. I don't mean romantic passion, though that could be part of it. I mean a marriage devoid of life. I want to help you steer clear of that.

A friend of mine and expert in the prevention of marital and family problems, Bill Coffin, has noted that when you combine dedication and constraint in marriage, it's like epoxy glue. You get a superstrong bond from the mixing of the two compounds. That's what married couples really need.

Two questions are of utmost importance. First, how do you *maintain* dedication over time in marriage? What does it look like, and how do you do it? Second, how do you *regain* dedication if you have lost some or all of it? The latter question is the one asked in marriages that have become distressed. The former should be asked in all others. Everyone in a marriage should find one or both of these questions relevant. Unfortunately, not too many of us think about what we can do to prevent our marriages from going down that path in the first place. *Please do! In the following chapters, the focus is primarily on preserving and deepening dedication.* We'll also explore how to regain lost dedication when you are feeling stuck in your marriage.

We'll touch on constraint again when it is important, but you can really do something about dedication. Dedication and the way it plays out over time will tell the most important story for the newlyweds mentioned at the beginning of the chapter. A great marriage is characterized by a sense of teamwork, a future together, deeper attachment, ongoing investments of time and effort, and sacrifice. Dedication is both the fuel and the essence of these things. The heart of dedication is expressed in the broad themes of *choice, permanence,* and *oneness*—the major themes of the rest of this book. *Stick* around, and let's go deeper.

Point of Application

In this chapter, I have laid out the theoretical foundation for the rest of the book. Spend some time thinking through what commitment means to you.

- What kinds of positive commitments have you seen that have impressed you?
- What kinds of failed commitments have you seen?
- What one point does Scripture make relating to marital commitment that you most want to take to heart?
- If you are married, how are you doing with dedication compared to constraint?

Sticking, Stuck, or Stopped?

Part I

CHOICES AND THE PATH OF COMMITMENT

. . .for better or for worse,
for richer, for poorer,
in sickness and in health, . . .
. . . and I promise to be
faithful to you,
forsaking all others, . . .

This first part discusses choices. So much of how commitments are made and lived involves daily, monthly, and yearly choices. Choices are fundamental to life. Commitment involves making choices, protecting choices from other options, and arriving at ongoing decisions that reflect the priorities of your commitments. Some people have trouble giving up anything; therefore, they can never make real commitments. But the richer paths of life call for choices to be made.

Commitment in marriage is based on choices on the wedding day and every day thereafter. At times, options not chosen can look pretty attractive, and the way these temptations are handled will affect your ability to be true to your commitment in marriage and to your mate. Since committing to choices means letting other options go, commitment can at times lead you to a sense of loss about what you do not have. At these times, you have to consider what changes are possible that are consistent with your commitment. When you have a loss over something that is not likely to change, grieving in healthy ways can be an essential part of maintaining a healthy grip on the important commitment that you have made. These are the themes of Part 1. The good news is that the whole matter of choices involves decisions over which you have some control. Let's take a look.

I shall be telling this with a sigh
Somewhere ages and ages hence:
Two roads diverged in a wood, and I—
I took the one less traveled by,
And that has made all the difference.

—Robert Frost

Chapter 2

MAKING THE CHOICE TO GIVE UP CHOICES

Better a handful with quietness
Than both hands full, together
with toil and grasping for the wind.
—Ecclesiastes 4:6 NKJV

About seven years ago, Nancy and I were in the market for a new car. We had two very old Toyotas, going back to graduate school days, and we were finally in a position that we could do more than dream about owning a new car. As we investigated every option, our choice narrowed to a Ford Taurus or a Honda Accord. The cost was similar for each, so we focused on features. The Honda was the smaller of the two. We preferred the greater room of the Taurus. Both cars had good safety records in terms of crash tests and insurance reports. We figured the Honda would be the more reliable of the two. After a bit of agonizing, we bought the Taurus.

Unless we had a lot of money, once we bought the Ford we couldn't also buy the Honda. Right? We could not commit to both—though we could buy a Honda in the future if we wanted to, and here is where you should not push this analogy too far once we get back to marital commitment. The choice of one precluded having the other. Many people make such decisions and then experience buyer's remorse. *What if I made the wrong choice?* they wonder. I think we all have this tendency, but some people experience it more intensely than others. When you commit to one path, you are often giving up another. It's true in car buying. It's true in marriage. It's true everywhere.

Here's a more emotional example. I met a couple who were in their late forties and had no children. All through their late twenties and into their thirties, Jane and Kelly tried and tried to have a baby. As many of you can understand, they went through years of the heartbreak of infertility. They prayed. Their friends prayed. They tried this doctor and that doctor. They tried most of the high-tech procedures. Still, no baby. After ten years of working hard at it, they decided they had better think about adopting. They were excited about it and began all the procedures needed to bring that about. Sadly for them, the process of adoption turned out to be just as wrenching as all the infertility procedures had been. At two different times they were within days of receiving a baby, but something fell through. One time the birth mother decided to keep her child after seeing him born. Another time, a relative of the baby they were to adopt objected and initiated legal proceedings that caused them to move on.

Finally, at the ages of forty-six and forty-seven, Jane and Kelly decided to give up on their plans to have a child. It was a very painful decision, but they could not stand it anymore, and they felt that they were getting too old to be parents. While they felt they had made the wisest decision, it was a big decision that affected them deeply. Sometimes they wondered, *What if?* or replayed all the factors that went into their decision.

Choosing to give up their dream of having a child was one of those choices in life where a lot is at stake. Jane and Kelly may be affected by their decision for a very long time. As we'll see in Chapter 4, commitments involve making hard choices and later can involve grieving for what was given up when the choice was made.

Some people fail to recognize that commitment means making choices among alternatives. Many people do not want to give up one option to have another, though they will have neither if they do not make a choice. The focus here is on the fundamental ways in which commitment, choices, and priorities are intertwined in our lives. The matter of priorities is the real heart of this chapter.

The Choice to Give Up Some Choices

For most people, marriage involves the choice to be the lifelong partner of one mate. It's certainly what most people want when they get married. I think this is even the case for people who have otherwise immature understandings of commitment. In marriage, you are choosing to *stick* to this other person through thick and thin. You are choosing to give up the other options, in the words of the vow, "forsaking all others." Hence, *commitment involves making the choice to give up some choices. Further, really sticking with your commitment will require you to protect the choice you have made in the context of life's demands.* Keeping commitments requires you to recognize that you have to give up some other paths.

Since commitment asks you to give up some things, it runs counter to much of what is valued and praised in our culture. Our culture values choice or, rather, having choices. "Keep all your options open," people say. Don't give up anything. Recently, I noted an advertisement for a book club that read: "Four books, four bucks, and absolutely, positively, no commitment!" You get, and you don't have to give up a thing. Perfect. I think the ad *is* perfect for a book club. That's the kind I might sign up for. The problem comes when you expect major commitments in life, such as marriage, to come with the same promise. You get, and you don't have to give up a thing. It is a lie.

COMMITMENT OPENS THE DOOR FOR INTIMACY

Commitment and the value of choice as expressed in our culture are often in a fundamental conflict. You cannot commit to one thing or person while keeping all of your choices open to you. Commitments go against the grain of our culture because commitments come with limits. Many people don't want to accept limits.

Some limits in marriage actually open the door to the deeper meanings in life. More specifically, the limits defined by commitment provide the opportunity for a deeper relationship in marriage. For example, research shows that when people are more dedicated in marriage, they report that there is more self-disclosure in their relationships.[1] That's because commitment in the form of dedication provides the fundamental framework of safety and trust that promotes closeness and openness.

Veronica and Tom have been married thirty-two years. They have two children, who are now in college. Like any couple, they have had their ups and downs, but they are devoted to each other. They know that each is there for the other, is supportive, and can be counted on to keep the marriage a priority. With such a commitment, each feels little risk in sharing deeply with the other, so they do. They know each other in very intimate ways. They are best friends because their dedication fosters trust. Far from limiting them, their commitment is freeing. This kind of commitment in action forms the basis of many years together as friends.

Hence, commitment in marriage—really sticking with full dedication—opens up the fuller depths of openness. Naked and unashamed. You are not likely to go to these places together if you haven't paid the full fare. Commitment gives you the security to risk greater levels of connection. Commitment doesn't guarantee that this will happen, but not committing virtually guarantees that it won't. You can hang on to everything and end up with nothing, or you can commit to someone in marriage and have depth. It's your choice. By the way, I recognize that some people do make a full commitment but their spouses do not, and then many of the deeper rewards for the relationship are not happening. For most couples, each partner tends to respond to the dedication of the other with increased dedication in return.

HAVING IT ALL?

Can you "have it all"? The title of numerous books implies that you can.[2] Personally, I have a lot, but I do not have it *all*. How about you? Most of us can think of something we lack, but maybe you think that you can eventually get there. It's a fundamental promise (even a premise) of our culture. Are there limits? Of course there are, but knowing this and living as if you believe it are two different things. It's a dilemma as old as the temptation in the Garden. There are many ways to think about that temptation. Let's review it.

If you have a Bible handy, read the third chapter of Genesis. God had made a perfect garden for a perfect couple in a relationship designed for total commitment and connection. They had many choices open to them, the whole garden, to be exact. We may sometimes think that God wants to place severe limits on our choices in life, but that's not the teaching of the Garden. Much is open; little is not. God said that they could choose from any tree—except one. As the serpent tempted Eve and Adam, he got them to focus on the very choice that was off-limits. That choice was the fruit of the tree of the knowledge of good and evil. Adam and Eve had many choices, but they most wanted to make the one choice that God said to avoid. Having free will, they made that choice.

We live out this ancient conflict all the time. Most of us really do not want to be told by anyone that we can't make any choice we please. Am I wrong? This rebellion against limits runs counter to commitment—always has, always will. Notice the swap Adam and Eve made. They were offered the mystery of oneness with God and in marriage. *They chose the freedom of choice rather than the mystery of oneness.* In reality, that "freedom" led to greater limits, but Adam and Eve were deceived and not able to see that. The deception lives on. That voice says, "You can have the most fulfilling life by keeping all your options open and not giving up a thing." That voice lies. Do you hear it? I hear it every day in the media and from people I meet. It's a loudmouth of a voice.

The paradox is that more freedom is to be gained when the limits of commitment are accepted. My sons love to play in our backyard, for good reason. We have a nice fence around the backyard. Within this fence, they have many choices open to them for playful enjoyment. They are free within the fence. There is plenty to do inside the fence too. It's not a small dog cage or something we're talking about here. They can swing, spray the hose, roll in the grass, run, jump, dig in the dirt, throw a ball, and fiercely battle imaginary warriors. Outside the fence are dangers: big dogs, bigger kids who might not be careful or kind, fast cars, and so forth. The fence allows them the freedom to fully relax and explore what's in bounds.

You can accept all the possibilities within the fenced area, or you can jump the fence to not be denied any options. That is not the path of commitment. A mature understanding of commitment accepts that some options are forsaken and some fences are built. However, the same fences that go up around a marriage because of commitment allow for pulling down barriers within it. Where is the greater blessing?

To summarize my point so far, real commitment means taking some choices off the table. Sometimes this reality is painful to accept, especially when people are very unhappy in their marriages. This pain can lead people to convince themselves that they didn't make their initial commitment freely. It is a form of rebellion against commitment expressed on the wedding day of full volition. When you choose a mate, you are making the choice to take other possible mates off the table. You're saying you're going to "dance with the one that brung ya." Did anyone really hold a gun to your head? Too many married people talk as if that were the case. I understand it. It's a fairly normal response to intense unhappiness. But it is most often a distortion of the past based in the pain of the present. It's rewriting history.

There are some arranged marriages in the world. At times, shotgun weddings have occurred. For most couples, however, it's not that they were forced into the commitment. Rather, it can be painful to own a commitment that feels like just being stuck. Please don't get me wrong. If you find yourself in such a place, I'm not saying, "You made your bed, now sleep in it." I have much to suggest that is more active in making your marriage all it can be. We humans have a tendency not to want to give up choices and sometimes not to want to take responsibility for choices *we* have already made. You'll note in Genesis 3 that Adam blamed Eve, and Eve blamed the serpent. "Wasn't me that made that choice!" Sometimes we want the option but not the consequences.

I don't want to imply that it's always easy to cope with this reality. Often, following through on your commitments is really very hard and not much fun. There are blessings to sticking, but it can feel a lot like being stuck at times. Furthermore, you give up some things when you make a commitment, and a sense of loss and grief is a real possibility. (We'll get more into these matters in Chapter 4.)

HE HAD IT ALL

There was once a man who had all of what this material life could offer. He had it all and he explored it all. He had few fences in his life and numerous choices. In the world of my sons' experience, you could say he had one really major backyard to play in. Listen to his description of what he had and what he did:

> *I made my works great, I built myself houses, and planted myself vineyards. I made myself gardens and orchards, and I planted all kinds of fruit trees in them. I made myself water pools from which to water the growing trees of the grove. I acquired male and female servants, and had servants born in my house. Yes, I had greater possessions of herds and flocks than all who were in Jerusalem before me. I also gathered for myself silver and gold and the special treasures of kings and of the provinces. I acquired male and female singers, the delights of the sons of men, and musical instruments of all kinds. So I became great and excelled more than all who were before me in Jerusalem. Also my wisdom remained with me.*
> *Whatever my eyes desired I did not keep from them.*
> *I did not withhold my heart from any pleasure,*
> *For my heart rejoiced in all my labor;*
> *And this was my reward from all my labor.*
> *Then I looked on all the works that my hands had done*
> *And on the labor in which I had toiled;*
> *And indeed all was vanity and grasping for the wind.*
> *There was no profit under the sun.*
> *Then I turned myself to consider wisdom and madness and folly;*
> *For what can the man do who succeeds the king?—*
> *Only what he has already done. (Eccl. 2:4–12 NKJV)*

That was written by Solomon, the man who asked God for an understanding heart instead of riches, and to whom God gave both (1 Kings 3:9–13). No king was greater in his time. He had it all in terms of what the world has to offer. Was he a happy man? Certainly not when he wrote the book of Ecclesiastes. Things he wrote throughout his journal made his feelings apparent: "For what has man for all his labor, and for the striving of his heart with which he has toiled under the sun? For all his days are sorrowful, and his work burdensome; even in the night his heart takes no rest. This also is vanity" (Eccl. 2:22–23 NKJV).

How could someone have so much and not be totally happy? I read

Ecclesiastes often, and I can't help thinking that it is the chronicle of Solomon's midlife crisis. What is a midlife crisis anyway? Do these crises really exist? I think they do for many people in various ways. Have you dealt with such a thing? Are you in something like that now? If you are going to have a midlife crisis, make it a wisely considered midcourse correction.

I think a midlife crisis is really about coming to the full realization that your earthly life is not going to go on forever, and that your options in the remaining years are limited by the choices you have already made. The future reality of death may be an impetus, but I don't think it's the driving force. The force of a midlife crisis is the realization of your limits. You are not going to get to do everything you wish you could do. You are not going to get to do everything you are capable of doing. You may come close, but you're still not going to do as well as Solomon. Note that not even he had peace at the height of his glory. Real contentment does not lie on that path. Solomon gets to that in his journal, as we'll soon see.

Priorities: The Right Choices

Your priorities are the things that are most important to you. The way in which you make choices among competing demands is a fundamental aspect of commitment. Making the right choices in your marriage is part of sticking. Making the wrong choices is part of getting stuck.

In my research on marital commitment, I find that placing one's mate and marriage as a high priority is a key part of dedication commitment.[3] No surprise in that, is there? The concept is simple, but living it is not. The fact is, even when you are fully dedicated to your mate, you have so many options competing for your attention that it is easy to let things slide at home. Options make you face your true priorities on a daily basis. Often, priorities are most revealed in the crunches of life, when push comes to shove.

This is not a comfortable topic for most of us because most of us are living with the pressures and pulls of life that tempt us to put our marriages on the back burner. I realize that you might like to light a fire under your mate's behind. Try your own first! I'd even go so far as to suggest that you are not normal if you do not often feel this tension between your stated priorities and your actual lifestyle. But things go seriously downhill when there is a chronic discrepancy.

GUILT TRIPS GO NOWHERE

Before we proceed, please understand that it does no one any good to read farther in this chapter and end up feeling massive guilt. Much of what is coming in this book will challenge you, but talking about commitment can stir up unproductive guilt. Please don't get stuck there. If change is needed and guilt is the impetus behind it, then fine. Feel bad enough so that you change, not bad in a way that merely gets you stuck in a ditch. If you read the rest of this chapter and feel guilt and nothing else happens, both of us have failed—you in a crucial task in life and me in my hope of encouraging you to live according to your priorities. If you are having a significant problem with priorities in your life, don't feel guilty; change how it works.

Now let's go deeper.

GETTING TO "NO" YOU

Rick and Margo married when he was twenty-seven and she was twenty-five. They worked for the same software firm, he in development and she in sales. She was very drawn to his intelligence and drive. She could see that he was going places in the firm. He was very drawn to her outgoing personality, her ways of approaching issues in life, her humor, and her comfort in talking with him—really, his comfort in talking with her. When they were dating, he worked hard to make time to see her. Even though the pace of the projects he was working on demanded tremendous amounts of time and energy, he found plenty of time for her. Ten years and two kids later, he was indeed the star of the software development team, and she was alone. His work required intensely long hours, frequent deadlines, and pressure from the highest levels of the company. He came home later every night, rarely before eight in the evening. She had shifted to working part-time for the same company years earlier in order to spend more time with their children, yet she was frazzled. She felt that she was raising the children by herself. That wasn't the vision she had for their life together.

Margo occasionally confronted Rick about his absence. Each time, he'd do a compelling job of convincing her that his real priorities were her and the kids. She wanted to believe him but couldn't see how it could be true. She asked him if he could attend their older child's school program. "No, Honey, sorry, I have to finish up a project this week, or I'll be in a real fix," he said. Or when she asked him if he could sit down and talk to her before she went to sleep, even then he'd say something like, "No, not tonight. I'd love to, but I have this crucial presentation in the morning." What amazed her most was his response when she'd ask him if he wanted to "get close tonight"—which was their way of saying "make love." He'd say something like, "No, I really can't. I am so wiped out and I have to get some sleep." *He was "no"-ing her but not "knowing" her.* She understood the pressure he was under, but she had married him to have a life together, and that's why he married her as well.

Although Margo was more disappointed than Rick was, neither was experiencing what he or she wanted when they said, "I do." To Rick, the conflicts between them and within him were no simple matter. He truly thought (and he was correct) that if he gave any less of himself to his work, he would lose his job. He was feeling trapped in a work situation where most of the people who were excelling were having terrible marriages or divorcing. The expectations and the pace were brutal. Slowing down would require him and Margo to rethink their entire lifestyle.

Consider this for a moment: you may too often put your mate last in your priorities precisely because your mate is committed to you for life. You believe that your mate will "be there" for you, so you don't have to pay as much attention as you do to others who really do not matter nearly as much in the long run. When you do this, you presume that your mate can take all sorts of neglect precisely because he or she is committed. Presuming on your commitment in marriage will erode the quality of your relationship over time. Do you see how twisted that is? The message to the person you promised to love and cherish is, " *You* can and will wait; *this* can't." At times, that is a very reasonable way to think. But when it's a chronic lifestyle, your chronic lifestyle needs serious reevaluation.

Choices and the Path of Commitment

When they talked about it, Rick was able to be reassuring about his priorities because he really believed what he was saying. He'd say something like this: "Honey, it will all get better later this year when I finish this one major project." He meant it too. But a prophet he wasn't, and certainly not one honored in his own home. Sure, there were times when it was better than usual, but not often enough. His *intended* priorities were for her and the kids. The problem was that his life exhibited *actual* priorities that differed from his intentions. He was aware of the difference and so was she. He found it so unpleasant to think about that he tried to put it out of his mind. Bad idea. He wanted to be more dedicated to Margo than to his work, but he couldn't stand to look too closely at all the evidence that he really didn't live that way. He wanted to stick by her side, but felt stuck in the pressure of work and the need to perform.

Many people in our fast-paced world struggle with the difference between intended and actual priorities every day. Spouses and children can handle the discrepancy for periods of time. They can make allowances. They can understand. In part, the ability to make these allowances is based on faith in the future. But when the pace never lets up, and what's on the back burner is rarely stirred or moved to the front, problems develop. In Rick's case, he made great money, he continued to advance and be a star at work, but his marriage became a shell. Although he provided incredibly well for his wife and children financially, that didn't seem to be very satisfying to either Margo or Rick. It was an empty life. If Rick hopes to change so that his intended priorities are more often acted upon, he'll have to learn more about setting apart the time for the essential experiences of marital life.

THE SANCTIFICATION OF EVERYDAY LIFE

Sanctification, consecration, and *holy* are words generally restricted to religious uses. They all are English words that reflect the same Hebrew and Greek root words throughout the Bible. The concept is that of something being "pure and devoted," "separate," or "set apart" for a particular use or purpose, particularly for the purposes of God. Great words. Powerful concept. Our modern word *dedicated* may come closest to the root meaning when what has been dedicated is dedicated to God. For now, focus on the notion of something being "set apart."

Nancy and I have some very fine china that belonged to my maternal grandmother. My mother gave it to us some years ago since she had so few occasions to use it. We are grateful to have this china. It's old, beautiful, and very special since it was my grandmother's. We rarely eat on these dishes. They come out maybe once a year for special meals. This china is *dedicated.* It's set aside only for use with special meals. It's not sanctified in the sense of being devoted to the Lord, but it is set apart for special use. It has been dedicated for a special purpose.

If your life reflects a high degree of dedication to your mate, you will live in ways that set apart your relationship. You will set it apart and make time for it—and more often than once a year! If it's really dedicated time, you'll jealously guard that time from the other options and choices in life. *Sanctification in this nonreligious sense of something being set apart is the secret to living your priorities when you have an abundance of options.* While the competing pressures can be many and varied, you gain a small victory whenever you set apart time devoted to your partner. This can be reflected in time spent doing something *for* your partner or, most important, time spent doing something *with* your partner.

In his book *First Things First,* Stephen Covey describes a powerful illustration that he and others have used in workshops to get a point across about priorities. Imagine this scene. You are at a time management seminar soaking up tips on how to use your time more effectively. The presenter sets a large jar on the table in the front of the room, placing beside it all sorts of softball-sized rocks. He says to the crowd, "How many of these rocks do you think I can fit into this jar?" Someone guesses thirteen. Another guesses nine. Still another guesses twelve. The presenter begins to place the rocks one at a time into the jar, counting as he goes: one, two, three, four, and so forth, all the while asking the group if the jar is full. The crowd keeps saying no until it's really near the top. Nine, ten, eleven, twelve. That's it. Twelve rocks fit in the jar. The audience agrees that the jar is full.

Next, the presenter brings out a bucket with a bunch of smaller rocks, and he pours them into the jar. They filter all around the bigger rocks. As he pours, he asks the audience, "Is it full?" "No!" they roar, because they know what's next. Sand. Then water. Now it's really looking full.

He says to the group, "What's the point?" As Covey relays the story in his book, a woman raises her hand and says something like this: "The point is that there are all these nooks and crannies and spaces of time in life that we are just wasting and not using to the fullest." The presenter considers the point, with hand drawn to chin, then says, "Nope, that's not the point." The audience, which has been focused on efficiency and organization, is taken back a bit. The presenter goes on to say, "The point is this. If the big rocks don't go in the jar first, they don't get in the jar at all."

It's a profound illustration. It's about setting apart time. No matter what size jar, almost everyone has a full jar. You cannot create more time. It's a limited resource. You see, the big rocks are the things that you believe are most important in your life. So, how often do you go through life with some of the most important, big rocks sitting on the table and not in the jar? The big rocks are your *intended* priorities. But if they are seldom in your jar, they are not your *actual* priorities.

I first read about this illustration in a magazine excerpt of Covey's excellent book while on vacation for a few days with Nancy and our sons. The boys were tucked away, asleep in bed, and Nancy and I were reading near the crackling fire in the fireplace. A nice, quiet setting. Good for reflection. I was so captivated by this illustration that I read it to Nancy. She likewise thought it wonderful. A few days later, we were back in Denver sitting in our living room and the boys were playing somewhere. I'm sure we knew at the time where we had left them—at least I'm sure Nancy did. I was still thinking about this image, and I turned to Nancy and said, "Honey, you know you are one of the big rocks." Nancy turned warmly toward me and said, "Yeah, but am I in the jar?" It was one of those times among many that she gave me targeted, tender feedback about my life. I heard what she said very positively.

It's a fair question. It's the question your mate and children are often asking about you, whether you are wife, husband, mother, father, whatever your role. The important people in your life want to be in the jar. They want in there before all the other stuff of life crowds them out. Is your mate in the jar? Are your kids? *If you are finding it hard to keep a lid on things in your marriage, maybe your mate is not in the jar.*

The principle of sanctification gets to the heart of the basic tension between various priorities in your life. You act on your dedication in marriage by setting apart time or place for your mate before everything else crowds out the time. Of course, this principle is conveyed throughout the Bible as it describes the level of dedication due to the Lord. That's how the Ten Commandments start out: "You shall have no other gods before Me!" Pretty direct, right? God is the biggest rock. He wants to be first in your jar. That is not because He loves to take up space in your life but because you were created for deep relationship with Him. After God, spouse and family come next. I think anyone would be hard-pressed to argue otherwise from any theological perspective. Get the irony? God wants all of you, then He wants to turn around and help you give all of who you are to your mate and children. It's His way.

I'm not claiming to know just what it means in *your* life to get God and your spouse into the jar first. I'm quite sure it can look many different ways in terms of how it's actually lived out. But it's clear that these two rocks need to be in your jar ahead of the other things. You may slip up at times, but that's what to shoot for. I find this all very challenging. How about you?

Allow me to list a few ways to enact this principle of setting apart special time in marriage, but recognize that there are thousands, and you must figure out which ones matter the most in your life. You might especially note ways that convey the message that "you are in my jar" to your mate.

- When you make regular time to take a walk together and hold hands and talk about interesting things (not all the problems of life), you have set apart a moment of connection together as friends.
- When you make it your business to be home at dinnertime so that the family can have dinner together, you have set apart a moment.
- When you schedule a date to have some fun, you have set apart time.
- When you make time in your schedules to work on problems and issues together, you have set apart some moments for keeping your marriage on track.

A friend of mine calls these times with spouse and children "holy" moments. You might think that is too strong a word for such time together. You might think the word *holy* should be reserved only for activities devoted to God. But God calls you to such things, so setting apart time and space for your mate can be thought of as an act of devotion to God—holy moments, indeed.

Have you begun to see the higher call on your priorities in your life? More important, do you see that if you do not treat such times together as crucial, they do not happen? "Time waits for no one," the old saying goes. It's true. It does not wait for you, and it does not wait for me. It will not make the spaces for you and your mate. That's up to you to do.

Moses was a pretty busy fellow. At some point in his life, he penned this verse: "Teach us to number our days, that we may gain a heart of wisdom" (Ps. 90:12 NKJV).

Moses made the profound connection between understanding that our days are numbered and living wisely. That wisdom comes from recognizing limits, not having a false belief in limitlessness. *If you can number your days, you can accept that they are limited, and if you accept that, you can accept the need to prioritize because there is not enough time to do it all.* Therefore, carve out the spaces for the best things. You can't create more time, but you can be more creative in making the most of the time that you have. And you have an Ally who has experience in creating time and space. Call on Him for help.

GETTING TO NO

A book on business negotiation is called *Getting to Yes*.[4] I think it's a great title and a fine book. However, I'd like to suggest that learning to say no is as important, if not more so, than learning how to get to yes. *No* is a word that you use when you recognize limits. If you are going to set apart time for your marriage, you are going to have to be good at saying no. You cannot protect time and energy for your mate and children without that little word. Life will pitch too many offers your way. "Wanna go play golf tomorrow?" "Wanna stay late and talk about that project?" "Wanna come in early and finish up that report?" "Wanna come over tonight and watch the game?" "Wanna come by the church and sit in on that planning meeting?" "Wanna . . . wanna . . . wanna . . . wanna?"

You get offers all the time. Some of the offers sound great and would, in fact, be great. That doesn't mean you were meant to say yes to all of them. Learning to say no can be liberating. To be sure, I am not saying that you should say no to things that God wants you to say yes to, not by any means. You have to discern. You have to listen carefully to God and to your family. No one can do that for you. Having said that, I think most of us need to say no much more often to many more people and then say yes to the right people.

You can say no more often. Try whispering it right now. Pray it: "Yes, Lord. I can say no!" You can do this. Your mate will notice. Your children will notice. There is liberation in saying no when it's based on a recognition of your true priorities and honest limits.

Trading Relationship for Stuff

The next point weaves together the threads of choice and priorities covered here. In our society, people are too willing to sacrifice important things such as relationships for what does not matter nearly so much. Many people want to "have it all," and the all that is most desired includes material goods or notoriety. Don't get me wrong. I'm not railing against a reasonable perspective on material needs or against capitalism, which I see as the way things really work. However, many people come to value *things and forms of success* over better relationships with others, including the ones they love most.

Stacey and Bert seem to have it all: money, cars, a nice house, three wonderful kids, and satisfying jobs. They have all the latest toys, they're up on the latest issues, and they are connected to the right people. They are pillars of their church. Both exercise a minimum of eight hours a week. He is a partner in an accounting firm, and she is a real estate agent. Impressive couple. Empty lives. They are rich in stuff and impoverished in relationships, including the relationship in their marriage. They have little time together or with their children. Sure, their children are involved in all the coolest activities. The kids need planning calendars as much as Bert and Stacey do, with their hectic schedules. However, the places where their lives overlap are minimal. Stacey sometimes wonders what they have more of: A family or an office together? They seem to have it all, but what do they really have?

One of the most negative consequences of the tendency to hang on to all options is that you may end up with nothing, especially in terms of depth of relationships. Remember the monkey who wants to eat the food that's in a jar? He likes the food in the jar—a lot. The trouble is that he grabs so much of it at a time that he can't get his food-filled fist out of the jar. It's too big to pull out unless he grabs less. He gets nothing until he figures out that less is more. Simple illustration. Profound wisdom.

Here's an irony for you. In our society we have more freedom to engage in deeper relationships than most people have had throughout history. We have more leisure time, or at least the possibility of it. While many low-income people do not have such freedoms, many others in our culture find it relatively easy to have a good standard of living. However, in wanting to have more goods and things, people sacrifice the time for relationships they could have if only they accepted somewhat less on the material side—*trading relationship for stuff.* How many couples, for instance, buy houses at the very limit of what they can qualify for only to end up working more and more to make ends meet and further reducing time to be together in marriage and family?

Solomon pegged the driving force behind how hard many of us work: "And I saw that all labor and all achievement spring from man's envy of his neighbor. This too is meaningless, a chasing after the wind" (Eccl. 4:4 NIV).

Ouch! I don't know about you, but this verse picks me up and slams me down to the ground. I hope you are not affected by envy, but I think most people are. Think about it. Do you envy certain people? Would you like to have what they have? Would you like to do better than they are doing? Would you like to beat them? Remember, Solomon was writing this verse. He had it all and did it all. No one beat him in his day. Many people must have envied him. Alas, he concluded that it's meaningless, a "chasing after the wind." You can't feed this beast enough to satisfy it. Being driven by envy does not lead to a life of meaning.

HAVING EVERYTHING AND NOTHING

Most people cannot have it all. In chapter 4 of his journal of Ecclesiastes, Solomon brought to life the story of a man who had everything but meaningful relationships. He had a great career, great wealth, but no close relationships or real meaning in life:

There is one alone, without companion:
He has neither son nor brother.
Yet there is no end to all his labors,
Nor is his eye satisfied with riches.
But he never asks,
"For whom do I toil and deprive myself of good?"
This also is vanity and a grave misfortune. (Eccl. 4:8 NKJV)

Solomon wrote those words without reference to a specific person, but I think he was writing of himself. He was a man with everything, all his options open, all his choices explored. He was also an empty man. He had it all, but he was not content. In this passage, Solomon described someone who is very popular in our world today. He is a tireless worker, has gained much success, and has a lot to show for it—a lot of stuff. He is toiling after the wind. But where have his choices—his commitments—led him?

In contrast to the empty life of this man who "has it all," Solomon wrote some of the most beautiful lines ever written about being in relationship:

Two are better than one,
Because they have a good reward for their labor.
For if they fall, one will lift up his companion.
But woe to him who is alone when he falls,
For he has no one to help him up.
Again, if two lie down together, they will keep warm;
But how can one be warm alone?
Though one may be overpowered by another, two can withstand him.
And a threefold cord is not quickly broken. (Eccl. 4:9–12 NKJV)

These lines are so beautiful that they are often incorporated into wedding ceremonies. On the day that I married Nancy, our pastor added a vow into the ceremony that we had not talked about beforehand. He had me promise to keep Nancy warm. Of all that was said and done that day, those were the words that stood out to me, Nancy, and my mother. Promising to keep Nancy warm encompasses so much. It's a powerful promise with far more potential for contentment than material goods can offer.

I know it's getting fashionable to question one's commitment to material goods at the expense of relationships. It's almost trendy. That does not diminish the fact that it's a very real dilemma most of us face. We can work harder to "chase after the wind" and try to "have it all," or we can cut back, pace ourselves, accept less on some fronts, and have more on the home front. These choices are not simple at all, especially in a culture that will not reward us for making them. Where are the examples of healthy, thriving relationships in marriage that are lifted up for all to see? Material success and wealth are glorified every day, all day, across our country.

If you are feeling this conflict and you begin to make certain choices toward marriage and family, expect a fight—a fight with the values of our culture and, much more troubling, a fight within yourself about what you value most in your life. Thinking about it is hard and painful.

TO THOSE WITH LESS MEANS

Before we leave this chapter, I want to acknowledge a type of couple and family for whom I have deep sympathy. These are the couples who don't have a shot at having it all in the popular sense, and they know it. They are far more worried about losing it all than having it all. These couples are so on the edge in terms of financial stress—read poverty—that thinking about cutting back or reprioritizing in terms of work demands and family needs is not dealing with reality. Sure, they can cut back on the extra part-time job, but then they do not eat or they end up dependent on the government.

If you are in this boat, I want you to know that some of this discussion is not for you. You really do not have some of the options right now that others have. However, even if your choices are more limited to begin with, you have some choices about how you act out your commitments. Within the range of the reality of your life, you can work to carve out spaces for your marriage and your children. It's the right thing to try to do. I want you to know that I think that much of what we're talking about in this chapter is all that much harder for you because of how tight things really are. That's a very tough spot to be in.

To those of us with greater resources and options, we could think a lot more about how to help such families do more than get by. It's beyond the scope of this book to develop this point fully, but it's surely a matter

Making the Choice to Give Up Choices

consistent with being committed and being a person who listens to the concerns of the Lord. You might take some time to note that in Ecclesiastes 4, which directly addresses ambition and priorities, Solomon deals directly with the topic of oppression. I don't think the linkage is accidental. It is some form of oppression when family members do all they can to support themselves, and the parents still cannot steal time for each other or their children. Give this some thought. I'm not arguing for a governmental solution. I'm suggesting that these people are all around us, and we with more means can help in very real ways if we look for the opportunities.

Solomon was pretty materialistic. He was not so much railing against money or comfort, but he was surely saying that it's an empty life to live for more and more stuff at the expense of relationships. We're called to something higher than material fantasies. We're called to experience the wonder of relationship with God, our spouses, our children, and those less fortunate among us. And if you don't know anyone less fortunate, get out and live a little. They are all around you if you look. End of sermon.

A Closing Note on Ambition

Solomon's depiction of the man with material wealth but no relationships is a vivid example of ambition gone awry. The man had achieved much. Solomon was not content to sit around and enjoy the day-to-day life of kingly pleasures. He went for the gusto. He was an ambitious man, blindly ambitious, because he was headed nowhere at 190 miles an hour.

Here's the key: *ambition of the sort that Solomon wrote about is winning over others, but commitment is sticking with others.* They are not the same. True confession: I am highly motivated toward both. These two dynamics wrestle in my soul. To be sure, not all ambition is wrong, and some commitments are unwise. However, focus for a minute on the distinction I am trying to make. Wrongly directed ambition has no sincere regard for the needs of people. Ambition will justify anything if it's strong enough. Ambition will justify the sacrificing of your mate and your children. Ambition whispers in your ear, "They'll wait for you. They'll understand." Dedication reins you in. Dedication asks you tough questions, such as, "For whom am I toiling?" It's a good question. What's *your* answer?

We've faced the fundamental fact that commitment means giving up some options in life and protecting others in terms of priorities. Here are some questions to think about and then act on:

- In your marriage, are you aware of options you have given up that have helped your commitment to your mate? What effect has that had?
- What are the priorities of your life? How do you live compared to your priorities?
- What are two specific steps you can take to make your actual priorities more closely match your intended priorities? Set aside a time to share your plan with your mate.

*Character is that which reveals moral purpose,
exposing the class of things a man chooses or avoids.*
—Aristotle

*It is only in so far as they reach the will and are embodied in habits that the
virtues are really fatal to us.*
Uncle Screwtape to Wormwood, the temptor
—C. S. Lewis

Chapter 3

THE THREAT OF
ATTRACTIVE
ALTERNATIVES

Guard yourself in your spirit.
—Malachi 2:15 NIV

Sharon and Steven were quite content in their marriage of nine years. Jennifer and Brad, both in their early thirties, were also a happily married couple. They had been married only a few years when Brad met Sharon. Brad had noticed Sharon at church, but didn't get to know her until they served together on a committee to find a new pastor. The committee meetings required long hours in the evenings, usually once a week, for months. To allow the committee to develop a close bond and work together as a team, the committee had been kept small, with just four people on it. As the months passed, the four developed a close friendship, two of the four in particular.

Sometimes friendship can lead to an attraction that can become a problem. Brad was in the midst of one of those times. He noticed that he really looked forward to the committee meetings because Sharon was there. While he felt some conflict about his feelings, he thought, *Nothing will come of these feelings, so what's the big deal?* The attraction seemed mutual, though neither spoke openly of it. Each was developing feelings for the other that both were uncomfortable having.

If Brad had perceived his feelings for Sharon as a threat and taken steps to guard his marriage, then the attraction might not have become a big deal. However, Brad disregarded the danger and started to dwell on his feelings for Sharon. He played out various fantasies in his mind—fantasies about being with Sharon, not Jennifer. They were not sexual thoughts as much as thoughts about just being with her, talking to her, or even being married to her. In some ways, because his thoughts were not explicitly sexual, he had a harder time seeing that his growing obsession with Sharon was any threat at all.

Brad was not unhappy at home. His feelings for Sharon did not grow out of that soil. Brad loved Jennifer, but he didn't feel as alive with her as he did with Sharon. He wanted to experience more of those "alive" feelings with Jennifer, but he didn't. Brad became dissatisfied with Jennifer as his feelings for Sharon grew. In his mind, he compared Jennifer to Sharon on everything. Sharon seemed more positive, more beautiful, more energetic, more insightful, more fun to talk with, more in shape, more this, more that, more everything. Whether Sharon was really superior to Jennifer in all those ways didn't matter much.

What mattered was the result of the comparisons. Brad grew more and more resentful with Jennifer. "Why can't she be more like Sharon?" he'd ask himself over and over. As he grew more unhappy with Jennifer, his unhappiness affected his marriage. He became more distant, more defensive, and more negative with his wife. Jennifer didn't understand what had changed between them, but she knew they were growing apart. She tried to talk to Brad about it, but he pulled farther away.

Brad continued to obsess over Sharon and berate Jennifer for not being someone else. He ultimately destroyed his marriage because he didn't take seriously the warning signs. He grew so unhappy with Jennifer that he decided to leave her. The situation could have been different if he had known what to watch for in his thinking, and if he had taken steps to protect his commitment to Jennifer. Though Brad had hoped Sharon would leave Steven, she did not. Sharon had kept her antenna up. She took the warning signs seriously, and she made different choices. She was sticking in her marriage. He stopped in his.

Like the previous chapter, this one is about choices. It's directed at the choices you make to protect your marriage from other attractions. While alternatives to marriage can include many things, such as divorce and living alone, I'll focus on attractions for people other than your mate. This issue is not talked about much, perhaps because of shame or embarrassment. Commitment involves choosing among options, but being committed doesn't make all the options go away. People are sometimes attracted to someone other than a mate. You can be very committed in your marriage and still experience this. It's what you do when faced with it that really matters.

Let's look at how you can deal with attractive alternatives in ways that honor and deepen commitment. If you are affected at times by feelings of attraction to another, you'll find much here to help you understand and deal with those dilemmas. If you have not ever experienced such attractions, you can gain insights here for keeping things that way.

Thinking About the Alternatives

Theorists and researchers use the term *alternative monitoring* for the degree to which people *think about what it would be like to be with people other than their mates.*[1] Studies show that when people are less dedicated, they spend more time thinking about the what-ifs. They spend more time thinking about the alternatives and the other people they might be happier being with. Thoughts such as the following characterize this process of thinking about alternatives:

- *What if I were not with my wife and could be with Sally instead?*
- *What if I left my husband to be with William?*
- *I'd rather be with her than the woman I married!*

As I said in the previous chapter, Nancy and I chose the Taurus and not the Accord some years ago when buying a new car. When you've chosen the Taurus, what might you think about sometimes? Let me give you some ideas:

- *There goes a nice-looking Accord.*
- *I'll bet that Accord would have fired up this morning.*
- *That Accord would not have left me stranded here in traffic!*
- *It sure costs a lot to keep this Taurus going.*

When you pick one path, it's natural to wonder about the others. This will be especially true when the path you are on becomes rocky. Nancy and I will not think much about the fact that we could have an Accord when the Taurus is running well. It's when things are not going so well with the Taurus that we'll ask the most what-ifs. Of course, the Taurus could work perfectly and be just what we need, and we could still wonder about having a particularly cool new Accord. The point is this: all the other cars in the world did not disappear when we bought the Taurus. The problems occur if we focus on the Accord and stop taking care of the Taurus!

Of all the dimensions related to commitment that I have studied, thinking seriously about alternatives is the most sensitive to how happy one is with a mate at the present time.[2] When you are less happy, you are more likely to have some of these what-if thoughts. If you are mostly always very happy with your mate, you may never have such thoughts, but that's not the case for most people. That's why commitment matters so much. It takes you through the tougher times. Not thinking about alternatives is a manifestation of dedication. You'll monitor alternatives more seriously when you are less dedicated, but when you are more aware of alternatives, your dedication will lead you to protect your marriage.

Sometimes the what-ifs are about people in the movies or people in books. Sometimes they are about people at work or down the street. Males are a bit more likely than females to think seriously about the alternatives. Either way, when these thoughts become more intense, they need to be treated very *seriously*. In general, thinking about alternatives is more serious if you dwell on the thoughts and the thoughts are about someone you know. They are the most dangerous of all when your commitment to your marriage is lagging and the thoughts are of someone who is potentially available (e.g., unmarried or in the process of divorce).

CINDY AND MARTIN—AND FRANK

Cindy and Martin have been married twelve years, and they have three children from the ages of five to nine. They've had a good marriage with some ups and downs, like most other couples. At one period of time they were having a rougher stretch than usual. Martin was working particularly hard, leaving him more tired and less available to the family.

Cindy felt very stressed and unhappy about Martin's being less available. Both were keeping up with the children and their needs, but they were not keeping up with their marriage. They had not gone out together, they had not been taking their typical after-dinner walks, and they had been increasingly irritable with each other. They had been growing apart. Almost everyone goes through this from time to time in marriage; it was one of those times for them.

Through this time, Cindy, a pharmacist, began to talk more and more with her coworker, Frank. She had worked with Frank at the same pharmacy for five years. They had a history of talking about many things together, and each had grown to appreciate the other as a friend. As Cindy became more unhappy at home, she was drawn to talking more to Frank at work. Frank was really listening to her, and she liked that. He seemed to have the medicine that her hurting soul needed, and he understood the stresses she was under at home. He had been divorced for several years, after his wife had left him for another man, so Frank was attractive, available, and nearby—a dangerous combination for Cindy.

In the context of her being unhappy at home, Cindy started noticing more about Frank than she had before, and she realized that her attraction to him was growing beyond friendship. She liked feeling what she felt, but it also scared her. *After all, I'm married to Martin, not to Frank,* she reflected. Frank seemed interested enough in her that she started to wonder whether he would date her if she left her husband. She started to play various scenarios over and over in her mind. She was having many great conversations with Frank at work, and she was having many more in her mind.

Cindy was becoming very aware of Frank as an attractive alternative, partly because she was unhappy at home and partly because Frank was a great guy. There was little not to like about him. She would have found him attractive even if she had not been upset about Martin, but because she was upset, the attraction was more intense and became more serious.

Seemingly insignificant events could trigger deeper turmoil for Cindy, such as an instance with a bee. Though Cindy was relatively fearless, she had a somewhat irrational fear of bees. Martin didn't have much tolerance for such a childish fear and typically rolled his eyes at Cindy as she squirmed whenever a buzzing bee approached her. When a bee flew into the pharmacy, Frank, who knew nothing of Cindy's fears, saw her recoil, and he swatted the bee away instinctively. Frank wasn't stung, but Cindy was, and the bee had nothing to do with it. Cindy's attraction to Frank had grown far more dangerous than any feelings she had ever had about a movie star she'd never know or any other male friends she did know.

Fortunately, Cindy was dedicated to Martin. She was not all that happy with him then, but she was dedicated. Because she intended to stick, she became conflicted about her feelings for Frank. She was not at ease about the feelings of attraction, but she was not sure what to do about them, either. She wished that the feelings would just go away; however, life is not that simple. The good news was that bells were going off in her head, and she was listening. At least she was aware enough of herself and her situation to appreciate that she was experiencing a real threat to her marriage, and the threat was not Frank himself as much as her attraction to Frank. We'll come back to Cindy and Martin and Frank in a bit.

ATTRACTION TO OTHERS AS A THREAT TO COMMITMENT

In addition to my and others' findings that people think less about alternatives when they are more dedicated, researchers Dennis Johnson and Caryl Rusbult found something even more interesting.[3] They found that when people were more dedicated, they seemed to perceive attractive alternatives as a threat to their commitment and their relationship. In response to this threat, those who were more committed began to internally devalue the attractiveness of the alternatives to protect their commitment to their partners. In other words, those who were more committed began to view the alternative person as less attractive over time, instead of dwelling on what was attractive about the other. Maybe they even looked for what might not be so good about the other in direct contrast to the strengths of their partner.

This study was conducted with college students in dating relationships, yet the findings are even more important in marriage. The key is the perception of threat. Instead of dwelling on the attractiveness of another, committed people perceive the attraction as a threat, as Cindy did. She was not at all comfortable with her growing attraction to Frank. It raised a conflict, and she was wrestling with it. Her feelings were partly enjoyable, but things would have been far worse if she had not appreciated the attraction as a threat.

You have the choice either to dwell on the what-ifs or to put that energy into nurturing your marriage and helping it become as rich as possible. After laying some theological foundations, I'll present specific strategies for protecting your marriage from attractive alternatives.

Scripture speaks directly and forcefully to the matter of alternatives and marriage in several key passages. Consider two of the Ten Commandments:

> *You shall not commit adultery. . . .*
> *You shall not covet your neighbor's house; you shall not covet your neighbor's wife, nor his male servant, nor his female servant, nor his ox, nor his donkey, nor anything that is your neighbor's. (Ex. 20:14, 17 NKJV)*

The Ten Commandments form the core of the moral law of the Old Testament. The first of these two speaks to the sanctity of marriage. It forbids adultery. Adultery occurs when a person fails to protect the marriage from an attractive alternative, even if the alternative was only momentarily attractive. As the vow says, "I promise to be faithful to you, forsaking all others." Unfaithfulness breaks this sacred bond of fidelity in marriage.

Thinking seriously about another could be an early warning sign on the path of breaking down the barriers to infidelity. It is God's design that sexual faithfulness be an essential—perhaps *the* essential—ingredient of marital commitment. In fact, sexual unfaithfulness is the most commonly accepted grounds for divorce in various Christian theological traditions.

Recognizing the danger of adultery is easy because it's such a fundamental breach of the marital bond. Short of adultery, actively thinking about alternatives can also damage your marriage.

Consider the couple presented at the outset of this chapter: Jennifer and Brad. Their marriage came apart because Brad didn't protect it from an attractive alternative. Sharon didn't do anything to break them up; she had no plans to leave Steven for Brad. But Brad's obsession with Sharon was the undoing of his marriage.

The second of the two commandments cited in this section also speaks to how we are to handle attractive alternatives. We are told not to covet anything of our neighbor's, including his wife (or her husband). The Hebrew word for "covet" is *chamad,* which means "to delight in," "greatly love," or "desire." The closest New Testament concept is lust, which is also a depiction of intense desire.

Jesus combined the prohibitions of both commandments into one statement that elevates the significance of protecting our marital commitments: "But I say to you that whoever looks at a woman to lust for her has already committed adultery with her in his heart" (Matt. 5:28 NKJV). The Greek word for "lust," *epithumeo,* means "to set the heart upon" or long for the object of desire—in other words, to covet. Jesus therefore likened coveting with the internal act of adultery. Much of what Jesus taught in the Sermon on the Mount moves our awareness to how the law matters in the internal regions of the soul. Here, He taught that it's important to be externally faithful in marriage, and that this faithfulness extends to the internal life.

I can't tell you exactly where the line is between being attracted to, and conflicted about, an alternative and being involved internally in adultery. But there's a line that you should be watching for. Sexual fantasies would obviously be over the line. Beyond that, you may have to be sensitive to God about when you are over the line.

Before moving on, I would like to clarify a teaching that is in error but that is common among Christians. It is the teaching that the external act of committing adultery is no worse than the internal act of lusting. This error stems from the notion that all sins are equally bad. That doctrine is *not* consistent with either the Old or New Testament.[4] I have heard people say that since they are already lusting after this other person, they might as well act it out because it's all the same sin, right? Wrong. It's far worse to commit sexual sin with another than to lust in your heart, but neither is good for your marriage and both are sin.

When you seriously think about an attractive alternative and do not appreciate this attraction as a threat to your marriage, trouble is brewing. You are responsible for your choices. However, this doesn't mean you have all the strength you need to always make the right choices. God stands ready to lend you His strength. You can ask Him for help. There are also some effective strategies to help you deal with these situations.

Tending and Mending Fences: Strategies for Greener Grass

Throughout the rest of this chapter, I will use imagery of the greener grass. When you are thinking a lot about someone who is attractive to you, you are thinking about the grass that appears to be greener on the other side of the fence. Before we consider specific strategies for dealing with attractive alternatives, ponder this passage from the book of Malachi: "Has not the LORD made them one? In flesh and spirit they are his. And why one? Because he was seeking godly offspring. So guard yourself in your spirit, and do not break faith with the wife of your youth" (Mal. 2:15 NIV).

In this biblical chapter, God says that He hates divorce. I hasten to add that He does not say that He hates divorced people—not at all. God loves all people. But divorce was not part of God's ideal for marriage. Note the phrase "guard yourself in your spirit." There is a profound point about the importance of the inner life in protecting your marriage. The word in the Hebrew for "guard" is *shamar*. It literally means "to set a hedge of protection around something." Practically, it means "to attend to" or "be aware" of something dangerous so as to protect your marriage.

Here in the United States, we're used to seeing fairly skimpy hedges, and I mean that practically as well as metaphorically. The hedges that came to mind for the Hebrew person of Malachi's time would have been large, thick, often thorny hedges that would have been nearly impossible to get through. It was not a three-foot-high row of bushes but an obstacle substantial enough to provide real protection.

There are many ways to guard yourself in your spirit. We'll explore these strategies: understanding the biased perceptions; looking for weeds; getting away from the fence; not dwelling on the greener grass; and taking care of the lawn where you live.

IS THE GRASS GREENER OVER THE FENCE?

Let's go back to Cindy, Martin, and Frank. Cindy had become very attracted to Frank. As they became closer friends, Frank seemed to embody many traits that Cindy believed that Martin did not. Frank was patient and kind. He listened with interest. He showed concern and compassion. He was being a good friend in those respects. Frank offered a refuge to the pain and distance Cindy was feeling in her marriage. She became focused on what Frank did well that Martin either did not do so well or had not done recently. That's what happens when you are seriously thinking about the alternatives. *You become focused on the things that the alternative appears to offer, usually failing to think clearly about the things that you already have in your mate or that the alternative does not have.* Hence, perception becomes skewed when you are intensely thinking about another person.

I like to use the metaphor of a checklist to describe some of the psychology of this biased process. The criteria that are important to them in a mate make up people's lists. When people marry, whether they think about it carefully or not, they have a checklist of some sort or another, and they have decided that this person they are marrying allows them to "check off" a certain number of characteristics on that list. Even for those who are not conscious of the list, I believe they have one. Some people's lists are vague, some are specific, but we all have them.

The items on the list come from your background, your expectations, your culture, your perception of what you have to offer, and your perception of what you need. Of course, some people are only slightly aware of what they are looking for or wanting when they marry. That's why taking your time and carefully thinking through expectations are crucial prior to marriage. Coming to terms with expectations is also crucial after marriage, especially if you did not do any of this work prior to marriage. Various books can help you examine your expectations.[5] So what do you do when you are married and you are attracted to another who appears to check off more items on your list than your mate does?

At these times you will tend to see most clearly the items on your list that the alternative appears to check off. However, you will *not* likely see the items that the person would not check off. Sometimes these are things that you still have in your marriage but have lost track of because you have not protected some elements of your relationship together. For example, Cindy thought that Frank was a better friend than Martin. In fact, Martin was her best friend for years, and he remained an attentive listener. But he was not listening much to Cindy. They had let their marriage slide and lost touch with many of the positives that drew them together. And they were paying for it.

Cindy became obsessed with what she didn't think she had with Martin while ignoring the things about him that she appreciated. *Remember, the ten-*

dency to emphasize more of what we are not getting than what we have goes all the way back to Adam and Eve. In the entire wonderful garden, they were focused on the one thing that they did not have—and that looked like a pretty attractive alternative. They lost their perspective on all that they did have. We tend to focus on what we're not getting partly because the negatives in marriage and in life are more salient than the positives; they stick out more.

There was much positive in Cindy and Martin's marriage, but the negatives were in the forefront. So Cindy was not thinking much about the negatives of Frank and the positives of Martin. It would be hard to convince her of the fundamental bias in her perception, but it was there. Frank and Cindy were on their best behavior with each other. They didn't have to work out budgets, discipline kids, or clean up the kitchen together. They didn't have to do anything hard. They could just listen and talk as friends do. That felt like compatibility to them, and maybe it was. But it wasn't a fair comparison. Cindy was really more compatible with Martin, but she had gotten very out of touch with that reality.

When you can't keep your eyes off some greener grass, you'll generally be biased in your perception. You'll not get far in battling with the temptations if you don't recognize and accept this. You have to doubt your certainty that this alternative could be good for you, all things considered. Even if you cannot find anything else wrong with the other person, you can recognize the sanctity of marriage in God's sight and His call to protect your marriage from attractive alternatives.

BUT THAT GRASS REALLY IS GREEN!

Before moving on, I'd like to acknowledge that you could become attracted to someone who would be more satisfying to you than your mate. I think it more often just seems this way because of the bias, but it could happen, so let's deal with it. You may desperately want something in your marriage at this point that is not there and may never be. Perhaps it's something you'll develop later, but perhaps not. It's painful to come to this realization. If that's your situation, I think it's better to acknowledge it to yourself than to ignore its meaning. I'm not saying you should dwell on it since that will get you stuck, but if you honestly recognize these things in yourself, you can at least make wise choices about how to handle the issue. If this sounds like something you are dealing with, you are going to have grief about the loss, and dealing with grief in marriage is the focus of the next chapter.

The result of focusing on the grass that looks greener is resentment and anger. You'll think you are not getting what you think you deserve or could have elsewhere. *I could have had a better deal,* you may think. *I* deserve *to have this,* you agonize. Unchecked, this thinking will erode your dedication to your mate. You'll be moving from sticking to stuck.

PROPER LAWN EVALUATION: LOOKING FOR CRABGRASS AND WEEDS

When you are attracted to another, you are not in a position to see clearly, and you'll concentrate more on what you *don't have* than what you *do have* at home. When the grass looks greener, you can put this strategy of recognizing your biased perceptions to work for you. You can do two things to guard yourself in your spirit. First, think seriously about what's not right with the alternative. There is the obvious—you are not married and covenantally committed to the other. Also, think of all the pain that would be caused to you, your mate, your children, and others if you did not make the right choices.

You can also look for more specific negatives about the other person. Perhaps he doesn't share your views on many issues that matter, such as faith, child rearing, and lifestyle. Your mate may not share some of these key views, either, but it's worthwhile to look for the weeds in the other lawn. The weeds are there because no one is perfect, no matter how right he appears to you now. Perhaps the other person doesn't handle money well or hasn't been responsible in his marriage. You get the idea. Can you notice some things that would not be so great about this other choice? Finding the negatives doesn't mean you have to demean the person, but it will help you to gain accurate perspective and move toward appreciating what you have.

You may wonder why sorting out the negatives in the alternative can be helpful. Finding some clear negatives helps you put the attraction behind you. You won't wonder so much for some time to come about what could have been because you'll realize it wouldn't have been a rose-colored picture after all. However, this strategy is not without its risks. If you spend some time trying but can't find negatives, that realization can add to your distress. In that case, you need to move on to the other strategies discussed here. Those of you with a history of struggling with attractions will be better off pursuing all these strategies anyway. In other words, you have much at risk here, so get moving on what you can do to protect your marriage.

A second strategy is to think about the positives of your mate and your marriage. Consider more carefully the good parts of your lawn. You are very likely to have many good things together, but you can easily lose track of them when your marriage has been neglected to some degree. Think it through. What things about your mate are just right for you and your life together? You may want to pull out old photos and other memorabilia to help you remember what was good. If you are at a low point in your marriage, be extra careful not to give in to the tendency to rewrite history and convince yourself that the positives were never there in the first place.

These strategies amount to changing your focus from one that is unfair and biased to one that is more realistic. It's a simple task, but simple doesn't mean easy. It takes discipline to take control of your thoughts rather than let them control you. I believe that we choose what we will dwell on, and we can choose wisely or poorly when attracted to others.

As Cindy began to think about it more clearly, she recognized that Martin did have many of the features she wanted—not all, but many. They had lost sight of much of what was important. She realized they could get those things back with some work. She also noted that Frank had told her that his wife had left him because he worked so much and was never home. Well, that was what she was feeling with Martin. *Why would that be any different over time with Frank?* she reasoned. In that manner, she started to fight back against the thoughts about the greener grass. Her dedication gave rise to the will to do that. If she had not been as dedicated as she was, she would not have been bothered by her thoughts of Frank, and those thoughts would have, at best, led her to further resentment in her marriage.

Brad, discussed earlier in this chapter, did not fight back when he was full of thoughts about how wonderful Sharon was in contrast to Jennifer. He let the thoughts roll, and the thoughts rolled right over him. He lost his sense of reality and became resentful to the point of ruining his marriage. You can't win a battle you don't fight.

GETTING AWAY FROM THE FENCE

When you are very attracted to the grass that *looks* greener, you can always decide to get farther away from the fence. When you are hanging around the fence, it's easier to see the lawn next door. We all have to trim by the fences at times, but we don't have to hang around by them waiting to see what will happen. In other words, you can't avoid being around others of the opposite sex, and some of them may be attractive to you or attracted to you. However, you don't have to linger any longer than necessary around those you may have trouble with.

There are a variety of ways to move away from the fence. It may not be reasonable or possible to completely remove yourself from the presence of an attractive alternative. Take Cindy, Martin, and Frank, for instance. To move completely away from Frank, Cindy would have to find another job. If her attraction to Frank was so serious that she could not resist the temptations, she would be wise to do exactly that. On the other hand, doing that prematurely might leave her with a permanent image of Frank as perfect and Martin as defective. If she could, working through her issues while continuing to work with Frank would be a more powerful approach.

This is a matter for great discernment. If Cindy is going to give in to temptations with Frank or grow in her resentment of Martin by being near Frank over the long term, she should move on. Otherwise, working it through to see what's not so perfect about Frank while strengthening what she has with Martin might be better. If you are in such a situation, you would be wise to get the help of a confidential friend to sort out what you are doing and why. There is plenty of room for self-deception, so be careful.

Let's suppose that Cindy decides to continue working with Frank. There are many ways to move away from the fence without leaving the situation completely. For example, Cindy can put a fence around certain topics—things she will not talk about with Frank. Talking with Frank about ways she is unhappy with Martin will be unwise. That not only will violate a boundary in their marriage, but also will amount to her sharing personally painful subjects with an attractive alternative. I have talked with many clients in my office who had an affair that began in this way. You cannot regularly share the most painful things of your soul with an attractive alternative and avoid developing deeper levels of intimacy. Resist that.

Frank and Cindy might be able to talk about many things that do not put added pressure on her commitment to Martin. Of course, they need to talk about work. Maybe they can talk about politics, sports, or fun vacations. That's all friend stuff, but it's not sharing the more painful parts, which often forges deeper intimacy that can grow to be a problem. Most important, if you are dealing with this, honestly consider what kinds of sharing add to *your* temptation.

I counseled a man who was very attracted to a woman he met at the gym. They were distracted from their workouts by talking to each other. Quite a friendship grew from their talks. That didn't seem to be nearly as much of a problem for him as when they actually worked out together. Doing aerobics together or lifting weights together really got to him. Upon thinking more about it, he was able to see that while he and his wife talked quite a bit, she had never been interested in working out the way that he did. It had become a source of deep resentment for him. He wanted her to do those things with him, but she was not interested. That the other woman liked to talk was not a big deal for him. That she liked to work out with him was a really big deal. He learned firsthand that it was more threatening to his marriage to work out with the other woman than to talk to her. He decided he needed to plan his workouts so that they would not have time to work out together. He could still say "hi" in the going and coming, but he *planned* for them not to be together in the way that caused him the most trouble. You have to pay attention to yourself in terms of what is threatening to your marriage. If you are honest, you can learn a lot about yourself and avoid much unnecessary pain. If you are not honest, and you have no trusted friends you'll talk with, you may end up in a heap of trouble.

Another way to get away from the fence is to decrease the amount of time spent together. Frank and Cindy have to work together a certain number of hours. They do not have to spend time together apart from work. Stopping for coffee on the way home from work, for instance, would be unnecessary and could only invite trouble.

CHOOSING NOT TO DWELL ON THE GREENER GRASS

The apostle Paul offered an interesting observation about sin and lust that is useful for our discussion here: "Therefore do not let sin reign in your mortal body, that you should obey it in its lusts" (Rom. 6:12 NKJV).

Most people will feel intense desires in life. Many of these desires will be good and right. Many will be temptations to fail in your major commitments. Sometimes these desires can be for partners outside marriage. Although having attractions to others from time to time is likely, the key is the degree to which you act on such attractions. As we have just discussed, you can act on these attractions internally in ways that can damage your marriage. For example, to *obey* some of these intense desires would mean to dwell on them, to give place to them, and to let them negatively impact your marriage. In Paul's words, to let sin *reign*.

The bottom line is that if you have these thoughts, you can decide not to allow them a comfortable home. It's really up to you what happens when you deal with these dynamics. It takes commitment and willpower to make the right choice. Either your will bends to your commitment, or your commitment bends to what you covet. You choose which path you take. To go back to the biblical words, *coveting* and *lust* do not refer only to being attracted to others, but suggest that one has allowed certain thoughts (or images or actions) to take up residence. When you regularly give in to these attractions in your mind, you allow destructive guests to be welcome in your home. That is most dangerous—having what-ifs that you do not choose to challenge, either in your mind or in your actions. *Guard yourself in your spirit, and do not let thoughts of alternatives reign in your mind.*

WHERE ARE YOU?

If you are not attracted to or thinking a lot about someone else at this time, work at keeping things that way. Watch the fences. Remain aware of how much you are thinking about others. The earlier your warning lights flash, the better.

If you are dealing with an attraction to an alternative right now, you should consider forcefully pursuing the strategies here. If the other person does not know of the attraction, you can do much without that person finding out that you are dealing with any issues about him or her. You can watch what you talk about, where you go, and what you do together. You can ask a good friend to help you plan how to be careful. I can't think up all the possibilities, but I can suggest that it's wise for you to do this. Take the time to consider what will help. That's an act of dedication.

If your attraction is out in the open between you and the other, you can consider and do all that has been suggested so far. These strategies are the same whether or not the other knows you are struggling somewhat with attraction to him or her. When it is out in the open, you may choose to take the extra step of being overt about what you are doing. For example, Cindy could say something like this to Frank: "I know that we are both dealing with some attraction here. I want to let you know that while I do find you attractive, I plan to protect my commitment to Martin. That means I have to pull back on some of the talks we've been having. I also need to pull back on some of the time we've been spending together. I enjoy it, but it's not good for my marriage. Really, I'm talking about keeping the boundaries clearer so I can protect my marriage. Please help me to do this."

It may not be wise to let another know you are attracted just to make this point. That could depend on how obvious your attraction is. In general, this open strategy makes the most sense when it's already totally clear that something is going on between you and another. In that case, you are making a very strong statement about protecting your marriage, and asking the person to help you honor that intention. Most people can respond appropriately to commitment stated so openly.

Occasionally, someone may not respond so well. That is, the person may not respond in a helpful way. In fact, some people may find you all the more attractive if you set your fences clearly. They may pursue you because they like the challenge of going over fences. When that's the case, you'll probably lose respect for the other person, and that may turn out to help you. Just don't let up on the fence on your side. If someone really pushes at your boundaries *and* you are tempted to pull the fence down, you'll have to get away from the person or risk ruining your marriage. It's your choice, but it's a big one. And there is a right and a wrong to these choices!

LAWN CARE 101

If you take really good care of the lawn where you live, the odds go down that you'll have to deal with being attracted to alternatives. That's because your marriage will stay much more rewarding, and most people are less aware of alternatives when they're happy at home. *It's not enough to have a fence around your lawn that protects it from the outside. You have to work within the fence to make the lawn green and lush.*

If you're attracted to someone in particular, this strategy is all the more important. You can use your feelings of attraction to another to your advantage if you are wise about it. Consider what your attraction to the other means for your marriage. What is it telling you about your marriage that you are so attracted to this alternative? What does the person seem to have that you want so badly right now? Is it really something you could not have at home? Is it something you used to have in your marriage that you've let slip away? As I noted, Cindy and Martin used to talk very well as friends. That's a big thing lacking right now in their marriage, but they are quite capable of having it together again. Perhaps she perceives Frank as being much more passionate than Martin could ever be. She could be misjudging this trait, or she could be correct; either way, it's something that she and Martin used to have much more of in their marriage. That can come back when two people work on it together. I've seen it happen over and over again. The spouses don't even have to have a lot of faith that they can rejuvenate their marriage. God can bless faith as small as a mustard seed when it's faith that acts.

To fully protect your commitment in your marriage, you need to consistently nurture your lawn. Water it; fertilize it; rake it; trim it carefully; pull some weeds. Most lawns (I admit, not all) respond well to tender love and care. There's often much life left in even the deadest-looking lawns. But you have to bring it out. And that takes us back once again to choices and priorities. If you are not consistently sanctifying time for fun, friendship, spiritual connection, physical intimacy, and other things that bond the two of you together, you're not taking care of your lawn as well as you could.

When Nancy and I bought our home, the lawn had been well cared for by the previous owner. We didn't have to exert much effort to keep it looking good. That's a lot like marriage for many of us. Early on, the lawn seems to do really well without having to work hard at it. That's a blessing of the early stages of marriage for most people. Over the years, it requires more effort to keep it looking the way it once did. That takes more time than it used to take. But it's time well spent.

A fulfilling marriage is not dropped in your lap from heaven. It is more often tended like a beautiful garden. It won't be perfect, no matter what you do. We live in a difficult and fallen world. Because of that, the things that matter most require protection. We all have these same challenges in our marriages. In the last chapter, I emphasized the importance of priorities in marriage and life. Keeping your marriage strong and growing takes time and attention—it takes making your marriage a priority.

Some Final Thoughts on Hedges and Fences

I have used the image of fences in this chapter because it fits in so nicely with the "grass is greener" metaphor. Before we move on to grief and commitment, think more about the biblical idea of setting a hedge of protection around your marriage. The nice thing about a hedge is that, while it functions like a fence, a hedge is a growing, living thing. A hedge is not a passive structure that you set and forget. You tend to a hedge. You water it. You trim it or let it grow larger in some areas for a reason. It's alive, and it can respond to the needs of the yard that it protects. I want to leave you with that powerful image. You need boundaries around your marriage that protect it and that are responsive to the current situation of your lives together. When you are tending the hedge, you are protecting your marriage as an active outgrowth of your dedication. You are sticking, not planning on getting stuck.

Point of Application

This chapter has covered the crucial issue of protecting your commitment to your mate from other attractions and temptations in life.

- At this time in your life, are you seriously attracted to anyone other than your mate? How "available" is this person? How much of a threat do you perceive this attraction to be?
- If you are attracted to another, do the work suggested here by taking a hard look at your biased perceptions. If this attraction is a serious threat to your marriage, get with a close friend whom you can trust to challenge you to build and maintain your commitment. You might also read carefully Proverbs 2–10 about staying on the right path in life. There are many very hard-hitting verses in these chapters regarding temptation. (And I recommend you apply the points about men and women equally to men *and* women *alike*.)
- Whether or not you are attracted to anyone else at this point in your life, what steps can you take to keep the hedges around your marriage strong and vibrant?

The Threat of Attractive Alternatives

To love at all is to be vulnerable. Love anything and your heart will certainly be wrung and possibly broken. If you want to make sure of keeping it intact, you must give your heart to no one, not even an animal. Wrap it carefully round with hobbies and little luxuries; avoid all entanglements; lock it up safe in the casket or coffin of your selfishness. But in that casket— safe, dark, motionless, airless—it will change. It will not be broken; it will become unbreakable, impenetrable, irredeemable.

—C. S. Lewis

Chapter 4

GRIEVING OVER THE LOSSES THAT COME WITH COMMITMENT

Hope deferred makes the heart sick,
but a longing fulfilled is a tree of life.
—Proverbs 13:12 NIV

On the day we marry, most of us believe we are gaining a best friend for life. Most of us are aware of gaining a lot on that special day. It would be far less typical to be thinking about what we might be giving up. For example, you probably committed to forsake all others, but when you got married, you probably had no "others" in mind. You didn't feel that you were giving up much of anything. Since so much of life together is ahead of you when you get married, it's nearly impossible to fully comprehend what will be forsaken when you say, "I do." I'm not saying that you can't make a full commitment on the wedding day, but you can't know all of what your commitment will mean to you in the years to come. Commitment does ask you to give up some things in life.

Even in a great marriage, you can become aware that your marriage is not *everything* you had hoped it would be. Maybe you've found your marriage falling short of your dreams, or perhaps you've found yourself face-to-face with an attractive alternative. When that happens, you'll likely have a sense of having lost something either that you really wanted or that you think you might have wanted. This realization can hit like a blast of cold air that takes your breath away, or it can feel more like a slow leak, leaving you feeling drained and flat. Being committed hurts at times. I think an occasional (or chronic, for some) sense of loss is a fundamental element of committing your life to one person. While some people seem to be deliriously happy together over many years, most people can identify in some way a sense of loss from time to time, even though they may not talk about it with anyone.

This chapter is about dealing with feelings of loss when they come up so that you can stick and not get stuck. These are the times when you fully realize what it means to be a committed person. Here's one couple's story.

This Is Not What I Had Planned On!

It was after midnight as Nicole paced up and down the hallway outside her bedroom. Her husband, Eric, and their two kids were fast asleep. Listening to the quiet, Nicole felt terribly alone. *At least no one is asking me to explain what is wrong,* she thought. She couldn't quite put her finger on the feelings. While everything was fine, she really felt that nothing was fine. She felt sadness and loss. She kept thinking, *How could he be so different now from when we met?* Those thoughts had been coming more frequently over the last few months. As she paced, a key thought took root: *It's not that I have a bad marriage, but what we have is just not quite what I wanted or expected.*

Nicole was grieving the loss of her dream, but she had not yet recognized that was what she was feeling. She loved Eric dearly, but she realized that he was a different person from the one she thought she'd married. She recalled the early days, trying to think through where she had misunderstood what life with Eric would be like. They met when they were seniors in college. Both had belonged to a Great Books discussion group on campus. They came to know each other through sharing their ideas. As they shared more, their attraction grew.

Dating had been a wonderful time of discovery for Nicole and Eric. The discoveries included both their similarities and their differences. They were thrilled to find that they had a similar Christian faith and church background. The discovery that they both liked to be physically active further encouraged their sense of compatibility. Nicole loved aerobics and Eric was an avid runner. They were surprised that they did not have the same political views but were delighted that it was so much fun to explore those differences. Even when they disagreed, it was fun to talk things out. They loved the similarities and they loved the differences. Throughout that year, Nicole and Eric made many discoveries, including the fact that they were in love with each other. Thoughts of marriage followed.

One aspect that Nicole especially loved about Eric was that he had plans for his future. She had plans, too, but it was particularly important to her that he knew where he wanted to go in life. Eric planned on a career in public relations. He loved to write and plan, and he figured that public relations would allow him to get paid for doing something that he loved. She planned on a career in counseling. That sounded great to him, and he really loved how engaging she was when they talked. He never felt more attracted to her than when they talked at length about something philosophical or theological. They could sit around having coffee and talk for days, it seemed.

Now, twelve years later, Nicole was pacing late at night. They had been married eleven years and had two beautiful children, Taylor, who was eight, and Briana who was five and a half (Briana insisted on adding the "half"). Nicole and Eric felt good that they had provided a solid, spiritually oriented home for their children. The kids were doing very well. Nicole and Eric had a decent marriage, for the most part. They were kind to each other and treated each other with respect. But neither was experiencing much joy in the marriage. Much of the closeness that they had felt when dating was no longer there. They were not so much connected as moving along parallel lines. They were not moving farther apart, but they were not getting closer, either, and both knew it.

Nicole realized with each passing year that she had become more disillusioned with her marriage. Eric was not turning out to be who she thought he'd be. While she was happy with the work she was doing at a community mental health center, he had struggled with his work. He had finished college with a degree in writing and public relations, but he'd never found a very good job in the field. Eleven years into his career, he was employed in the same job he had accepted right out of school: working in the public relations department of a company that made tires. Although

Nicole appreciated that Eric held a steady job, it was relatively low-paid work that didn't offer him opportunities for advancement or intellectual stimulation. That showed too. He was not at all interested in what he did eight hours a day, and it seemed to be sapping the life out of him. From Nicole's perspective, the worst part was that none of this seemed to bother Eric—he had given up.

On the positive side, Eric was around the house more than many of her friends' husbands. "At least he's home," Nicole would console herself. However, as Eric's despair grew, he became far more interested in watching sports on TV than either had ever imagined possible. Nicole became a football widow (not to mention baseball, basketball, hockey, and power badminton). The remote control seemed to be permanently attached to his hand. "He certainly is good at that," she noticed.

Eric was no longer running, and he was gaining weight from sitting around all the time eating chips and drinking beer. She wondered if he was depressed, but he denied it when she asked. Nicole could not see any ways in which he was all that sad. Since she worked in mental health, she could tell that he had few symptoms of depression. That puzzled her, perhaps because she knew her feelings were running that direction at times. He had become more passive and unmotivated than she had thought he would be. The person Eric was becoming was not someone to whom Nicole was very attracted.

Nicole was losing respect for her husband. She was ashamed to have those feelings too. She loved him, but she didn't like a lot about him at that point in their life together. Her feelings of loss and loneliness grew daily. She noticed that she felt the way she did when her father died, and that puzzled her. *No one's dying here,* she thought. Then the thought stunned her: *My dreams for this marriage are dying.* The thought scared her. Worse, because of shame about her feelings, she was reluctant to talk to anyone about her feelings. "Until death do us part" seemed like a long, lonely time.

For his part, Eric had been aware that his work was pulling him down for some time, but it was much less painful to accept the situation and quit trying to change it. He couldn't think of anything he could do to make his work more meaningful or to advance. He had prayed about it, but he felt that God had let him down, so he quit praying. There was plenty of football and baseball to get interested in. *Life is really not so bad,* he'd think. Both Eric and Nicole were gaining an awareness that Eric might be much more passive about life than either had thought. Whether or not he was really that way deep inside was beside the point. He was living that way, and Nicole didn't like it.

Eric was also grieving over his marriage in his own way. Although he had initially loved talking to Nicole about anything, they never talked that way anymore. All they talked about were problems with money and problems with the kids. It was too threatening to talk about problems between them. As he thought more about it, he began to believe that she had deceived him while they were dating. "I don't think she was really all that interested in talking about things that interest me," he'd say to himself. After all, they no longer talked about politics, philosophy, or religion and faith. They went to church together and read Bible stories to their children, but they never talked together about deeper things anymore.

Note how easy it was for Eric to think Nicole had deceived him while totally failing to notice the ways he was no longer the same guy she had dated. While Eric was thinking that Nicole was not interested, she was thinking that he had become a pretty boring person. Both stopped trying to talk about anything beyond the necessities.

For Eric and Nicole, what had started as a marriage with promise had become something more painful. Neither, especially Nicole, was happy with who the other had become. Both also believed in unconditional love—sacrificial love—and in so believing, each felt a sense of shame at knowing they were having trouble completely accepting who they had married. They were on the way to being stuck, not sticking. What each was experiencing might be called many things. I call it grief because both felt sad about something that was lost—or that seemed to be lost.

COMMITMENT AND LOSS

As I plow into what may be the most difficult and sensitive chapter in this book, I want to make one thing very clear. I believe that people who live out their commitments generally end up with far richer lives and relationships because of it. In other words, the gains of commitment far outweigh the losses that come from making—and sticking with—choices. However, the portrayal of commitment is not complete without discussing the losses that can come with making choices.

It is inevitable to have times in marriage when you will become aware of what you do not have. These may be things you once had or things you only *thought* you had. I think that even if your marriage were almost perfect, what you want may change enough to cause you to feel a sense of loss. For some of you who are reading this, the sense of loss may be deep and chronic. Just as with anything else, some people experience this a lot, and some a little or not at all.

When you are feeling the loss of something in your marriage, it may seem that the feelings are too big or tangled to work through them productively. You have five options:

Option One: Stop (quit).
Option Two: Become stuck.
Option Three: Change your expectations.
Option Four: Change the situation.
Option Five: Actively grieve for losses.

Since this book is about sticking and not getting stuck or stopping, I will focus on the latter three strategies. If you were not committed, you might be tempted to leave your mate and find someone who seems to offer you what you now feel as a loss. Many people leave one spouse only to find that they have exchanged one set of gains and losses for another. However, it would not be honest to ignore the fact that some people leave a mate and find someone with whom they are happier. Still, that's not our focus here. We're also not focusing on becoming stuck and demoralized in marriage. We're talking about commitment that sticks. Productive grieving can help you stay on the right path.

While I will discuss the three choices as separate strategies, there are times when you'll end up doing all three. Here's the way I suggest you approach these issues. First, identify your expectation that is not being met. Second, determine if it's reasonable or not. If it's a reasonable expectation, work for changes in you and your marriage to bring it about (change the situation). If it's reasonable but it's not something that's likely to change, work on the grief model (actively grieve for losses).

If you have an unreasonable expectation that you feel loss about, work to change the expectation to something more reasonable (change your expectations). Some expectations can easily change upon closer examination and thought. Some don't change easily, even if you fully recognize them as unreasonable. Either way, you may need to work productively with your grief, since you can feel a loss whether or not the expectation is reasonable.

There are variations on all of these themes. It is easier to discuss the key points if we keep them separate for now, but real life is not as neat as a book outline.

Expectations and Loss

In addition to conducting research on marriage at the University of Denver, I have counseled hundreds of couples in my office and in workshops, so I hear directly from many people about concerns in their marriages. People have longed for the following:

- A more financially responsible mate
- A more emotionally sensitive mate
- A more athletic mate
- A more (or less) sexually responsive mate
- A more active parent in a mate
- A more musically sensitive mate
- A more physically attractive mate
- A more spiritually active or sensitive mate
- A more effective housekeeper
- A better listener
- A less emotionally volatile mate
- A more emotionally expressive mate
- A mate who shares specific interests
- A mate who shares more tasks around the home
- A mate who loves to go out on the town

- A mate who loves to stay at home
- A mate who is more protective
- A mate who is more encouraging of talents
- A mate who is handier around the home
- A mate who makes more money
- A mate who works less (or more)
- A mate who . . . well, you get the idea

This list reflects the kinds of things people expect in marriage. When people do not get what they expected, they are disappointed. As the writer of Proverbs said, "Hope deferred makes the heart sick, but a longing fulfilled is a tree of life" (13:12 NIV).

The Hebrew word for "hope" in this text is *towcheleth,* and it means "expectation." The Hebrew word for "sick" is *chalah,* which has the root meaning of "rubbed" or "worn"—by implication, "grieved," "pained," or "made sick." To put it simply, unmet or delayed expectations and longings grieve the heart. They rub at it; they wear it down. Can you think of a time in your life when something you longed for did not happen, and consequently, you felt grief over the loss? How about something that you really wish was in your marriage but is not—not at this time or perhaps not ever?

MANAGING EXPECTATIONS

We all have expectations for life, including expectations for our mates, our families, our work, and nearly everything else. Some expectations are very specific, but others are not; we are aware of some of our expectations, but we are not aware of others. Though expectations are not the primary focus of this book, expectations are a significant topic with regard to grief and commitment. If you would like to further examine your expectations and how to handle them in your marriage, I encourage you to pick up one of the many books available to help you.[1]

In marriage, expectations affect everything. You probably have expectations for who does what around the home, whose work outside the home is more crucial, how children should be raised, ways you'll be physically intimate, what closeness means in your marriage, how you'll make decisions, and on and on. *The losses you feel in your marriage will be made up of the difference between what you expected and what you have.* When what you expect is, for the most part, not going to happen, it's a cause for sadness and grief. Expectations can be reasonable or unreasonable, but that doesn't matter to feelings. Even if you expect the unreasonable, you'll feel a sense of loss. It's important to think about what's reasonable and what's not. It's also very important to talk with your mate about what you expect. One of the most unreasonable expectations of all is that your mate will know what you expect without your having to say anything.

Both Eric and Nicole were grieving over the loss of what had been a great part of their friendship—the ability to talk about a variety of interesting topics. Their expectations were based on their dating relationship and the deeper desires of their hearts. Sure, they had let something slip away, but there was nothing wrong with the expectation that they would continue to have great talks from time to time. We'll look more at what they could do about this in the next section on changing the situation.

Nicole also felt loss about Eric's being far more passive than she *expected* he would be. He might not be able to change it much, and if he could, he might not be willing to at this time. In other words, what she had expected about Eric might not be reasonable in light of who he had become at that point in their lives. If so, Nicole needs to grieve over Eric's present passivity. Of course, something can be lost at a particular point in time but not lost forever. People do change. You don't know the future until you get there, do you? Nicole strongly suspects that Eric will be more passive than she expected, throughout the rest of their lives together. But she does not know that for certain.

If Nicole changes her expectation about Eric, her sense of loss will be lessened. If Nicole adjusts what she expects of Eric, she will be less disappointed, but that's not the whole of it. Changing the expectation also involves grieving, since she is giving up something that had been part of her vision for their marriage. At other times, changing an expectation does not so directly involve grieving. For example, if you had expected that your marriage would be free of conflict, and you now find that it's not, you would be wise to conclude that your original expectation was unreasonable. You could grieve over that, but it's an expectation that can go away once you see how unrealistic it was. It's easier to give up expectations when you realize (accurately) that things are not much different in any other marriage. If all couples have similar struggles, and you come to understand that, you can reorient your expectation in line with the realities of life. Life is turbulent at times (see John 16:33 if you want to read Jesus' opinion on this).

CHANGING THE SITUATION

Before we delve into grieving, let's consider what you may be able to do to attempt changes when they seem possible.

CHANGING WHAT *YOU* DO

Most of us look in the wrong place when we want change in our marriages. I'll bet you've heard the story of the man out on the street late at night, bending over looking for something under the street lamp. A stranger comes up, offers to help, and says, "What did you lose?" The hunched-over man says, "I lost my car keys." "Did you? Right in here somewhere?" the good Samaritan asks. The first man replies, "Why, no, I lost them over there, but the light is better here." Before looking for what's missing in your mate, try putting yourself under the lamp and taking a good look.

The most productive move you can make when you are not pleased with the way your marriage is going is to change yourself. Instead, most of us have a tendency to want—even demand—change from our mates. After all, it's so easy to dwell on how the other is failing. Please consider two passages from the Bible. Here is the first: "If it is possible, as much as depends on you, live peaceably with all men" (Rom. 12:18 NKJV).

This is a profound verse. *First,* Paul said, "If it is possible." Some things in relationships are not possible. It's not always possible to have a relationship, especially marriage, be just the way you want it to be, even when what you want is good and right. *Second,* Paul said, "As much as depends on you." You are responsible only for the part that depends on you. You can't control the other people in your life. You can't make your mate into your ideal woman or man. You can pray that God makes the person into *His* ideal, though. It takes a bit of humility to accept your limitations, but you know it's true. *Third,* Paul said, "Live peaceably with all men." The end goal in our relationships is peace and harmony. Does what you do in your marriage usually promote peace or strife? Much strife is generated when one spouse tries to force the other to make a change.

Let's go back to Nicole and Eric for a few thoughts. Neither can really make the other do anything. Nicole cannot drag Eric away from the television. She cannot make him be more active about his work. She cannot force him to take better care of himself physically. She can decide to take better care of herself, though. Perhaps he will become more interested in physical fitness again if she sets an example. Eric cannot force Nicole to take the time to have the kinds of talks that they used to love. He can decide to start reading good books again. If he misses having those discussions with Nicole, he can first show himself and her that he is still interested in reading great books and talking about issues and ideas. It's not reasonable for him to expect Nicole to be interested in doing that with him when Nicole sees only that he is interested in watching the games on television.

As I said, it's so easy to focus on what your mate is not doing that you don't think enough about what you could be doing to develop your marriage. Jesus spoke forcefully about this tendency to become focused on others. This is the second passage of the two that I want you to think hard about on this subject:

> *Why do you look at the speck in your brother's eye, but do not perceive the plank in your own eye? Or how can you say to your brother, "Brother, let me remove the speck that is in your eye," when you yourself do not see the plank that is in your own eye? Hypocrite! First remove the plank from your own eye, and then you will see clearly to remove the speck that is in your brother's eye. (Luke 6:41–42 NKJV)*

Jesus urged you to "first remove the plank from your own eye" before trying to do anything about changing the other. What specks are you focused on in the life of your mate? What planks are you missing in your life? Go for the planks.

CHANGING WHAT YOU DO *TOGETHER*

Eric and Nicole could best change some things if they worked together. They could recapture the connection they had gained from talking about interesting topics. Both were still capable of that. A change would involve one or the other daring to speak up, and that means taking a risk. The risk comes from admitting gently but openly that one has a deep desire for something that is not happening. It's not wise to grieve about a loss when it's a loss that you don't have to accept. There is nothing wrong with what Eric and Nicole expect in this area. They had merely stopped setting apart time for such things, and they were paying a price for it.

You can work together to change the way things are in your marriage. If your mate is not the way you wish he or she was, you can talk about it and work to see what can be done to make your marriage more mutually satisfying. It takes trust to have such a talk and teamwork to see what can change to make your marriage more fulfilling. (Many strategies that can help you make such changes will be presented in Chapter 6.)

Working together as a team in your marriage is a powerful asset to bring to a discussion of changes you'd like to see happen. Eric and Nicole do not have this kind of oneness going for them at the point where we left them earlier. They are doing fair in many ways, but they do not have a sense of teamwork. Each is feeling quite alone with a sense of loss. Without being more connected, trying to make changes happen as a couple is not likely.

If either of them wants to try changing as a couple, the starting point is for one to come to the other and ask for help. This is best done with humility and gentleness, not angry demandingness. For example, Nicole could choose a quiet moment to say to Eric something like this: "I've been thinking about how things are going for us. I think we are far more distant from each other than is good for our marriage. I have missed being close to you and wonder if you miss that too."

Or Eric could say, "Nicole, I've been thinking about how our life together is going. I think we've lost something we once had. We used to talk so much about things that drew us together. I realize that I've been pretty distant for some time, and I'd like to try to change that. I'd like to see if we could get back on track."

Note the liberal use of the words *we* and *us* in these statements. For either to start a conversation with the other in this manner would be ideal; there is no sense of blame or hostility. That gives the most room possible for the other to respond positively and to develop a sense of being a team, looking together at what can be done to rebuild their relationship. Contrast that with statements that are all too common:

- "Why can't you get off your behind and do something with your life?"
- "You are such a negative person. Who'd want to talk to you about anything?"
- "You're so lazy. Look at what's happening to your body. You have a beer gut, for goodness sake."
- "You know, I used to think that you were an interesting person to talk to. I was wrong. You are very boring."

You get the idea. These statements do not bring you closer to what you want. They amount to questioning the character of the other. They also portray a pessimistic view of what's possible in the marriage. These statements do not promote peace. No one opens up and wants to work with his mate if he is on the receiving end of such comments.

Let's suppose that Eric and Nicole draw together to bring about changes. They can resume talking together about fun and interesting things. They'll need to make that a priority and set apart the time to make it happen. They can do it. They've only misplaced, not lost, their ability to talk on these personal levels. They can also resume working out together. All kinds of good things could come out of feeling better physically. None of this should be taken to mean that the changes would be easy to make or that they could happen overnight. They will find obstacles in their way. For one thing, they are far busier than they used to be. Making time for conversation or working out together will be harder now—with kids' schedules, work, household tasks, and so forth—compared to when they were in college. But they can make the changes if they put their minds to it. One of the most powerful things they could do *together* would be to pray about these issues.

Let's suppose that one major problem area cannot really change: Eric's passivity about his work situation. Of course, it could change, but let's assume that it's not likely to change at this point. Since this is important to Nicole, she is going to have to deal with the reality of the situation. She can examine why it's important. Perhaps she sees their economic future as more dependent on Eric than on herself. Perhaps finances are not the issue at all. Maybe she has trouble respecting someone who just lets life happen. Nicole could decide that what she expects is not realistic with Eric—and that may help some—but she is still going to be left to grieve about the loss. Let's explore active, productive grieving in marriage.

Grieving: What It Is Not

The word *grief* usually refers to painful feelings associated with a loss that we cannot replace, no matter what we do. For example, most of us grieve when there is the death of a loved one because we cannot do anything to reverse the loss. Some of you who are reading this may be thinking that you have no grief over losses of any sort in your marriage at this point. That's terrific! However, please read on since some of the ideas in the rest of this chapter may be helpful to you in the future.

For what follows, I define grieving as the active process of working through feelings of loss in ways that are consistent with one's integrity and commitments, and in ways that promote healing of the soul. Before we go farther, I want to suggest what grieving is not.

FLOATING DOWN DA NILE

You've probably heard the joke: "Denial is not a river in Egypt." Clever line. Denial is different from grieving, and it is a very real option when dealing with the pain of unmet expectations. When you live in denial, you push out of your awareness painful memories, feelings, or thoughts—and do so in a way that usually fails to acknowledge the pain. When you grieve, you acknowledge the pain you feel, and more important, you do something to work through it. Denial is passively floating down a river of pain while not acknowledging that the pain is there. Grieving involves setting a course and paddling through to it. It's active. You take note of the currents and the rapids, and you set your mind to get to a place that's consistent with your commitment and integrity.

I worked with a couple who argued over everything, for example, the way the toilet paper should go on the holder. If you struggle over this, try what works for Nancy and me. We think toilet paper was meant to go vertically on the countertop. More efficient. Mike and Deanne also argued about what brand of paper towels to buy or about whether the kids should clean up their rooms before or after dinner. Major stuff, right? They had so many petty arguments that it did not take long before I presumed that deeper things were wrong. You can't argue intensely about stuff that doesn't matter unless something that does matter is behind it.

They were chronically irritated with each other about various silly things. It took a while, but as the trust in each other grew, I could hear anguish about loneliness, distance, and failed dreams. Both were deeply disappointed that their marriage had not turned out as expected. Mike and Deanne had difficulty talking about their pain.

Usually, such conversations do not happen well unless there is some real emotional safety. For most couples, it's anything but safe to talk about deep pains associated with deeper desires and losses. For many people, it's not okay to look at what the pain is about. That's a form of denial. Maybe the pain will go away if you don't look right at it.

The problem is that such deep anguish tends to leak out in other ways. For Mike and Deanne, it leaked out in silly arguments. The deeper wounds fed the conflicts for them. Denial didn't work well for them, and it probably won't for you.

When you engage in denial, you fail to acknowledge what you feel. You don't allow yourself to notice it, or you distract yourself with other things. Therefore, you cannot actively work on it. That means denial can push the feelings to come up in other ways, such as distance or hostility in your marriage. In contrast, when you keep yourself from dwelling on certain thoughts or feelings, you accept that the thoughts are there, but that you will treat them in ways that honor your commitment to your spouse. That's being active and taking control over your thoughts and feelings.

GRIEF VERSUS DESPAIR

Whereas grieving is a process of actively feeling and dealing with a loss, despair implies a complete loss of hope. Despair is the end result of a growing sense of futility—the belief that nothing constructive can be done with your circumstance. Therefore, despairing is *passive*, and grieving is *active*. Grieving is something you actively engage in and learn from. Grieving improves you. Despair grinds you into hopelessness.

In marriage, a sense of despair would most likely come from a combination of three factors: (1) a sense that things are miserable; (2) a sense that things cannot change; and (3) a sense that the suffering involved is meaningless (i.e., that it is not good for anything, including spiritual growth).

Consider Eric's situation with his work. He has fallen into despair. He may not be clinically depressed, but he has given up. He no longer thinks about what he might do to improve his work situation. Nicole is seriously affected by his despair. In fact, despair is infectious in a marriage. If each falls into a long-term pattern of despair—about his work, about life, about their marriage—they will truly be stuck. Their marriage will grow colder and colder until all life is frozen for them in it.

Here's the story of another couple who underwent a terrible loss, but didn't give in to despair. Betsy and Samuel had been married twenty-seven years. The last of their three children had just left home to live on her own. Sam had worked for a parcel delivery service for more than twenty years, and Betsy ran her own bookkeeping business. They had done well over the years. They were happily married, had remained close friends, and were involved in all kinds of activities. They had managed their money well. With the children launched, and money being ample, they had looked forward to traveling more at this new phase of their life together. They had plans for trips to take in the future. They could see many years ahead of sharing their desire to see parts of the world.

Two months after their youngest moved out, Sam left for work on Monday at 5:00 A.M., just as he had done for many years. Betsy kissed him good-bye, as she had done on thousands of mornings. Neither knew that the events of the day would change the rest of their lives. Betsy didn't have to leave for work, since she did her bookkeeping for her clients from her home office. But she did have to get some things for her business from the office supply store. She showered, dressed, and headed off. As Betsy was driving to the store, she went through a green light at a major intersection. She never saw the eighteen-wheeler coming from the right, with its brakes out, at fifty miles per hour. If it had been on the left, Betsy wouldn't have lived. As it was, the truck demolished her car and her body, but she wasn't killed.

Betsy was so severely injured that Sam didn't recognize her when the doctors finally allowed him to see her. She was badly bruised and swollen. Her pelvis, shoulder, and back were broken. She lay unconscious for days, and Sam never left her side. She remained in the hospital for three months and had unending physical therapy following that. One year later, Sam's and Betsy's lives were still turned upside down. Betsy had made excellent progress, but she was racked with chronic pain. The doctors told her that they had done all they could do with conventional medicine, but the pain remained. She began to try a variety of less-conventional healing strategies, but nothing worked all that well. Her constant and tremendous pain limited her movement, affected her concentration, and made it hard for her to enjoy life.

The losses began to pile up. Not only did Betsy lose the ability to get up every day without pain, but she could no longer work. There was no way she could concentrate with either the pain or the pain medications. Sam never openly complained, but he certainly experienced a tremendous amount of stress. It was hard for him to see his wife suffer, and he had all the extra financial concerns and everyday, routine tasks to take care of without the help of his lifelong partner. And they missed just being "normal." One of the most painful losses for both Betsy and Sam was that Betsy could no longer endure making love. Something about intense physical experiences made the pain far worse.

Their losses were multiple and great. Their friends prayed for them regularly. Their church helped them in many ways to get through all the disruption of their lives. They had a good settlement from the insurance company. But life would never be the same again for Sam and Betsy.

They started to talk openly about how the accident had changed their life together. It changed their present, and it changed their future. They wouldn't be able to travel and otherwise enjoy some of the activities they had looked forward to. Their dreams had to change and were, in many ways, limited by the effects of the accident. It was an irreversible loss. There was no way short of a miracle that their lives could go back to the way they were.

They were in agony, but they were in agony together. Ironically, there was joy in that aspect of it. Betsy and Sam had commitment that remained strong and vibrant throughout their ordeal. There was no question in Sam's mind about whether he would stick with Betsy despite the changes. He did not feel stuck, but he did feel a horrible sense of loss. So did Betsy. But they did not give in to despair. They fought, hung together, and grew closer.

When such a loss occurs, it's obvious that a grief model is appropriate. The accident and the fact of the chronic disability were nonnegotiable.

They had to accept some loss. The loss with Betsy is one that Sam chooses to endure by remaining committed to Betsy. But because their future is affected entirely by this loss they must grieve for what they have to give up. They must adjust their dreams, but they don't have to give in to despair.

Life works this way. Things don't turn out the way you expect them to, and sometimes in dramatic ways. Committed couples hunker down and plow along in their commitment. There are benefits to doing this, but at times it comes with serious pain.

GRIEF VERSUS REGRET

While grief involves struggling with a loss, regret involves a desire to change a past decision. With grief, we struggle with the loss of something in the past, present, or future. To regret is to wish we had never gone down that path in the first place and suffered the loss that came with that path. In marriage, regrets are often poorly informed. The assumption most people make when entertaining regrets is that the choices they could have made would have turned out *much* better. Few people are unbiased enough to face the fact that other choices might have turned out far worse. Hindsight only tells you how a decision worked out, informing you that you might not make that decision again. But it usually tells you little of the road not taken. Foresight might reduce some pain in life, but I don't know anyone who can truly predict the future. Do you?

Strategies for Grieving Productively

Most cultures don't "do" grief very well. At least here in the United States, I think we try not to grieve since we work so hard at not incurring any losses. Many act as if they will get through their entire lives without suffering loss. They will accept only gain.

I think the longings God created within us will always exceed the reality of this fallen world. We will grieve at times, and the grief can drive us closer to the heart of God. The fact that God understands grief perfectly is recorded throughout Scripture. He is grieved about sin, lack of faith, oppression, and hardness of heart in the people He has made.

Of course, you can live only so long before you are completely humbled when something that matters to you goes wrong and you can't change it. We will all be humbled by death if by nothing else. So let's not pretend that we will never incur any losses. It's wiser to grieve productively. What follows are some tips about grieving.

ACCEPT THE FEELINGS

If you are sad or upset at some point about what you don't have in your marriage, you will do better to deal directly with these feelings than to pretend they are not there. As I said before, if you ignore such feelings, you may find them popping up in other ways in your life. Feelings of loss that are not being actively dealt with may show up as either withdrawal and distance or resentment and irritability. When you allow your feelings to take you in these directions, you will hurt your marriage. On the other hand, if you deal with feelings of loss honestly and openly within yourself, you can take control of these feelings to some degree. You may not make them go away, but you decide to actively work with the feelings in ways that can benefit rather than harm your marriage.

Accepting these feelings in a healthy way does not mean dwelling on them in an obsessive manner. That could cause malaise and inaction. Instead, accepting the feelings of grief could include a number of active strategies, such as praying through your sense of loss and grief, praying for your marriage and your mate, and talking with a good friend about your sense of loss.

King David understood loss, grieving, and how to have a deep relationship with God in the midst of it all. The Psalms describe his inner struggles and journey to the heart of God. Other books in the Bible describe the external circumstances of his life. I encourage you to read about his life. It's powerful, real stuff. You might start reading from 1 Samuel 16. In one of his psalms, David directly linked walking with integrity with speaking the truth in your heart:

> LORD, who may abide in Your tabernacle?
> Who may dwell in Your holy hill?
> He who walks uprightly,
> And works righteousness,
> And speaks the truth in his heart. (Ps. 15:1–2 NKJV)

Grieving Over the Losses That Come with Commitment

Do you speak the truth in your heart? Are you honest with yourself about your struggles? It's hard to be honest with others and with God if you can't face what's inside you.

DON'T BLAME YOUR SPOUSE FOR BEING WHO HE OR SHE IS

You may feel grief in your marriage in the areas where reality is less than the ideal that you carry within your head. Part of productive grieving is accepting the loss, and part of accepting the loss includes accepting your mate for who he or she is. Like everyone else, you need to keep working on loving and cherishing the one you married. Remember the vow "to love and to cherish"? There is no more powerful way to do that than by showing acceptance, and that starts inside you. That's why my coauthors and I, in the book *Fighting for Your Marriage,* stressed that the desire for acceptance—and thus, the fear of rejection—is the root issue from which springs much conflict in marriages.[2]

It will do Nicole and Eric little good to be chronically upset for being who they are. There is no way one can know all about a mate before marriage. Further, people really do change over time. When your mate is not exactly who you thought he was when you said, "I do," you have a choice. You can be resentful and punish him or her for changing your dream, or you can become more accepting. Please understand: you don't accept wrongs or irresponsibility without challenge, but you can choose to accept your mate more fully in many areas. It requires patience, contentment with what is, and an active commitment to forgiveness—forgiveness for who your mate is not, including real sins and the garden variety failures to live up to your dreams. God wants to help you with that tall task. You cannot overestimate the importance of prayer in this journey.

GRIEVING TOGETHER

This idea may seem a bit strange to you, but I have observed something in some couples that is an amazing picture of grace and commitment: *some couples have marriages that are so strong, with such a level of trust, that the partners are able to talk openly together about grief and unmet expectations.*

As I was writing this chapter, a colleague told me of a couple she was working with. The couple shared their deep sense of loss for how their marriage was turning out. Each could describe ways in which what they had expected or dreamed about was not happening. Each could see that they desired some things from each other that were not going to happen, at least not at present and perhaps never.

My colleague talked candidly with them about grief and acceptance—and that some couples were able to share these things in the marriage. I wish all couples were so responsive. This couple immediately acted on these ideas. Of course, that's how a counselor can tell that counselees have taken something in.

At the next session they told her how they had already incorporated the concept into their private language. For example, during the week when he had hoped that they could talk more about what was going on in his work, and she had not been able to listen without being critical of something he said, he closed up and pulled back a bit. After giving him some breathing room, she walked over and sat down beside him and said, "Grief?" He replied, "Yes, grief." That's powerful validation rooted in acceptance and forgiveness.

The couple fully understood that each was disappointing the other and that each felt grief. However, *they had begun to convert their individual experiences of grief about what didn't happen at times between them into a vehicle for drawing closer together.* The effect for good on a marriage is so powerful that it's hard to put in words. I've seen it happen only in the most committed marriages. It's not safe to do if the commitment is not clear.

SPIRITUAL GROWTH AND GRIEVING

Now for the profound part. Very good things can come from loss and grief if you are willing to accept the experiences as lessons in life. That would sound trite, I know, if it were not the story of faith throughout the ages—and throughout Scripture. Pick any major biblical figures and meditate on the losses they experienced, often as a direct result of being committed: persecution, ridicule, long periods of time without seeing God really at work in their lives, and more. Think about how God used their losses to make them all they could be in Him. We tend to become complacent when we have everything just the way we want. Loss, not gain, drives us closer to God.

Look at David again. Scripture records God's assessment of him as a man after God's heart. But David experienced many losses, such as the loyalty of many in the kingdom, the support of family, a baby, and on and on. Some losses were the direct result of his sin. Many others were the direct result of his commitment to God. Isn't that comforting?

At the time that David was fighting the Philistines in front of him and running from Saul behind him, he was very fearful, full of uncertainty and loss. After all, God had anointed him king, but things were not going smoothly. At that time of overwhelming pain, he wrote these words: "The LORD is near to those who have a broken heart, and saves such as have a contrite spirit" (Ps. 34:18 NKJV).

The word for "broken" here is the Hebrew word *shabar*, which means "crushed." The word for "contrite" is the Hebrew word *dakka'*, which means "reduced to dust"—literally "powdered." You may not experience such painful times in your marriage or in life. If you do not, thank God. If you do, thank God. Life can be very hard. Marriage too. God wants to be near you and comfort you when you feel that your dreams are crushed and your life is crumbling to powder. That's why there is real power in powder. That's not the world's conception, but it is God's.

So here's the secret of the power of loss when you handle it well. Loss humbles you. Loss reminds you that you are *not* God and that you need God. In the Psalms, you see the very intimate struggles of people driven to God by the hard circumstances of their lives. There you see complaints, gripes, deep anguish, grieving, fear, and anger; and also fantastic levels of praise, humility, deep connection with the Lord, and peace. The former drive us to the latter. It's the same in marriage when you have the perspective that God can use it all to draw you closer to Him and to each other.

SEARCHING FOR MEANING

Viktor Frankl died while I was writing this book. He was a Jewish man who survived the concentration camps of the Holocaust. As a psychiatrist, he became noted for his theory that one of the most basic human needs is for meaning in our lives. In his study of Jewish survivors of the Nazi extermination camps, he found that the ultimate despair for human beings is the loss of meaning.[3] He found that people could survive just about anything except the pervasive sense that their suffering was meaningless.

That's despair. Grieving is more about finding the meaning in the midst of the sufferings of life.

Ultimately, what meaning is there apart from God? Either He is, and He is the rewarder of those who seek Him (Heb. 11:6), or nothing, including the pains in your marriage, really matters much. Going to God with the pains (and joys, don't forget) of your life is the most powerful way I can think of to keep in touch with meaning in the midst of your struggles. Your pain and struggles have meaning because your life does, and it matters to the One who gave them to you.

SOME CLOSING THOUGHTS ON REALITY

Nothing happens as neatly in life as it can on paper. The suggestions presented here are solid, but that doesn't mean these sorts of things are easy to work through. If something is bothering you enough that this chapter really hits home, it's something that may take a long time for you to work through. When someone dies, the loss is so immediate and absolute that you are more able to move into grieving without wondering if it's the right thing to do. With losses in marriage, things won't happen that quickly, no matter how actively you apply yourself. You could work for years to change an expectation. Grief can go on and on, even if you actively deal with it. Many times, the right thing to do is not all that easy. Most of these times occur when you are dealing with things that deeply affect your soul.

Even though life is messy, an active, moving, lively respect for the losses as well as the gifts prepares you to live it to the full.

POINT OF APPLICATION

I doubt that this chapter has been easy for those of you currently struggling in your marriage. If some significant thoughts and feelings are stirred up by what you read, use that energy to make improvements in your marriage.

- Are there significant areas in your marriage where you have a sense of loss? What are they?
- Spend some time reflecting about your expectations related to areas

of sadness, loss, or frustration in your marriage. What is reasonable; what is not? What can change; what cannot? If you are deeply affected by these dynamics at this time, consider working through your expectations in more detail with one of the resources mentioned in the notes for this chapter at the back of the book.

- If areas of loss in your marriage fit into the grief model, commit yourself to doing that work. Pray about it. Set aside time to reflect on the thoughts and feelings. You might even plan time to talk over these things with a trusted friend—someone who is totally supportive of your having a strong marriage.

Part 2

DEVELOPING AND MAINTAINING THE LONG-TERM VIEW

...from this day forward, ...
...until death do us part.

In this part, another fundamental aspect of commitment takes center stage: the long-term view. In addition to the matter of choices, commitment in marriage is fundamentally about staying the course. The short-term view is not compatible with a fulfilling marriage. The long-term view gives you confidence to invest in your marriage. The long-term view gets you through the ups and downs in life together. In this part, you'll find advice for how to nurture and act on the long-term view in your marriage. The goal isn't simply to stay together in your marriage, but to thrive and grow together over the years. That takes some work and some investment. It also takes some vision for the future. These are the key topics here.

The way we conceive the future sculpts the present, gives contour and tone to nearly every action and thought through the day. If our sense of future is weak, we live listlessly.

—Eugene Peterson

Chapter 5

SHORT- AND LONG-TERM VIEWS

For wherever you go, I will go;
And wherever you lodge, I will lodge;
Your people shall be my people,
And your God, my God.
—Ruth 1:16 NKJV

*B*arbara and Luke were in their late twenties, and both had dated around but had not yet found anyone they would want to spend their lives with. They met each other one night at a party at a mutual friend's home, and their attraction was immediate. They could not tell you exactly why, but each heard a whisper in the soul that said, "This is the one." They talked for two hours that night. They saw each other again the next night, going out to dinner. By the end of that dinner, each was fairly certain that they would marry, although neither spoke a word of that so early in their courtship.

Barbara was attracted to Luke's gentle confidence and comfort with the inner regions of his soul. She thought, *This guy can really share what's on his heart.* That had a powerful effect on her. She had not seen that in any of the men she dated. Luke was similarly attracted to how Barbara handled herself. He felt invited into her life. He felt accepted by her. Each had been attracted to others before, but this was different. It was somehow more complete. It helped that both had a better sense by that time in life of what they were looking for, and both were thinking the same thing: *This is it.*

Not very long into their dating relationship, Luke began to notice a slight panicky feeling. He couldn't quite place it at first. Something felt ill at ease about the relationship. It wasn't that anything wrong was happening in the relationship; things seemed nearly perfect. They did have a few moments when things began to fray, but the moments were infrequent. However, it did seem to him that he felt more anxious during the periods when they would not see each other. They talked every day on the phone, but between work and other responsibilities in life, many times they would not see each other for a few days.

Luke began paying more attention to his feeling that something was not quite right. Finally, about three months into the relationship, it hit him what the odd feeling was—it was anxiety about the relationship. The thoughts crystallized for him: *I really love Barb. But what if she doesn't want to be with me for the rest of her life? What if she decides that I am not the one for her? I know what I want, and it's her. What does she want?*

Luke didn't know that Barb was going through the very same feelings of anxiety. She had identified her feelings for what they were a few weeks earlier than he had. She knew she was becoming anxious because the relationship was so good and she did not want to lose it. Luke knew he was in love and was thinking about how to tell her. Neither had said, "I love you," yet. Each had said, "I love you," many times to others in their lives, to others where the relationship had been much more shallow. As a result, both had decided they were not going to use those words casually. But theirs was not a casual relationship.

The next night when they went on a date, Luke told Barb over dinner that he loved her. She told him the same. In that simple act, they took a step forward in declaring the attachment and growing commitment they had for each other. One month later they were talking openly about marriage. Of course, marriage is *the* major step of commitment in a relationship. But many other steps made prior to marriage increase the clarity of commitment between two people. Each incremental step in commitment reduces some of the anxiety that each potential mate can feel about whether the other will remain in his or her life.

Just talking about the possibility of marriage was a step in commitment for both Luke and Barb. Both felt more at ease about "their future" by talking about it together, though neither spoke directly about the earlier and occasional feelings of anxiety. Other common steps in moving forward in commitment include telling friends and family how serious the relationship is, talking about plans for the long-term future, becoming formally engaged, and working together on wedding plans.

For most couples, this is the way commitment develops over time—in steps, with each step going farther to secure the sense of permanence and a clear future for the relationship. Marriage was created with the long term in mind, and without the long-term view, much will go wrong. This chapter is mostly about the damage done when the short-term view is dominant.

The Anxiety of Attachment

As we saw with Barb and Luke, when a person becomes very attached to another and falls in love, the person tends to enter a period of anxiety about the future of the relationship. It's an anxiety that becomes greatest after intense satisfaction is experienced but before commitment is secured. It happens when there is an attachment but without enough glue to make it feel secure. From a psychological standpoint, various forms of commitment tend to spring up to make this anxiety go away. It's scary to be in love with someone when you don't know whether the person is going to remain in your life.

There are many incremental steps in forming commitment. When teenagers pledge to go steady, that's a form of commitment. When teenagers give a "steady" a class ring to wear or hang around the neck (Do teens still do this? If not, they do something with the same meaning, I'm sure!), they are pledging a higher level of commitment. The emblems publicly say that "you are mine and I am yours." Though these commitments are often immature in many ways (because young people are making them), they are real commitments, and they are intended to get rid of the anxiety of loss. The force of these commitments, simple as they are, is both internal and external to the relationship. Internally, they communicate a sense of allegiance, that "you can count on me to be here for you." Externally, they convey a sense of exclusivity. Each is publicly identified as "belonging" to the other, at least for a time. These messages have many levels, but the root of them is "you have me; you can relax."

Before moving on, I want to indicate that there can be unhealthy levels of anxiety over losing someone—anxieties that go beyond the normal range of what most of us experience. Extreme jealousy is an extremely negative form of this otherwise normal anxiety. It moves people not to commitment but to control. Mutual commitment is not about one trying to control or coerce the other to avoid the possibility of a loss of love. Extreme jealousy is usually destructive over time in a relationship.

If you are very jealous, you should start facing the probability that you have such a big void in your soul that you could destroy the relationship to fill it. Most people don't experience such levels of jealousy, although some jealousy is not unusual, especially during courtship. Research shows that premarital couples are more likely than marital couples to report jealousy as a problem.[1] This makes sense because during that period of time, a lot about commitment is still being established between the two.

Most young adults who fall in love and desire a future together will move toward marital commitment. Historically, commitment in marriage has been understood as lifelong, "until death do us part." This is commitment that says (or at least used to say), "I'm with you for life. You can count on me." God had this long-term view in mind when designing what marriage is to be between a man and a woman. A commitment formed around the long-term view reassures both parties that the relationship will continue. Using the terms from the first chapter, there is a culmination of dedication and constraint in a belief that there is a secure future. In fact, this is a chief benefit of being committed. Commitment says you can put anxiety about loss aside and trust the other to be there for you.

YOU'VE GOT THAT PANICKY FEELING

Contrast the calm assurance of committed couples with the panic, fear, and anxiety that come when one person loves another but cannot be sure of the other's desire or commitment. That's a lousy feeling to have, no doubt about it. You know you *want* this person in your life, but you are not sure you can *keep* him or her in your life.

It's probably good to experience some breakups in dating relationships because they can help you learn that you can endure some of this anxiety and live. However, those who experience too many losses as children can carry wounds and anxiety into adult life. For example, people who were children when their parents divorced are more likely to believe that they may not be able to make their marriages work. Although that's quite realistic (given the high divorce rates), that belief can develop into a form of pessimism: "Nothing I do will really make a big difference." While most people truly want the long-term, committed relationship described in the biblical model of marriage, many people now believe this to be an unrealistic expectation. They end up living out a self-fulfilling prophecy of loss. That's sad.

Barbara Dafoe Whitehead has written a marvelous book on the changes in society that have affected marriages. She argues that the twin engines of prosperity and a focus on self have shredded the traditional meaning of commitment in marriage. In her book called *The Divorce Culture,* she writes, "Perhaps never before in the nation's history has there been such pessimism, even cynicism, about the ability of men and women to live together in lasting marriages and to share a common life."[2]

That hits the nail on the head. Our culture is now infected with a short-term view of marriage, and the short-term view is destructive to marriage. In the rest of this chapter, I will develop the theme of permanence guided by thoughts about long- and short-term views. We will take a pretty hard look at the negative consequences of shortsightedness.

Two Views: Short and Long

We are all affected by the cultures in which we live. Cultures reinforce certain mind-sets. Unless we stop and think about the views surrounding us, we may internalize mind-sets that are both destructive and contrary to what we believe is right. In other words, the dominant view of the culture will automatically become our view unless we give it careful consideration.

It's like an autopilot in an airplane. Once it's set on a heading, that's where everyone in the plane is headed. That's great if it's a good destination but not great if the plane is headed toward the side of a mountain. When it comes to commitment, the autopilot of our world is set on the heading "short term." Our world is so prone to focus on the short term that you'll tend to be that way, too, unless you stop to think about it.

I'll come back to this problem of worldviews in Chapter 7, but for now, I want to investigate specifically how it affects thinking about time.

EVIDENCES OF A BASIC HUMAN PROBLEM

Failing to consider the long-term implications of our actions gets us into all sorts of problems. Part of this tendency comes from an unwillingness to delay gratification. Most people would rather live for today at the expense of the future than be more careful with resources today in order to make the future more secure. Living for the moment, not for the future, drives our world today. I've included here a few of the more obvious examples of short-term thinking.

The Government. Here in the United States, as in many industrialized nations, we have great wealth. We have more as a people than any nation has ever had in the history of the world. Though ours is a land of prosperity, our government lives from year to year with immense debt. The deficit has been going down at the time of this writing, but our government still owes a horrendous debt from overspending in years gone by. Our children will inherit an enormous debt as a result of the shortsightedness of our generation. Whenever we as a society or as individuals splurge with money we really do not have to buy more things in the present at the expense of the future, we are living for the short run, not the long run. We are living for the moment.

Personal Economics. Most of us hope to live to a ripe old age. However, too few people save much money for retirement or emergencies long before that time of life. To be sure, many people find it very hard to save anything at all because they find it hard enough just to get food on the table every day. However, our country is an example of the fact that even when there is a generally high level of prosperity, the tendency of most people is to consume all their financial resources in the present rather than save anything for the future. Recklessly spending and neglecting to save is a failure to think long-term about one's future needs.

How about you? Do you have more debt than you could possibly pay off in a month or so (and I'm not counting a housing loan, just good old credit card debt, car loans, and the like)? The amount of personal debt of the average American has continually gone up over the past few decades. That's strong evidence that people are thinking more about the present than the future. One result is that many people have no resources to cover emergencies. When an unexpected illness occurs or the car quits, too many people have to rob Peter to pay Paul.

The Environment. I don't personally subscribe to some of the more radical notions in the environmental movement—notions that could lead to actions that go way beyond reason to address the problems of pollution. Having made that little disclaimer, I must acknowledge that many industrialized and preindustrialized societies make many decisions that harm the environment for the sake of short-term expediency. The long-term consequences of such actions are often not considered or acted upon.

As I am writing this chapter, I am sitting in a hotel room near the Cuyahoga River in Cuyahoga Falls, Ohio. The river is beautiful. It also has a somewhat infamous past since it caught on fire decades ago. The sight of a river burning was so bizarre that it served as a wake-up call to Americans about how we treated our land and rivers. There is no fire now, and the river is much cleaner than it was then. But what causes people to put so much pollution and garbage into a river that it could catch on fire? The short-term view. "Waste from factories, sure. Chemicals from farming, sure. Dump it all in. We can worry about it later, but for today, that's the easiest thing to do."

The long-term view is more about taking wise care of resources and preserving what we can for the future. The short-term view is about immediate gratification and consumption of resources at the expense of the future. When there is no future, why not consume all the resources today?

Business. How many businesses have failed from a persistent, exclusive focus on the short term? It's a big number. Companies that fail to consider what will happen in the future are destined to fail. Long-term strategic thinking is necessary in business to balance the needs of the moment with the needs of the future. For example, any business could pay out all its current profits to the owners or the employees. However, without money to invest in new products, new marketing, or training for employees, most companies would go under. Everyone who got paid right now might enjoy it for a time, but the shortsightedness will kill the future of the business.

Crime. There must be many reasons why people commit crimes. Some people steal because they see things they want, things that they are too impatient to wait for or that they believe they will never be able to buy for themselves. In the absence of a strong ethic against stealing, the desire for immediate gratification wins out over any fear of punishment or internal sense of wrong. A lot of people get away with crime, but it's usually a better life only in the short run.

In many ways, making decisions based on the short term is like stealing something you cannot really afford to have. It's stealing from the future for the sake of the present. Such thinking can harm everything, especially marriages.

CHARACTERISTICS OF SHORT-TERM THINKING

Before returning our focus to commitment, I'd like to list some characteristics of short-term thinking. No matter what area of life you think about, these factors reflect nearsightedness. After discussing some of these general problems of the short-term view, we'll consider the impact of these factors on marriage.

Give-it-to-me-now-ism. If there is no tomorrow, why not focus on today? When you have little sense of a future, it's quite rational to get all you can right now. "There's no time like the present," you say. But the statement that many really live by is, "There's no time *but* the present." Why protect current resources for a future that may not exist? It's truly not a rational thing to do if there is no future. So you live for today. You go for the gusto. It's about "having it all" right now. In marriage, this attitude creates performance anxiety. It's as if one mate tells the other that their commitment is only as secure as how well the other can perform right now.

Scorekeeping. A specific extension of the short-term orientation is scorekeeping. If there is only the present, and all you are ever going to get in life is in the present, you'll keep pretty active score on how you are doing. You'll feel that you need to do this because of your sense that all you are going to get is what you can get right now. Things can even out if there is time. When two mates have made it clear that they will stick, the commitment carries with it a sense that there is time to grow.

Scorekeeping feeds on and is fed by a consumer approach to life. If our highest priority is to be satisfied right now, that's how you'll evaluate your marriage. That means keeping score, and its effects are devastating. Once couples start seriously keeping score, they are in real trouble. The problem with scorekeeping is that it not only represents a short-term perspective, but also is fundamentally biased in favor of the scorekeeper. Let me explain.

If you do a lot of scorekeeping, you are sure to score many more points than your mate. There are many reasons for this; I'll note two. First, you see everything you do for the marriage and only a fraction of what your mate does (since you are with yourself all the time). It's easy to "run up the score" from this bias in point of view. Second, you'll give yourself the perfect benefit of the doubt while hardly ever giving your mate the same courtesy. When things are going downhill in marriage, you may attribute the good things your mate does to chance and the bad things to character. He forgets to buy the ice cream you like, and you think, *He hates me. He did that on purpose just to make me mad.* Or she goes out of her way to pick up a book you've been wanting at the bookstore, and you think, *Okay, what does she want now? She must want something from me.*

In books my colleagues and I have written, we call these *negative interpretations* and warn couples that they are powerful destroyers of goodwill in marriage.[3] The bottom line is that negative interpretations make it likely that you will score little in favor of your mate once you start seriously keeping the tally. Your mate can't possibly win, and your marriage will inevitably be the big loser.

Impatience. How's your patience? How well do you wait for things in life? Do you become irritable when things are not happening the way you want them to happen right now? If you have mostly a short-term focus, you're likely to be impatient. After all, you have no time to lose. Every second that things are not going your way is time wasted. Things better happen soon because there is no counting on the future for them to happen.

Most people think that there will be a future, but two few really live as if they believe it. Patience used to be considered a virtue. I don't think it's glorified too much anymore, except in Scripture. Consider this passage:

> *The end of a thing is better than its beginning;*
> *The patient in spirit is better than the proud in spirit. (Eccl. 7:8*
> *NKJV)*

I could have it wrong, but I think that Solomon was linking the long-term view with patience and the short-term view with pride. I can see this in two ways. First, when someone is more focused on how things look now than on how he will end up in the future, it's often because of pride. That has to be one reason why he buys nicer things than he can afford. He has little concern for how things will be in the future, but it makes him look good or feel good now. Second, the proud person sees his immediate needs as a higher priority than the needs of others. He acts this out with the attitude, "I don't care about what these other people need or want. I want what I want right now! I deserve better than this."

There is nothing wrong with wanting to improve your life in various ways, but when your desires need fulfilling at the expense of others or the future, you will experience problems. It's better, Solomon said, to be patient and more focused on how things will turn out in the end.

Paul wrote that the fruit of the Spirit is love, joy, peace, *patience,* kindness, goodness, faithfulness, gentleness, and self-control (Gal. 5:22–23). Walking in the Spirit and being mature will be reflected in patience. In contrast with pride, patience requires humility with others when they are not doing things just the way we want them done right now. With a longer-term view on a relationship, especially marriage, it's more natural to have patience. Everything doesn't have to happen right now. There is a future.

Selfishness. Running as a theme beneath the surface in all this is selfishness. Note that the short-term view encourages selfishness—and selfishness encourages the short-term view. A short-term view reinforces a commitment to getting your way right now, making you more a taker than a giver.

This orientation toward taking now and not giving for the future hurts economies, damages the environment, and wreaks havoc in relationships. Let's see in more depth how these dynamics play out in marriage.

SHORT-TERM MARRIAGE

Commitment develops between two people to secure faith in the future. The long-term view that comes with commitment reassures both partners of the permanence of the union. I want to devote the rest of this chapter to a detailed picture of how a short-term view kills the chances of having a good marriage.

In the example given earlier, Barb and Luke developed their commitment into a full and deep sense of permanence. They left the initial anxieties behind and moved toward building a life together. Everything worked out quite well for them, not perfectly, but well. Each had a relatively mature idea of commitment, and they dated long enough to make wise decisions about their life together. By the way, the research backs up the wisdom of a longer courtship[4] because you are more likely to know the person you are committing to when you do marry.

DESTROYING THE LONG-TERM VIEW

Ben and Pam met in high school. They went to rival schools and met in their senior year at a homecoming dance. As with Barb and Luke, the feelings of attraction were very strong from the start. Ben and Pam dated several years. Both attended the same local college, thinking all the time that they would eventually marry—and they did. However, they never achieved the same degree of settled commitment, the kind of security, that Barb and Luke had. They got engaged and broke it off several times before actually tying the knot. On the day that they got married, things were good. Each was confident that they were making a good decision. They were not a bad match, but they were more "here and now" oriented than Barb and Luke. They had trouble maintaining a clear view of a future. It didn't help that they couldn't handle conflict well. Just when it seemed that things were going well, something would blow up and put more distance between them.

Ben and Pam had been married ten years when things really began to unravel. They had a seven-year-old son named Josh who heard their frequent arguing. They regularly argued in ways that are associated with the breakdown of a marriage over time.[5] Most damaging was their threatening their commitment to each other when their arguments escalated. Serious arguments often ended like this:

> PAM: (*with a note of irritation in her voice*) Why can't you get our bills paid on time? Here's an overdue notice from the phone company.

> BEN: (*with an angry, defensive tone*) You know, I really resent that tone. I did pay that bill on time. Why do you assume that I screwed up?

> PAM: Why do you assume that I assume that you screwed up? Are you insecure or something?

> BEN: (*turning away, muttering*) Yeah, I'm real insecure. It's no use ever talking to you.

> PAM: (*sarcastically*) Oh, I can't hear you. Can't handle a little conflict?

> BEN: I don't know why I ever married you.

> PAM: No one's forcing you to stay. We could get along just fine without you.

> BEN: (*as he was leaving the kitchen for the basement*) Maybe that's a pretty good idea. I don't see any great reason to stay with you!

Note what happened here. In the midst of their frustrating arguments, one or both would threaten the whole future of the marriage. This is, unfortunately, not an uncommon pattern. *Do not threaten your future just because you are very frustrated right now.* That is very destructive.

Josh heard most of these arguments. Like many couples, Ben and Pam kidded themselves that Josh didn't notice their conflicts. He was acutely aware of them, and they were starting to affect his behavior at school. His teacher noticed that he was acting out more in class, becoming more defiant, and getting in more fights with other boys and girls. His parents didn't realize it, but such behavior is fairly common for boys who are regularly exposed to poorly handled conflict between their parents. Little girls are more likely to become withdrawn and depressed, and they are less prone to acting out their anxieties than little boys are.

Josh was particularly wounded by hearing his parents talk about breaking up. As far as he could tell, they talked about it every few weeks, always when having a big argument. He began to feel insecure about his future because of his parents' fights. Ben and Pam would make up at times, but that was always done more quietly and often behind closed doors. So even when they were doing better in their marriage, Josh was not reassured since he saw none of the work to repair the damage done during the fights. Further, the damage kept accumulating beyond Ben and Pam's ability to repair it for their marriage or for Josh.

"WHAT HAVE YOU DONE FOR ME LATELY?"

Over time, Ben and Pam chewed up whatever commitment they had developed through the earlier years. Their repeated arguments were a big factor in their renewing thoughts about divorce. Their conflicts were leading to both a growing sense of unhappiness and a weaker sense of commitment. Like most people without a strong sense of the future, they became very focused on the here and now. Each tallied up what the other was doing—or not doing—for him or her. Each began scorekeeping with a vengeance.

Ben resented how little Pam appreciated what he was doing to make an income for the family. Sure, she worked outside the home, but he felt that he was killing himself to get ahead in his work as an insurance agent—to provide for the family. *She's not doing nearly as much for this family as I am,* he thought. Such thoughts went through his mind over and over again.

For her part, Pam was often thinking about how little Ben seemed to do around the home. She worked full-time in marketing for a software company, yet she felt that she had to do everything around the home. She thought more about how she could get along just fine without him. *What's he doing for me anyway?* she'd wonder. *He doesn't wash clothes; he doesn't cook; he doesn't do anything!*

Ben and Pam were really rolling with the scorekeeping. Each was closely watching how the other was "performing." Because of the biased perceptions, neither was scoring many points on the other's scorecard. The reality was that each was doing a great deal for the marriage and family. He did much more around the home than she gave him credit for. She did more, but she didn't do "everything." He certainly wasn't the only one working hard to provide for their family, either. Although he worked more hours, she worked full-time and worked very hard. Both were doing so much that neither had extra time to relax, but each thought the other found plenty of time to take it easy. Their perceptions were so biased that their interpretations of each other's motivations and actions were growing chronically negative.

As you can imagine, the combination of these forces puts a tremendous amount of pressure on a marriage. No one will fare well in the biased perception of a mate once things go this far downhill. Waves of anger, resentment, and bitterness flow. Scorekeeping is virtually guaranteed to increase resentment. While it is sometimes very fair for one mate to push another about an imbalance in the workload, it's otherwise a sign of a marriage headed downhill when scorekeeping takes over.

Ben and Pam were coming close to giving up. Meanwhile, little Josh was bewildered and hurting. He didn't understand what was happening between his parents, but he was aware that many children didn't have both parents living with them. He was very afraid. He was not sleeping well, was crying more often, and was getting into fights at school.

When the present is unpleasant and people see no future together, they think a lot about divorce. People with more conservative views of divorce think about the death of a mate—not as in murder, but as in what-ifs: What if a car accident took her? Or what if he died of cancer? These amount to little fantasies of freedom from commitment. Obviously, they are not good signs.

In the story just presented, you saw how Josh was suffering as a result of his parents' problems. There are no greater casualties of shortsighted marriages than children. Children become the innocent victims of high marital conflicts and of divorce. Much of the damage that's done comes from the glorification of the short term. Of course, parents don't usually *want* divorce for their children. I know many people who have divorced, and not one was happy to make that decision. The choice to divorce is usually made with agony about what it will mean for the children. In the language of the first chapter, concern for the welfare of children acts as a major constraining force in keeping marriages together.

There is much misunderstanding and debate about the effects of divorce on children. I'll give you my view of what the current research asserts. Let's start out with the obvious: *children will fair best when living with both parents in a loving home where there is a clear commitment to the marriage and the family.* People argue about many things in academic circles, but no researcher or theorist seriously doubts that children do best when raised by both parents in a loving home. The hot debate concerns whether children do better when they live in a divorced household or when they live with parents who have chronic, serious conflicts. The answer depends on the kind of social scientist you talk to.

On the psychological side, there are clearly documented negative effects on children from being exposed for the long term to parents who do not get along, especially when there are significant levels of open conflict between the parents. Both boys and girls do not do well under these conditions. That's why many people advocate divorce "for the sake of the children." Of course, one major problem for children whose parents do not get along well is that many parents don't suddenly start getting along well after they divorce. The children remain exposed to the open warfare between the two most important people in their world.

That brings me to some advice for those of you who are married, have children, and have a lot of conflict in your marriage: learn to handle it better. You can do it, and many resources are available to help you do it.[6] You have to swallow some pride and work at it, but it's important for your children. Even if you cannot muster the motivation for the sake of

Short- and Long-Term Views

your marriage, do it for your kids. All the better if you can do it for your marriage as well. Couples can learn to manage conflicts better, and in doing so, they can turn their marriages around and help their children.

The other kind of research relevant to how marriage and divorce affect children is sociological. In that literature, compelling data show how much better children do when living with both parents. They live better economically, do better in school, are less likely to engage in precocious sexual activity, are less likely (especially boys) to become criminally involved, are more likely to stay physically healthy and have access to good health care, and are much more likely to retain a relationship with their fathers.[7] And as many of you know, stepfamilies are not exactly easy to negotiate. That's a tough way to go, though many couples manage it very well. There are also many single parents doing a terrific job. I'm not criticizing single or blended-family parents who are doing their best to raise their children well. But I do want to appeal to parents to understand the fundamental ways in which marital stability (commitment) and harmony (getting along) provide the best environment in which your children can grow.

If you are divorced and have children from that marriage, one of the best things you can do for your children is to make your peace with your ex-spouse. If you are still battling over things, do your best to compromise and quit fighting. If you are not battling, you do your children an immense service. I realize that you may believe you are right in a major dispute regarding your children, and you may feel compelled to fight for certain rights or arrangements. Or there could be some abuse involved so that it would be unwise to make peace with an abuser. Unless it's really very clear that what you are disagreeing about will greatly impact your children, it would be better to quit battling. There is no doubt that the battling will harm your children over time. Obviously, this is most possible when both of you agree to "bury the hatchet." I return to that powerful verse Paul wrote: "If it is possible, as much as depends on you, live peaceably with all men" (Rom. 12:18 NKJV).

It's not always possible, but go as far as you can to control or end the conflict. And if you cannot end it, go as far as you can together to shield your children from it. It's essential.

If you are in a marriage where the soil has gotten rocky and hard, it's time to do all you can to change the condition. Get help from your pastor or a counselor known for helping couples make it work. Read books that are targeted at helping you with the problems you are having. Find ways to redevelop your dedication to each other. I have suggestions about that coming up later in the book. These are the best things you can do for your children's future as well as your own. In the next chapter, I will give you specific advice about investments that can keep a marriage strong or turn one around. If you value the future, there is no time like the present to start acting on it.

When things get as bad as they became for Ben and Pam, a lot of work is necessary to turn things around. It can be done, but it's tough going. Take note that for many couples, things get bad precisely because no one is acting on the long-term view. When you take the long-term view, you are more inclined to use resources of the present to make a better future.

When I was much younger, I saw an oil filter commercial that still sticks in my mind. A mechanic was about to deliver the bad news to a car owner that he needed a new engine. The owner had neglected the regular maintenance that an engine needs to run well. He had neglected to regularly change the oil and oil filter, causing greatly increased wear on the parts of the engine—hence, the need for a very expensive solution. The punch line for the oil filter commercial was "You can pay me now or pay me later." When you don't spend the time to keep your marriage in good shape today, you'll pay a far greater price tomorrow for your shortsightedness.

The Spiritual Basis of the Long-Term View

I cannot overstate the importance of the long-term view for marriage. Marriage is meant to be a lifelong relationship. In that framework each mate is released to grow, invest, and trust. Marriage can be hard work at times. It's just not worth the work if the marriage is not going to be there for you. It's worth all the time and effort when you know it will be there in the future.

In closing this chapter, let's consider two specific issues about the long-term view related to a Christian worldview.

I think that a fundamental erosion of a sense of eternity has occurred among people living today. This sense of eternity was originally placed within us by God Himself (Eccl. 3:11). It's pretty hard to explain in any other way why anyone should have developed any sense of something like an eternity. It's just not something we experience in this life. Paul noted that directly:

> *For our light affliction, which is but for a moment, is working for us a far more exceeding and eternal weight of glory, while we do not look at the things which are seen, but at the things which are not seen. For the things which are seen are temporary, but the things which are not seen are eternal. (2 Cor. 4:17–18 NKJV)*

We cannot see the things that are eternal. That's why some people find it hard to believe the eternal exists at all. It's a matter of faith, but again Solomon said it was a faith that God started within us. My impression is that industrialized societies have fewer people who really believe in eternal things compared to people of days gone by. We have a growing and all-encompassing short-term view as a society. It's the *big* short-term view. And if fewer and fewer people believe that there is anything to eternity, more and more people are living for the moment. If there is no eternity and no God, there is no larger meaning to anything that we do. I'm sure an articulate atheist would disagree, but if this moment in time is all there is, there is simply not a lot of meaning in life. Here today, gone forever.

In Dostoevsky's *The Brothers Karamazov,* this point is brought out. A minor character recalls the reasoning of Ivan, the brother who is the most philosophical and skeptical, in this manner:

> He solemnly declared in an argument that there was nothing in the whole world to make men love their neighbors. That there was no law of nature that men should love mankind, and that, if there had been any love on earth hitherto, it was not owing to a natural law, but simply because men have believed in immortality. Ivan

Fyodorovitch added in parenthesis that the whole natural law lies in that faith, and that if you were to destroy in mankind the belief in immortality, not only love but every living force maintaining the life of the world would at once be dried up. Moreover, nothing then would be immoral, everything would be lawful, even cannibalism.[8]

This is compelling logic. If you destroy a person's appreciation for the immortal, you destroy any realistic basis to love. There is no reason to defer gratification. There is no right or wrong that matters much. Why wouldn't someone want to get all he could right now if there is no future? And if there is no eternity or accountability, why not choose the things that work out best for himself and do it right away? Paul reached the same conclusion: "If, in the manner of men, I have fought with beasts at Ephesus, what advantage is it to me? If the dead do not rise, 'Let us eat and drink, for tomorrow we die!'" (1 Cor. 15:32 NKJV).

If there is only death tomorrow and there is no eternity, have a good time now. That's what Paul stated. My point is that this sense that nothing in the future really matters drives an emphasis on the here and now. I see it as the root of a more pervasive sense of meaninglessness.

So it is in such soil that our marriages now grow or die. The loss of the long-term view and the emphasis on the here and now (in its selfish meaning) are everywhere. These attitudes adversely affect marriage as well as everything else. The result is an ideal of getting all we can now. We are encouraged to live for the moment. This is not the only societal trend that negatively affects marital commitment, yet I think it's a big part of what tears at the fabric of marital permanence.

THE LORD'S COMMITMENT TO YOU

If you have studied Scripture and the history of God's people, you can see God's long-term commitment consistently and firmly expressed. God knows that this life is hard. He realizes that people will become disillusioned in this life without a clear sense of His commitment to us. The belief in the ultimate meaning of life and the greater long-term view of Scripture reminds you that life matters and your marriage matters.

Stretching out your view of time in this way can help you battle the pervasiveness of the short-term view in the world today.

The writer of Hebrews repeated a phrase uttered by God to His people throughout the history recorded in the Old Testament: "Let your conduct be without covetousness; be content with such things as you have. For He Himself has said, 'I will never leave you nor forsake you'" (Heb. 13:5 NKJV).

Your contentment in the present will be enhanced by having clarity about the long-term commitment of the Lord toward you. The more you are sure of His commitment, the easier you will find it to be content in the circumstances of life. Instead of trying to grab it all, you realize you already have it all from an eternal perspective. That's stretching out your view of life. That's living in the present but in the shadow of eternity, with the knowledge of a God who is fully devoted to a relationship with you. He reaches out His hand to all of us. It's a hand into the future—into eternity.

POINT OF APPLICATION

At the outset of this section on long- and short-term views, stop and think through broader implications in your life. Here are some thoughts to push you along in that:

- How anxious are you about the security of the commitment in your marriage (or with the person to whom you are engaged)? If you are anxious, what about? What is unclear about the commitment between you and your mate?
- How secure do you feel in God's commitment to you? Spend some time this day reflecting on what Scripture reveals about God's love and commitment to you. Write down one verse that is particularly powerful to you. Share it with your mate.
- In general, how good are you at delaying gratification and planning ahead for the future? Do you tend to have a short-term or a long-term outlook? Why? Discuss this issue with your mate. How do these tendencies affect your marriage?
- Pick one specific way in which you could do something this week

that is good for your future. One way to get focused here is to ask yourself: "In ten years, what will I wish I had done now that I am not doing to protect and build my marriage?"

Patience and tenacity of purpose are worth more than twice their weight of cleverness.

—Thomas Henry Huxley

Goodness is the only investment that never fails.
—Henry David Thoreau

Chapter 6

INVESTING FOR THE LONG HAUL

He who observes the wind will not sow,
And he who regards the clouds will not reap.
—Ecclesiastes 11:4 NKJV

A friend of mine recently shared with me what she had written about one of her camping experiences:

Our family takes an annual camping/fishing trip to the Rocky Mountains. By our family, I don't just mean my husband, myself, and the two kids. I mean Grandpa, uncles, aunts, cousins, brothers- and sisters-in-law, nieces, nephews, and usually a few friends besides. It was the first night of the trip. The fire had died down, and we were all snuggled into our sleeping bags, the kids' flashlights had long burned out. Finally, all was still, and except for the sharp rock in my side, I was comfortably dozing off. Then we heard voices and rustling in the tent next to ours. It was our friend, Chuck, and some guy whom he'd brought along. Chuck is one of those bighearted people who just kind of picks up strays—animals and people, and he simply loves them back to health. Well, this guy wasn't the most congenial person I'd ever met. I'm ashamed to admit it, but we were not very gracious to this man. I'm sure he had a name, but the family secretly named him "Jerk." I won't go into why we thought that name was appropriate, but trust me, it fit.

Well, we heard Jerk whining, "There's a big rock poking me, I can't sleep." Chuck offered to trade places with him, which they did. Rustle, rustle, grunt, uh, . . . rustle. There. Ten, maybe fifteen seconds of silence then, "Now, I'm lying on a hill, I can't sleep, I feel like I'm falling."

I started to giggle (until my husband elbowed me) when we heard Chuck, a veteran camper, offer to move the tent. Now, if you're a camper you already know what a generous and ridiculous offer this was. If you're not a camper, let me explain. Chuck was generous in that moving a tent full of gear, in the middle of a cold, starless night is no easy task. The tent stakes have to be located and pulled up, the rain flap removed, the tent dragged with all the stuff inside, the rain flap repositioned and the stakes driven into the ground once more—all with numb fingers and in blackness that would be tough on a bat. Ridiculous in that no tent site is comfortable—it doesn't matter where you set the tent. It will not be level and there will always be sharp objects under the occupants. It's the first rule of camping. If you want comfort, you stay in a hotel. Well, Jerk was a rookie and he took Chuck up on the offer to move.

I fell asleep listening to Jerk whine about how cold he was while he stood around watching Chuck move the tent by himself. Later the next day, Chuck and I had the chance to share a canoe and fish for a bit. Contrary to most fishing stories, the fish were not biting. So we had time to talk. I asked Chuck why he hadn't just told Jerk to quit whining and go to sleep instead of going to all the trouble of moving the tent. He said that of course it had been a lot of work to move the tent, but it was an opportunity to be a friend, to demonstrate that he valued the man enough to try to meet his needs. He was investing in their relationship. I felt a bit convicted, but quickly recovered. "You're not going to get a return on your investment," I told him. "The guy's a jerk." "Yeah, he kind of is, isn't he?" Chuck said with a knowing grin. "But God doesn't hold me responsible for the return on my investment. My job is to invest. The results, or returns as you call them, are up to Him."

Well, this statement left me feeling more than a little convicted, and I hope I never recover. The idea that we are called to invest in relationships, even with people who sometimes act like Jerks, (which frankly fits most everyone at times) and trust God for the results was a new and powerful concept to me. Pretty Christlike, actually.

It's not always wise to move the tent. Sometimes it's a better investment not to move it. It depends on the relationship and what you're trying to accomplish. Chuck was operating from a redemptive mind-set about the relationship with the unhappy camper. He was making an investment in the unhappy camper that might have returned nothing in this life, but Chuck could sleep with the knowledge that he had tried to positively impact the life of another.

Sometimes it's hardest to make investments with those we live with every day. We get to thinking that it's just not worth it or that they'll wait, but marriages need regular, steady investments to thrive. That's the point here. I'll start with a little history and some elementary financial concepts to explain why investing in your marriage over time is so crucial. Although you may not be as interested in money as in your marriage, wise principles for investing work in marriage just as well as they do in the money world.

CRASH

The year was 1929. In the late 1920s, more people than ever before were investing their savings in the stock market. For those of you who do not study such things, buying stocks is a way for anyone to own a small (or large) piece of a company. In the years leading up to 1929, most people in the stock market were speculators, meaning that they had a short-term view on investments in stocks and were going for quick profits. They were looking for the killing in the here and now, not steady, long-term growth.

A popular speculative strategy at that time (and it's still popular) was to buy on margin. When you buy on margin, you don't have to have all the money to pay for what you are buying. You put up a percentage of what the stock really costs so that you can own the stock without having to invest the full price. It's like taking out a loan from a stockbroker instead of a banker. Through the 1920s, many people investing in the stock market were used to buying on margin, and life was good. The market kept going up, and the investments didn't seem very risky. There is no problem buying on margin if the market keeps going up.

In 1929, as economies across the world started to decline, the market started to come down—way down. It became an out-of-control train careening down the mountain. People who were used to the good times and quick gains were shocked. When you "want it now and want it quick," you don't tolerate any loss very well. People began to sell out in droves. However, few wanted to buy, and that brought the prices tumbling down. Those who had not bought on margin did poorly. Those who had bought on margin were totally wiped out. They lost money they had, and they lost a lot of money that they didn't have. They were falling with no net to catch them.

Imagine you were one of those investors. You jumped into the market because all your friends were doing it, and it seemed to be a quick way to make a buck. You bought a lot of stock—far more than you could really afford—using a margin account with your broker. Then you saw the prices of your stocks plummeting. You got a margin call from the brokerage house that said, "You are losing a lot of money on your investment, and we're calling you in to make up the difference." You didn't have the difference to make up. You lost all of your financial assets in a very short time, and you melted into cold panic and nausea.

That's the way it is for many couples in marriage. They are thinking short term, not long term. They are focused on the immediate return, not what's a good value. Part of really sticking and not getting stuck is learning to be a wise investor in your marriage. Let's evaluate the kind of wealth that matters most in marriage; then we'll look at how to invest to build it up.

RELATIONSHIP CAPITAL

A definition of *capital* is "wealth that is used to produce more wealth." The term is usually used in connection with money or other assets of a business to help it grow. There are various kinds of assets in life. Some people are rich in money. Others are rich in relationships. If you've been wise, you have built up *relationship capital.*[1] *Relationship capital is what comes from the investment of emotional and spiritual resources in key relationships.* In marriage, relationship capital is your reservoir of resources, including positive bonds, trust, confidence, support, and spiritual connection—the sense of oneness, "we're in this together," and "you can count on me." Priceless treasure.

Many problems in marriages come from mistaking material gain for true riches. That was a major point in Chapter 2. You cannot buy relationship capital with money. The theme "money can't buy me love" hit home for the Beatles, but Solomon was onto the theme quite a bit earlier:

> *Many waters cannot quench love,*
> *Nor can the floods drown it.*
> *If a man would give for love*
> *All the wealth of his house,*
> *It would be utterly despised. (Song 8:7 NKJV)*

You can buy U.S. savings bonds, but you gain the deeper *bonds* in marriage only from steady and wise investing. Time and energy count most at home. Those who invest the most in their marriages are also those most likely to have a long-term satisfying marriage. Ironically, those who continue long term in a marriage are also the most likely to end up with the greatest financial security.[2] Divorce wastes resources,[3] and the failure to invest wisely in the relationship of a marriage contributes to divorce in the first place. In many ways, the deeper riches of relationship and the blessings of financial security are most likely to come to people with an active, long-term commitment in marriage.

When you invest wisely in your marriage, you also build relationship capital that can take you through the tougher times. Have you ever seen married friends go through a horrendous stress, such as the loss of a child or the diagnosis of cancer? Perhaps you've dealt with such things firsthand. When faced with such a crisis, some couples fall apart, but others hunker down and draw closer together. The ones who draw together are the ones who have built up some capital in their marriage. They have something to draw upon. Couples who have not built capital together, or who have squandered it, have no reserve. When the wave hits, they are washed away and the marriage drowns, like a house built on shifting sands can be washed into the sea.

How do you invest and build capital? Let's look first at how it happens with money, and then apply some principles from finance to marriage.

MARRIAGE AND THE STOCK MARKET

I am not a financial adviser, but I know what you are likely to hear if you go to a financial adviser and say this: "I would like to save up for retirement. Where should I put most of what I am saving?" Unless retirement is virtually upon you, you'll likely hear that you should put a great deal of what you are saving in the stock market. Why? Because in the United States, the stock market has been the single best place to make long-term investments over the past half century. On average, nothing else has come close over the past fifty years. Of course, investing in stocks is somewhat like taking a roller-coaster ride, and some are more rolling than coasting. That's what makes the stock market seem so risky to people—that and the problems back in 1929.

I believe there are some telling similarities between marriage and the stock market. Marriage is a great long-term investment. Satisfaction in marriage, however, goes up and down all the time, kind of like the Dow-Jones industrial average—a major indicator of how the market is doing. Some stocks see fewer bumps and dips than others. Some days and months see less ups and downs. Same for marriages. The "happiness rating" in some marriages has more volatility than others. Some couples bounce around a lot more than others in terms of satisfaction. Either way, the long-term view of commitment carries you through ups and downs in marital happiness over many years. Investing in marriage is like investing in the stock market in that while it may be one of the best bets over the long term, it is also risky. You are not guaranteed that your investment will yield the return you are hoping for. Some people have suffered significant losses in their marriages. But, by far, most who consistently invest in their marriages will do very well in life.

Most important, without the long-term view, people do the same things in marriage that people with short-term views do in the stock market. They try to time it. They move their investment in and out, trying to get the best deal over the short run. They cash in when it's going down and try to buy back in when it's going back up. Like short-termers in the market, they are looking for the immediate gain, they closely watch the score, and they move their investments around based on the winds of the day. These short-term investors tend to buy and sell at the wrong times, losing a little or a lot in each transaction.

Those with a long-term view in marriage behave differently. First, they don't pay excessive attention to the short-term dips. The long-termers don't react very much to the downs because they expect them. It's part of the long view. The following advice is typical for financial magazines and books written for those who want to save for their future:

> Investing for long-term prosperity is fundamentally different from trying to win at the short-term game. Indeed, Wall Street's measures for forecasting near-term results can be useless compasses for an investor whose horizon is ten years off. But it is the long view that will have the greatest impact on your worth. Now more than ever, investing for the long haul means screening out extraneous noise.[4]

The long-term view helps you be less reactive to the "noise" of day-to-day life. The long-term view limits your risk because it steadies your investing. Only the future will tell if the accepted financial wisdom of today holds for money in the decades to come. Whether it does or not, I am certain that those who will do best in marriage—no matter what happens in the economy—are those who approach marriage as a long-term investment.

There is one important limit on the real risks of investing in relationships. That's God. Scripture makes it very clear that Chuck's attitude toward investing with the unhappy camper is a solid one. Even if there is no temporal reward in some of our investments in relationships, we are ultimately investing with the Lord. He honors genuine investment in others, even if we cannot see any returns on the human level. As Chuck said to my friend, "God doesn't hold me responsible for the return on my investment. My job is to invest. The results, or returns as you call them, are up to Him." Paul said something along the same lines: "Whatever you do, do it heartily, as to the Lord and not to men, knowing that from the Lord you will receive the reward of the inheritance; for you serve the Lord Christ" (Col. 3:23–24 NKJV).

That's pretty clear, isn't it? We ultimately serve the Lord when we invest in service to others. Do you believe and act on that?

The second thing that long-term investors tend to do is to invest even more when the market goes down. Why? Because they know that they will get even more stock for their money when the market is down. It's one of the best times to invest more, but only if you have the long-term view.

When your marriage hits a slump, it's the very best time to invest more. Investing in the relationship is the most powerful way to tell your mate that you're here and you're sticking. When you stick with it, you'll usually see a favorable response. I know there are exceptions to this, but most marriages are not the exception.

TRUST AND RELATIONSHIP CAPITAL

When you hold and act on a full commitment in your marriage, it not only helps you to develop the attitudes of a good investor, but it also helps you to develop trust in your relationship. When you trust, you place your confidence in someone who has been there for you. For anyone or anything that you trust in life, you've come to that trust because you've seen that person or thing come through for you time and time again.

In marriage, trusting means having confidence in the commitment, actions, and follow-through of your mate. Trust is a fundamental type of relationship capital that you can build. When you have trust to bank on, you are more able to make it through the low points. You have confidence together that you'll keep moving forward and not get stuck in the present. Trust makes it safe to keep investing, even when things don't feel quite right.

Trust builds slowly over time. Because of this, you cannot regain trust in one day when something has happened to deplete it. Furthermore, you can't make your spouse trust you. You can consistently show yourself to be trustworthy by acting on your dedication and investing in the relationship. You can also grow in your trust for your mate by taking risks. Try making some investments and watch what happens. If things go pretty well, you'll gain more trust. When trust based on a solid commitment is really rolling between the two of you, you'll experience the best blessings of marriage together. Can you honestly say to yourself that you are consistently showing your mate how dedicated you are—that you are sticking and not stuck or stopping?

Nancy and I have had our blowouts over the years. I suspect very few married couples get through life without having some. But I have a very deep trust for her and her instincts in life. This trust comes from observing her handling of things over many years. She once confronted me in a way that highlights the intersection between trust and the long-term view of commitment. I had been in yet another period of working too much. (I'm trying to manage that tendency, but it's a long-term project.) Nancy thought I was looking particularly ragged (departing from my natural good looks and youthfulness, no doubt), and she was concerned. It's worth noting at this point in this story that she has no good reason to be concerned unless she loves me and is committed to me. She does and she is. I love her and am committed to her.

Anyway, she found me in front of my computer one day, working, of course, and took the opportunity to voice her concern. She said, and I quote, "You have to slow down because I'm the one that's going to be changing your diapers when you are old." Okay, that's one way to voice the concern. Sometimes I don't hear Nancy's concerns as well as I should. That time I got it right and didn't become defensive. First, she said this gently. I cannot tell you strongly enough how important that is when you plan to confront your mate about something. The research confirms how crucial a gentle approach is at such times.[5]

Second, we have some trust built up. We don't have a perfect marriage. What I do for a living can make it trickier at times. But we do have relationship capital to draw on. At the moment I just described when she confronted me, her gentleness combined with my trust for her helped me to hear what was most important. Here's what I heard: "Dear, I love you and I am going to be here for you all the way—until you or I fall apart—but I'm worried about how much you work. I'll be here for you when you're old and gray, but I want you to leave something for me!" Long-term view with love. She made a deposit that day.

MARRIAGE ON THE MARGINS

Whether or not investing on the margin is a good economic strategy for you in this day and age, I want to suggest that it's a bad investment strategy for your marriage. When you invest on the margin in your marriage, you are essentially risking only a fraction of your resources in exchange for what you are hoping to get. You aren't totally buying in. Investing on the margin in your marriage means you are trying to get a great return out of your relationship, but you are willing to put up only a fraction of the real cost. The rest is borrowed from somewhere, usually the future, which means that resources you really do not have get consumed, leaving you in debt as you move into the future together. If the debt keeps building, you're headed for bankruptcy. You can't build the relationship capital in your marriage by devoting a small portion—the marginal amount—of your effort today. Marriage does not thrive on the margins. Marriage takes the full investment of time and attention to thrive.

Richard Swenson wrote a book that became very popular a few years ago. Its title says a lot: *Margin: Restoring Emotional, Physical, Financial, and Time Reserves to Overloaded Lives.*[6] This medical doctor discusses the fact that in our fast-paced, give-it-to-me-now world, we leave little margin between the text of our lives and the end of the page. This is a different metaphor from what the financial term *margin* implies, but note that it goes the same direction. Swenson argues that we don't leave much room for dealing with stresses. Essentially, in spiritual, emotional, and financial realms, we tend to have few reserves because we consume everything in the present and set nothing aside for the times we are squeezed.

In marriage, many of us do not build up enough relationship capital, and when the stress hits, there is not enough to get us through without serious damage. There is no margin. To increase a healthy degree of margin in our lives, Dr. Swenson prescribes *simplicity, rest, balance,* and *contentment.* These values are not sustainable with the short-term view. They are values inspired by patience and an understanding of time and the long term. What about you? What kind of reserves do you have in your marriage to cope with the inevitable strains of life?

RELATIONSHIP BANKRUPTCY

Remember Pam and Ben from the last chapter? Like many couples, they started out without much in their relationship bank account. However, both were relatively short-term oriented, which put a fair amount of pressure on the marriage for immediate returns. Instead of making deposits and building capital in their relationship, they eroded their positive feelings with intense conflicts. Marital researchers, such as Clifford Notarius and Howard Markman, have indicated how greatly these eat up the reserves in the bank account of a marriage.[7] After so many years, Pam and Ben had completely consumed every relationship asset they had. To have no relationship capital can be devastating to a marriage. Pam and Ben might have turned things around, but they were repeatedly threatening divorce. There was no future in view, so there was no future to save for together. It was all now or never, and never was looking pretty much like where they would land. A marriage like theirs ends up in bankruptcy, with nothing left and no trust for how anything could be rebuilt.

As is fairly typical for women in tough marriages, Pam became more depressed over time. Life is not easy, and feeling utterly alone in your marriage makes it harder. Ben wasn't finding happiness in his home life, and he sought it in his work. But his work was pretty stressful, too, and he had no resources with Pam to help him cope with it. Despair was setting in for both. They were bankrupt. They had nothing left to give each other, and they were building nothing for the future. Incredibly sad, isn't it? That's how it ends for too many couples who at one time were excited about their life together.

Investing for Growth in Your Marriage

There are many ways to invest in your marriage. Caryl Rusbult, a researcher who has extensively studied commitment in marriage, has pointed out the crucial role of investments.[8] If you are married, you are probably aware of the obvious investments of money and possessions that you have made. There are also the less tangible investments of time, effort, talent, and self-disclosure. Even teaching your mate how you like the toothpaste tube squeezed is an investment. Some of these things represent a real expenditure of effort over many years!

Past investments become part of the basis of constraint commitment that I described in Chapter 1. If things are going well, either you'll not think a lot about all that's been invested, or you'll think of it all with settled satisfaction. If things are not going well, you're more likely to think about what you have invested in terms of what you might lose by leaving. That's the concern of cost that comes with constraint. In the present, what you invest is more determined by your dedication than by constraint. *You invest more time and effort because you are dedicated. It's dedication based in the long-term view that moves you to put more effort into your marriage today.*

TAKING THE RISK

Just about any kind of investment carries some risk. In life, you cannot control everything. You can't make it all turn out for the good. You could do your best and have married someone who does not try to keep the marriage strong, and end up lonely and distant. That's the scary part. You may be thinking, *What if I put in all this effort and nothing comes back?* I often hear that concern. When it's based mostly in scorekeeping and shortsightedness, it needs to be dealt with as a poor attitude that harms marriages. But sometimes this fear is based on a realistic appraisal of one's mate. Your marriage has the best chance of doing really well when you choose to invest yourself in it. Choosing not to invest guarantees your marriage will get stuck or stop altogether. No matter what your partner does, you can make investments.

My father-in-law is a retired farmer, and my mother-in-law is a retired schoolteacher. They always knew how to save money. Like many other couples, they've gone through tough financial times, but they kept saving. You cannot be a farmer without frequently facing uncertainty. The weather reminds you of your inability to control it all. Have you ever noticed how much farmers talk about the weather? There is a good reason.

In the past couple of decades, these wise folks have been plowing more of their savings in the stock market. They aren't the kind of people you would think of as risk takers. They are very careful, but they came to understand something that many people never do: it's riskier *not* to invest at all than to invest and risk something. On the day after the stock market experienced the largest one-day decline in recent decades, they made another sizable investment. That's taking the long-term view. That's acting on commitment.

Stocks and other long-term investments have some risk, but all of life is that way. If you don't invest and instead consume all your resources today, you will surely lose in the future. Solomon understood this point very well, and he used the image of farming to do it: "He who observes the wind will not sow, and he who regards the clouds will not reap" (Eccl. 11:4 NKJV).

People who are always watching out for what might go wrong and don't risk end up with nothing. If you want to reap good things in your marriage, you'll have to take some risks. If you go through your married life thinking, *I'll not take any risks; I don't want to suffer loss or pain,* you will surely suffer loss and pain. Even Jesus reserved some of His harsher words for the servant who took what was entrusted to his care and buried it in the ground (Matt. 25:14–30). The servant didn't want to lose anything, risked nothing, and ended up losing everything. Life is not without risk. But trying to avoid all risk in marriage guarantees only that you'll not invest wisely.

If you really want to build relationship capital in your marriage and family, take the long-term view on what you are doing, and keep investing, no matter what. That's a central part of what it means to be truly committed to each other.

LIFESTYLES OF THE RICH AND HUMBLE

A book published in 1996 became very popular. It is called *The Millionaire Next Door* by Thomas J. Stanley and William D. Danko.[9] This book really got people's attention. Its main point is that the people who are building financial wealth in our country are not usually the people who flaunt their money and possessions. Rather, they seem ordinary in every way, but they worked hard and are careful with their resources. You might want to read such a book if you want to learn what these people know about managing money.

I bring it up because the secrets to their financial success are the same secrets to the relationship success in healthy marriages. In other words, what these millionaires did to gain financial wealth is based on the same secrets that you can use to build relationship wealth in your marriage.

These authors identified six keys to building financial wealth. I remind you that I am not concerned with your financial capital as much as with your relationship capital. But these six things are parallel to the keys that I see in research on successful marriages, and I'll use these keys to organize the advice in the rest of this chapter. Stanley and Danko found these six keys:

1. Thriftiness
2. Disciplined investing
3. Aversion to debt
4. Serious tax sheltering
5. Sharp financial advice
6. Hard work

Let's look at each key to building relationship capital in your marriage. I'll define how each one can be reflected in marriage.

1. *Be Thrifty.* What does it mean to be thrifty with relationship resources? It means not to waste them. For example, time is the number one resource that couples squander. You don't have an unlimited amount of time. Nope, not you and not me. Yes, if you are committed, you are very clear about intending to have a future, but that doesn't mean you can waste the time you have today. In fact, one of the few downsides to having a well-developed commitment to the long term in your marriage is that you may act unwisely *because* you have a sense of a future. I mentioned this in Chapter 2. At times you may make the wrong choice about priorities because you presume your mate will be there for you. So you squander the opportunity you have right now—tonight—to build something in the marriage. When you are more thrifty, you see that bit of time in the here and now as an opportunity. You spend your resources wisely.

For example, how many hours of television watching are logged in the United States and other industrialized nations when some of that time could be invested in marriages? Our marriages need this investment more than our entertainment industry. Are you thrifty with the amount of time you have together? Being thrifty doesn't have to mean being cheap. It can mean knowing when to spend more and when to spend less. So to spend less time watching television and more time taking walks and talking like friends is a very wise choice to make. If you are going to overspend your time, do that in areas to build your marriage.

2. *Discipline Your Investing.* The people who develop true wealth (in any sense of the word) have a strategy. They understand the long-term view and make commitments based on it, and they invest *regularly.* If you talk to a financial adviser about how to do well in the stock market over time, the adviser is likely to tell you about a strategy called dollar cost averaging,

or DCA for short. With DCA, you decide how much you are going to invest in the market, and you send in that investment in regular intervals, whether the market is up or down, soaring or crashing. Let's say you decided to save $1,200 for retirement, invested in the stock market, per year. With DCA, you'd send in $100 per month. *You invest no matter what.*

This strategy keeps you from reacting to the state of the market. It is a rational approach only if you believe that the stock market is fundamentally a long-term investment. As I said, I think marriage is such an investment. It works out well only with a solid long-term view. The long-term view with a plan accompanying it keeps you from bailing out in a short-term dip and losing what you have already invested.

What does DCA look like in marriage? First, let's determine what investments in marriage might be. Only you know the most tangible investments for your marriage, but I can list some of the more potent investments for many marriages. Any of the following could add to your relationship capital over time. You'll note that all of the following investments require time. If you do not carve out time, they do not happen. So, carving out the time for any of them is the most important investment you can make and the most tangible expression of priorities. I beat that point to death in Chapter 2—and with good reason. Nothing else happens without the investment of time:

- Praying together
- Doing something fun together
- Talking like friends
- Leaving small notes of appreciation
- Planning a special date (together, or as a surprise for the other)
- Working on a budget together
- Resolving a conflict about money as a team
- Planning a vacation together
- Going to church together (worshiping together, engaging in a ministry together, etc.)

I'm sure you can expand on this list. Doing that in itself is an investment in your marriage. Make a list of the things that matter most to the two of you in staying close and bonded in your marriage. Each probably knows the kinds of things that the other can do that really mean a lot.

I once cleaned the spiders out of the window wells of our home because Nancy really wanted me to do it. I must admit, I didn't do it right away when she asked, which would have been more impressive to her. Nevertheless, I did it, and Nancy was pleased. That might not seem like much, but such little things are investments in a marriage. Just goes to show, it might not be obvious to you what things you can do as tangible investments in your marriage. Share what matters to each of you. Then work at regularly making these investments.

Keep in mind—and act on the fact—that wise investors stay at it, even when the conditions don't look right. Regular, steady investing profits a marriage. Again, Solomon nailed the point:

> *In the morning sow your seed,*
> *And in the evening do not withhold your hand;*
> *For you do not know which will prosper,*
> *Either this or that,*
> *Or whether both alike will be good. (Eccl. 11:6 NKJV)*

Keep sowing your seeds. You don't know which will return the best growth, but when you stick to it and keep investing, the harvest will be plentiful.

I know some of you who are reading this have been thinking, *But what about diversification?* Thought you had me, didn't you? Yes, financial professionals say it's important to diversify. It's important in marriage, too, but you don't diversify by multiplying spouses. To be sure, some people hedge their bet by being married while keeping a competing relationship going on the side. Clearly, that's not good for a marriage. So what is?

Diversify in the ways in which the two of you stay connected. There are various avenues of bonding in marriage. You can develop a close bond in your spiritual lives. You can make your sexual relationship more fulfilling. You can engage in fun activities together. You can do things together that benefit your children, and these can often tie you more closely together in your marriage. See where I'm going with this? I doubt that most couples can have every type of connection smoothly rolling along all the time.

Some things go better than others at different times—and in different times of life together. The more avenues of connection you have up and running, the stronger your marriage will be. That's diversification.

I have seen many couples with almost no connection together other than sexual. One couple I worked with had sex and only sex going for them as far as I could tell. Don't get me wrong. It seemed to me that they had a lot going in terms of their physical connection and this kept them close together on a number of levels. But they were not diversified. When complications came up sexually, for example, in the latter stages of pregnancy or after a baby had just arrived, their marriage would take a huge nosedive. These can be stressful times for marriage anyway,[10] but weakening the only connection spells trouble. Other couples who regularly invest in more ways of connecting are going to be less vulnerable to the setbacks of one area that falters for a time.

In the work I have done with my colleagues on how couples can preserve and protect their marriages over time, I have come to believe that the most powerful investment is to *make time for friendship in your marriage* and to protect that time from conflict.[11] Being able to stay connected is crucial for building relationship capital in your marriage. Over the years, too many couples quit making time the way they did early on. Early on, they tend to go out of their way to make room for the relationship. When life gets busy and demands on time grow, friendship time together is usually sacrificed. That's short-term thinking. You need the basis of friendship in your marriage to stay strong to make it in the long term. The time together as friends can be a two-hour date or a twenty-minute walk around the block, but it needs to happen regularly.

Now for the second part. When you have made time to invest in friendship, keep in mind the nature of friendship. Friends talk about things in ways that are different from ways married couples tend to talk over the years. Married couples who are not investing in friendship direct most of their talking time to problems to solve and problems between them. It's important to have these conversations and do them well, but it's also important to have talks as friends. Friends talk about interesting topics: dreams, fun things, philosophical issues, beliefs, experiences, spiritual impressions, prayer requests, you get the idea. Friends talk about what draws them closer together, not about problems and conflicts. Therefore, make time for friendship to happen, but agree to keep conflicts and problems off-limits. Doing this establishes some time in your marriage when you can relax from the pressures of life. That's a powerful way to preserve and deepen the bond you have together over the years to come.

3. *Avoid Debt or Get Out of Debt Fast.* There are many ways to go into debt in marriage. Basically, anytime you use up more resources than you have in the bank or than you can make up in the present, you create debts for your future. As with investments, you probably know better than anyone what factors are putting your marriage in debt. I recommend that you sit down and talk together about what's putting your marriage in debt—if it is in debt—and work together to reverse the flow of red ink. That means forgiving each other. The less debt you build up, the better. Work together to stop the actions causing debt to mount.

Since you are not perfect, getting rid of the debts that will accumulate in your marriage is vital. You will hurt each other from time to time. That causes debt to build. These debts chew up your marital relationship capital in the worst way. It's crucial to work toward making forgiveness a regular investment in your marriage. Whole books have been written on forgiveness, so I'll not try to go into detail here, but I will stress the need for forgiveness in your marriage. Whenever Jesus taught on forgiveness, He used the financial metaphor of releasing another from a debt (e.g., Matt. 18). Even when He did not directly refer to financial concepts, the Greek word for forgiveness used in the New Testament portrays the picture of a debt released. You give up your sense of a right to hurt each other when you are hurt. Forgiving each other doesn't mean that you are not responsible for your actions, but it does mean that you work at keeping debts from accumulating between the two of you. If you need more specific advice on how to move forward with forgiveness, I recommend that you check out resources that cover the subject in more depth.[12]

4. *Seek Tax Shelters.* You may be thinking that there is no tax on relationship capital. You are correct, so I'll settle for a play on words here. Couples who are building a strong base of relationship capital over the years in marriage are avoiding things that unnecessarily *tax* the marriage. Just as with the government, there is no proper way to avoid taxes that are due, but there is also no reason to pay more than you have to pay. In marriage, people often allow their resources to be taxed more than need be.

For example, you may be overinvolved in activities outside your home. There's nothing wrong with activities, of course, but if you have too many commitments there really isn't time to otherwise invest in your marriage. You cannot avoid all taxing situations. However, you can reduce how much you are taxed. The life in your marriage depends on your doing this.

What activities, relationships, or things add a tax to your marriage? If you work on it together, I bet you could make some decisions to limit or release some things that get in the way of your marriage growing in the years to come.

5. *Use Sound Investment Advice.* No one knows it all. People who have managed their finances well turn to others for advice at times. They realize that others can offer fresh or unbiased perspectives. Similarly, people who do the best over time in their marriages take advantage of sound advice for making the marriage strong.

What are sources of information on how to invest wisely in your marriage? Two stand out to me. One is God. Scripture presents many ideas for ways to improve your relationships. I think that's a primary way that God has shown us what works and what does not when building a great marriage. Perhaps you've seen how good the advice can be with some of the passages I've referred to in this book. You can also ask God directly for help. I believe that God is truly interested in helping you make your marriage strong and satisfying, and that He delights in receiving your prayers for help. You can pray for wisdom in your marriage. You can pray for God's guidance in being the best mate possible for your mate. It takes some humility to ask God for anything, because in doing so, you admit that you don't know everything and you certainly don't control everything. Where better to go than to God?

A second source of sound investment advice for your marriage is others who have something to say. You can read books on how to build your marriage. You can ask questions of friends you trust—those who seem to know what it takes. You can ask a pastor or a counselor who specializes in helping marriages. People around you know a thing or two about how to have a great marriage, but you have to seek out the insights that they can share with you.

6. *Work Hard.* The steps I have been suggesting in this chapter are not necessarily easy to accomplish. They require effort—sustained effort. I've

never seen a really good marriage where the two partners didn't work at keeping it that way. It's true, though, that when you are preserving and adding to relationship capital in your marriage, the work does not seem so hard. That's because the positive bond stays strong, and it's easier to keep the motivation. It's harder to do the right thing when you are in a downturn, but as I said earlier, that's the most important time of all to put in the effort. You'll experience fewer downturns if you keep up the work of a good marriage.

Happy Camping

I started this chapter with my friend's camping story. I'd like to end it with one from my life with Nancy. I can personally vouch for the interesting conflicts that can come up when camping because we've "been there, done that." Nancy and I had one of our biggest arguments the first time we went camping together. Nancy grew up in a family of campers, but I did not. I confess that I used to be camping challenged.

We arrived at our campsite after driving all day. It was late, and we were tired and hungry. I was just standing around not really knowing what to do. Nancy became a little frustrated with me. Actually, a lot. Nancy is usually patient, but as I said, we were tired and hungry, and I guess she wasn't in the mood for the helpless male thing. I decided to help matters by becoming frustrated with her for being frustrated with me, and we managed to have a nasty argument.

However, after we finished our argument, we got down to learning to camp together. She taught me how. That's an investment all in itself. She taught me how to pitch a tent, how to cook with little stoves, and how not to grumble about little stones under my sleeping bag. Of course, I also learned to try to remove the stones before I put up the tent. These days I'm great at building campfires. Most important, *we've* learned how to camp together. Getting there took work and patience and time. Now it's fun. We're reaping the reward of the investment of time to learn to camp together. You can do it too. Invest in how to be happy campers *together.*

It's time for a review of your investment strategies in your marriage.

- How are you doing at making regular investments in your marriage? What things do you do that you consider investments (big and small)? What things does your mate do that you recognize as investments? Spend more time on this last question because it's too easy to miss ways in which your mate gives to you.
- Schedule time to meet with your spouse. Talk about two specific things. First, what kinds of investments does each appreciate most from the other? Be open and nondefensive. It's a good thing to hear from your mate about the kinds of things that mean the most to him or her for showing love and commitment. Second, what specific investments can each agree to try to increase in the marriage? Review the specific ideas in this chapter to help you identify some areas to work on.
- Do what you agreed to do! This is the most important step in investing.

Love does not consist in gazing at each other but in looking together in the same direction.

—Antoine de Saint-Exupéry

Chapter 7

A Lasting Vision, A Vision to Last

Where there is no vision, the people perish.
—Proverbs 29:18 KJV

It was a time of unparalleled darkness. In 1929, the Great Depression shuddered and shook the lives of both the rich and the poor for the decade to come. Then things got worse. The financial uncertainty of the depression gave way to a greater fear—uncertainty about war. The whole Western world seemed to be coming unglued. I want to recall those days to highlight the importance of vision in life and the importance of the right sort of vision in marriage.

Most of the time when we think of vision, we think of something positive. But it's also possible to have a dark vision. Adolf Hitler was a man of vision. He rose to the height of his power with the help of the depression. The German people had been suffering terribly. Their economy was in shambles; fathers and mothers could not work hard enough or fast enough to feed their children. The people also continued to feel the sting of defeat from World War I. The road was paved for Hitler's vision of national glory and domination. Among other things, he convinced many Germans that their suffering was the result of a Jewish and Communist plot. He captivated the nation with his powerful vision of blinding hatred, raw power, and superiority. A vision can be powerful, but that does not mean it is good.

Adolf Hitler had a dark heart and a dark vision. They're clearly revealed in his various statements, for example:

> Any alliance whose purpose is not the intention to wage war is senseless and useless.

> Success is the sole earthly judge of right or wrong.

> A violently active, dominating, intrepid, brutal youth—that is what I am after. . . . I will have no intellectual training. Knowledge is ruin to my young men.[1]

Imagine living through those years. Perhaps you don't have to imagine; you only have to remember. The economy of your land was in rubble. All around there was nothing but uncertainty. Within that culture of fear, Hitler and his vision arose in one of the most powerful nations on the earth. From 1933 on, Hitler rebuilt Germany into a military powerhouse. Nearby nations feared his ambitions while other countries took comfort in their distance. Within Germany, Hitler's foes were defeated easily, and he steadily gained political power.

Where would you look for hope? Perhaps you would look to the United States, but the country was in isolation from the world at that point in history. England, led by Sir Neville Chamberlain, had an official policy of appeasement with the slogan of "peace for our time." Although I am sure many people had the foresight to see where things were headed, one man in history spoke out—loudly. He had a different vision from that of Hitler, but he, too, understood the power of a vision. He saw what was coming and he saw what was needed. His name was Sir Winston Churchill.

Churchill argued for years that England needed to rebuild and vitalize its military, especially its navy. He could see the storm coming from Europe, and he openly criticized his nation's policy of appeasement while Chamberlain and too much of Europe tried to ignore Hitler as he amassed power to devour entire nations. Churchill said of appeasement, "An appeaser is one who feeds a crocodile, hoping it will eat him last."[2] In essence, Churchill took the long view while other world leaders held on to the short-term hope of appeasement.

Germany began World War II at a tremendous advantage in both military and material might. But Churchill inspired his people. Though the country was outgunned, he gave the British people a vision for a future of victory, freedom, and honor. His vision provided the free world with something more powerful than military might. He inspired people to overcome fear and to fight and to die, if necessary, for what was right.

The contrast between Churchill's words and Hitler's is striking. Earlier in his career, Churchill stated, "Sure I am of this, that you have only to endure to conquer. You have only to persevere to save yourselves."[3] Later, Churchill declared, "Let us therefore brace ourselves to our duty, and so bear ourselves that if the British Empire and its Commonwealth last for a thousand years, men will still say, 'This was their finest hour.'"[4] Churchill made the last statement in a speech to the House of Commons at the beginning of the Battle of Britain. During the following months, the people of England found within themselves the ability to fight far beyond their obvious resources.

Hitler knew the power of a vision of domination, but he vastly underestimated the power of England's vision of freedom from oppression. The people of England were inspired, both by the immensity of the task at hand and by the words of their leader. *That's what a good vision does—it inspires you to live at your fullest potential. A good vision helps you transcend what keeps you from living abundantly.* It pulls you toward the higher objectives in life.

Hitler had a vision that was dark and evil. Churchill had a vision filled with confidence, hope, and resolve. Churchill understood dedication. Each leader pulled his nation forward by the power of vision. Both visions were powerful. One was right.

What does it mean to have a right, powerful vision for your marriage? That's what I hope to explain in the rest of this chapter, because having the right vision in your marriage can help you conquer the forces working against the two of you living life to the full. Want to really stick? Nurture a vision for your life together.

What Is Vision?

A vision is an image or ideal that guides people, often providing meaning, motivation, and inspiration for the tasks ahead. A good vision includes elements of foresight, idealism, and dedication. A vision is more than seeing a certain kind of future; it is seeing the future so clearly that you act on it.

In case you're thinking it, I'm not about to say that marriage is like war—at least not a war between the sexes. Though I realize that war is an image of marriage that comes to the minds of many people, that's not why I chose the illustrations from World War II. I used Churchill and Hitler as examples of the power of vision. Nevertheless, building a strong and happy marriage is a bit like waging a war in that it takes dedicated effort over many years as you deal with the various challenges. Having the right vision is an essential element in living out your commitment. You can also have the wrong kind of vision in marriage, one that keeps you from a strong and thriving marriage.

While partners are not at war with each other in a strong and healthy marriage, the culture most of us live in is at war with the institution of marriage. The prevalent vision of marriage today is not one that inspires many people.

POSITIVE VISION OR CYNICISM?

Without a vision, Solomon asserted, we perish (Prov. 29:18). Why perish? Because *the larger view gives meaning to the details of life that otherwise can diminish your soul.* Grand visions inspire us to higher ideals and ethics, without which we are all vulnerable to the ravages of cynicism. The Hebrew word used for "vision" in Proverbs 29:18 speaks specifically to guidance from God. How does God's view of marriage compare with the cynical view dominant in our culture?

Cynicism is reflected in a mocking, disbelieving pessimism within much of our culture. Cynicism cries out that our efforts are meaningless because nothing is certain. Why bother? Cynicism is alive and well in Western cultures. Indeed, consider American culture. Never before have a people had so much wealth and so many opportunities. But do we see a land flowing with optimism and goodwill? No, the pervasive attitude says believe nothing, trust no one, and live for the moment. That's not a positive vision to inspire people. It's a selfish, cynical vision that kills the soul. It is the essence of bad vision for marriage. The most cynical view shouts out the following:

- Marriage does not work.
- Marriage is temporary.
- Marriage is for romantic fools who think they can make love last.
- Marriage makes people miserable.
- Marriage is a trap used by men to confine women to lives of slavery.
- Marriage is a trap used by women to confine the energies of men.
- Marriage constrains your capacity to enjoy and express your sexuality.
- Marriage will keep you from realizing your full potential.
- Marriage institutionalizes men's abuse of women.
- Married people are less satisfied in life than unmarried people.

The message underlying all of these comments is that commitment in marriage is unrealistic, if not completely stupid. Have you heard these messages—in the news, in the movies, in popular music, from your friends?

COUNTER YOUR CULTURE

You cannot avoid having your perception affected by your culture, but you can work actively against the views of your culture when the views are contrary to commitment in your marriage. Think of it this way. Living within a culture is like living in a fish bowl. A colleague, Janice Levine, says that how we see things is affected greatly by the water in which we swim.[5] We get so used to the water in which we swim that it becomes very easy to think of "our tank" as reality. We become accustomed to it. So in regard to marriage, the cynicism around us is the dirty water in which we swim.

You are probably familiar with Simon and Garfunkel. They were a popular duo when I was in junior high. Once they were trying to get the perfect photograph for an album cover. They found just the spot they wanted, which was near an iron post at the Fifth Avenue subway station in New York City. They went out one day and took five hundred pictures. Satisfied that they had gotten the perfect shot, they packed up to leave. Then they looked up and noticed the writings on the wall behind them—the wall in the background of all five hundred pictures. Sage writings they were not. If you have been to any big U.S. city, you know what these messages look like, except back in the sixties, I think they were more legible. And they didn't have computers that could easily edit the photo images back then, either.

Later, they could laugh about it, but I doubt it was funny to them at the moment. *They had to redo the shoot because they hadn't first stopped to carefully consider what was framed in their vision.* That's how it is with vision in marriage. If you aren't careful, it can include elements that you hadn't really thought about or planned on. When you fail to think about the vision for your marriage, you will likely include many messages from your culture that may not be helpful or positive.

Here's Paul's warning to pay attention to the background of the cultures in which we live, as described in Eugene Peterson's translation of the Bible, *The Message:*

> *Don't become so well-adjusted to your culture that you fit into it without even thinking. Instead, fix your attention on God. You'll be changed from the inside out. Readily recognize what he wants from you, and quickly respond to it. Unlike the culture around you, always dragging you down to its level of immaturity, God brings the best out of you, develops well-formed maturity in you. (Rom. 12:2)*

We can become well adjusted to the vision of our culture about marriage (and other things), or we can become attuned to the vision of God and be changed from the inside out. To grasp the higher view, we must reflect on God's design and nurture it within our lives.

WHAT IS A REALISTIC VIEW OF MARRIAGE?

The view that marriage is irrelevant at best and harmful at worst is common, but it's not the view that we should accept. Nor is it a view that we should ignore. Such cynicism about marriage has some validity—it reflects what all too many people have actually experienced or seen others experience. While the cynicism is understandable, marriage *does* have immense value, and marriages are worth the effort they require.

Sure, there are some marriages that virtually none of us would think it wise to continue. But far more often, marriages are the very best long-term investments that people make. Marriages can be risky for people, yet life is even riskier without marriage—riskier for individuals and for society.

If you are inclined toward the cynical vision of marriage, I want to ask you to reevaluate it. Think through the impact on society and on your life of keeping this view. God's view is that marriage is important and worth the effort. Given the prominence of marriage in God's plan for humankind, it should hardly be surprising that there is a mountain of scientific evidence on the beneficial effects of marriage. Before moving on to specifics about God's view, stop to consider some basic, often little known facts about marriage.

Glenn Stanton wrote *Why Marriage Matters* to bring to light the evidence for the benefits of marriage. Taking a predominantly sociological perspective, he has compiled and summarized the extensive literature showing the overwhelming benefits of marriage to the individuals in them and to society as a whole.[6] It's not a how-to book about making your marriage better. It's a solidly reasoned argument for why marriage matters at all. Stanton catalogs the benefits of good marriages, ranging from documented positives for child well-being, social connection, financial security, mental health, physical health, and even sex. Yes, married people tend to have more sex, and more satisfying sex at that.[7] Not exactly the dominant worldview, is it? While the overall benefits of marriage are greater for men (on average), the benefits are clearly in evidence for both men and women. But on that note, I have something to say to my male readers: it is particularly important that you act out dedication in your marriage so that you are as much a blessing to your wife as she likely is to you.

Most people who stick with it experience huge benefits of marriage. There are great and lasting benefits to a grander view of commitment in your marriage. *Unless you work to the contrary, the vision you are likely to have for your marriage is the one handed to you by culture.* Is that the vision you want to guide you in your marriage?

One more concern before moving on. I fear that we can develop views of marriage that are wildly unrealistic, almost fantasylike, and thereby encourage greater feelings of disappointment. I also believe that if we accept a lower, more cynical view of marriage, we virtually guarantee that our marriages will be hollow shells of their real potential. Be careful. I think it is best to have a *positive,* full vision for what you can develop together in your marriage that is also *realistic.*

Please take a few minutes to reflect on these questions: What is the view of marriage that dominates the culture in which you live? What is the view of marriage you have gained through all your experiences in life?

WHAT ARE YOU BUILDING?

Winston Churchill spoke on many subjects, not just war. Given his understanding of vision, consider this quote: "We shape our buildings: thereafter they shape us."[8] Building a marriage is much like building a house, and the plans you follow are shaped by the vision you have in mind. The vision you construct for your marriage will shape the life you have in it.

All couples have some model in mind for marriage. In fact, each individual in a marriage has a vision, and the vision each holds may or may not be shared by the other. Some couples have a shared vision that guides them in wisely constructing their relationship. Others have more of a vision infected by our culture—a vision of foreboding and helplessness. While it's hard for me to imagine, I suppose there are some couples who have no vision at all, not together as a couple and not as individuals. I don't mean to say that they have no expectations. We all do. But they have no view of life and marriage that's bigger than the events of the day. The ideal is to have a shared, positive vision for the future of your marriage.

Let's go back to the two couples we met in the beginning of this book. Take a few minutes to read again about Jeremy and Suzanne, and Lisa and Steven. Jeremy and Suzanne came to their marriage with a strong, positive, and committed vision for their future. He had absorbed some of this from what his parents had modeled over the years. Suzanne and Jeremy shared this vision together, and they began to build their life together girded by a vision of stickingness.

Contrast that with Lisa's vision of foreboding. She had a vision, but it was more of a nightmare to fear than a vision to propel her forward. The real problem is that her vision is perfectly realistic in the world today. She wanted desperately to have hope and a positive vision, but even her mother had little hope to offer her. In a way, her vision was mixed. On the positive side, she knew what she wanted: the fuller, lifelong commitment in marriage. But her positive vision was hampered by dark clouds from the failed dreams of so many couples around her. She knew more couples who had divorced than who were making it work. She wanted to believe the higher view was possible, but she was neither sure nor easily reassured.

I think Lisa and, I hope, Steven have more going for them than those without any vision at all. The couples who concern me the most aren't even thinking about vision. They aren't thinking about what they are trying to build. They are plodding along with whatever model of marriage was given to them by their backgrounds and culture, and they are not particularly inspired to anything beyond that. For more and more couples, the vision of being together doesn't include marriage, just living together as long as it's convenient. But the commitment levels of those who live together and are not planning on marriage are much more like dating couples than married couples.[9]

Lisa was troubled in a way that is good. She was struggling with her deeper desires for what marriage can be in comparison to the realities of the marriages she had seen. Struggling is good because thoughtful people make considered choices. From all the work I have done in the field of marriage, I am convinced that if the average couple would wait six more months prior to marriage and think more carefully about the commitment they are making, the number of divorces would go down substantially. Too many people don't reflect enough on what they are doing and why they are doing it.

You can be different. You probably are different, or you wouldn't be reading this book. Having said that, I want to encourage you to work at fully developing a positive vision for your marriage. Such faith and vision for your future hold in check the cynicism of our day. You are reminded that your marriage is meaningful, worth fighting for, and worth working on. That's a powerful way not to get stuck.

Nurturing a Positive Vision in Your Marriage

Mates who consistently nurture a vision for their life together are the most likely to have lifelong, happy marriages. Fran Dickson at the

University of Denver has studied couples who have been married fifty years and more.[10] In her research, she found that happier couples reported talking regularly about their future over the years of their life together. This sharing of hopes and dreams is a tangible expression of vision. Furthermore, this sense of vision separated those who were together and happy later in life from those who were merely together but relatively unhappy. In essence, those who were sticking over many years nurtured their sense of their future, and those who stayed together, but were stuck, did not have this quality about their marriages. You and your mate can maintain dedication to each other by keeping a positive vision for your future.

Contrast this with what chronically unhappy couples do. They nurture an obsession with the past rather than a vision for the future. How many couples spend far more time talking about their past than their future? And most of the time when talking about the past, they talk about failures, conflicts, and disappointments. Of course, you sometimes need to talk about the past to better understand something that happened or to work through forgiveness. Also, just to be clear, talking regularly about wonderful times in the past is a good thing to do to remind you that your marriage is bigger than the present circumstances.

My research indicates that the desire for a future together is a central component of dedication.[11] It's not just a view that says, "Yeah, sure, we'll probably be together." It's a vision that says, "My future is with you, and I *want* to grow old with you!" Many couples *expect* to be together in the future. Dedicated couples *want* to be together. When couples have the "want to" of dedication, talking regularly about the future together comes more naturally. Couples who had the best marriages over the many years do this regularly.

Now for the good news. You can *choose* to do things in your marriage that couples who have great marriages tend to do. In other words, if lifelong happy couples nurture their vision, you can do it too. Become a self-fulfilling prophecy of blessing to each other. In the rest of this chapter, I want to give you some tips for increasing your sense of vision in your marriage. I don't know which ideas may work best in your marriage, but I'll bet one or more is worth a try. Some of them are closer to fostering the grand vision of your marriage, which includes a sense of future, meaning, and hope. Other ideas here are not so lofty, but they can be part of an overall strategy to convey hope in your future together.

One very specific way to develop your vision together is to talk about your goals for the future. It's a familiar but true adage: "If you fail to plan, you plan to fail." Most of us know goal setting is wise, but too few of us do very much of it in marriage. Solomon described planning ahead as the path to blessing (Prov. 21:5). This is as true in marriage as in anything else.

It doesn't take an hour each evening to keep future goals clear in your marriage. I know couples who do this in a structured way once a year. For example, Wendy and Glenn carve out a couple of hours every New Year's Day to talk about their goals for the year. Sure, there is plenty to do on that holiday, but they have found that they can make this happen. What better day? When they meet, they talk about goals in major areas: spiritual, financial, relational (marriage), and children. One year they agreed to spend thirty minutes, two days a week, to nourish their spiritual relationship, and they picked out devotional material to read to each other. They didn't perfectly keep to their agreed-upon plan, but having the plan led them to find the time together far more often than they had ever done before.

They also worked on how they were doing financially and where they wanted to be in the upcoming year in terms of savings. They didn't follow that plan perfectly, either, but having it helped them save more than they otherwise would have. I am intentionally pointing out that they did not perfectly, legalistically strive to achieve their goals. Yet they achieved them in that the goals were reasonable and the goals stretched them beyond where they would have otherwise been. People can take something good and apply it so rigidly that they sap the life out of it.

Wendy and Glenn are not slaves to a formula, but they recognize spending this time together is valuable. The actual goals they set are helpful to them, but talking about their future together is even more powerful than setting good goals. It reinforces the overall sense that they have a future and that they have a vision for it.

Short-term goal setting is valuable too. When you plan and set goals for the week to come, you alleviate the pressures of conflicts that come in the day-to-day routine. *The blessings of long-term goal setting, however, have*

A Lasting Vision, A Vision to Last

more to do with enhancing and realizing your vision for the future. A solid vision that includes goals keeps you headed in the direction that you want to go. Among God's many challenges to Israel, God said through Amos, "Can two walk together, unless they are agreed?" (Amos 3:3 NKJV). The point is simple: two can't walk on the same path together unless both are agreed on the destination. This is as true in walking with God as in walking with your mate. Goal setting helps you do that.

One more thing. In marriage, like much of life, clinging rigidly to goals when the circumstances change is unwise—unless God has somehow given you specific direction on a goal or task. There are times for flexibility about the plans we make. Remember Betsy and Samuel from Chapter 4? They had a goal to travel more as their children grew up and left home. That part of their vision was shattered by the accident that left Betsy with serious physical limitations. Strong couples rise to the occasion and move ahead through the trials of life. Part of being able to do that is knowing when to be flexible. Betsy and Samuel had to redefine what their future was going to be like, and they did. Their future was together, they knew that, but they needed new goals that reflected the changes affecting their lives. If you develop a routine for goal setting in your marriage and you keep at it, one goal should be to reevaluate goals set in the past based on new circumstances. That's not wishy-washy; that's wise.

SHARING DREAMS

Sharing dreams is a lot like sharing goals in terms of the benefits to your marriage. It's one more way to demonstrate the reality of a future together. But dreams are different from goals, so sharing them is somewhat different. *Goals in marriage are what you plan to accomplish together while dreams in marriage are what you hope to experience together.* Hence, dreams touch the deeper hopes of your heart. Sharing dreams can be positive; however, you won't do much of it if your marriage is not going well. That's because dreams reveal more about who you are than goals do. In marriage, people are less likely to share their dreams when conflicts are not being handled well and when there is not a strong sense of safety founded on a commitment. As I said earlier, research we have conducted at the University of Denver shows that couples with greater levels of dedication are the same couples who disclose more deeply in their marriages.[12] An atmosphere of mutual dedication, along with a sense of a future, makes it safer to share dreams. As with many things related to commitment, this dynamic works both directions. Sharing your dreams can reinforce the atmosphere of mutual dedication and a future.

If you already share your dreams together, keep it up. It's healthy for your marriage. If you don't share dreams but would like to try, I have a word of caution for you. Be careful to handle the dreams of your mate as something precious, coming from the deeper regions of the soul. If you stomp on your mate when he or she is sharing dreams—or you demean the dreams that are shared—you'll seldom hear your mate's dreams again. That's the most unfortunate part of handling issues poorly in marriage. Destructive conflicts and invalidation shut down the pipeline through which the deeper connection flows.

For this reason, it can help to agree to have such talks in a certain way. I suggested this in the previous chapter: set aside some time just for this (such as taking a walk or going out to dinner), and both agree to keep conflicts and issues off-limits. It's another powerful way to make a positive investment in your marriage.

Jennifer and Antonio have been married thirty-three years. They are one of those couples whom others envy. They fell in love in college, and although they've had some falling-outs, they have not fallen out of love or dedication. They have raised two children, have many friends, and are known as people who tend to be a blessing to others. Better yet, they have a deep sense of being partners in life. They even work together. They own a dry cleaning business and Laundromat. It's hard work and they are not rich. But they enjoy the work together and it shows. People like to come around their shop because what they have together is infectious.

Some people who know Jennifer and Antonio think, *How can they pull this off? Are there couples who are really this happy together?* The answer is yes. There are couples who have something that's as good on the inside as it appears to be from the outside. Some people falsely believe that these couples were born under a lucky star and that it's their lucky lot. Some couples have a much harder time than others, from the very first day. They have a harder time through no fault of their own, but life throws them a series of curveballs. However, no matter what life throws, great marriages are created over time and don't just happen to unsuspecting travelers.

Jennifer and Antonio work at it. They make the investments we discussed in the last chapter, and their efforts pay off.

For example, they dream together. No, they don't have a Vulcan mind-meld while they sleep at night. Rather, they talk about what they'd most love to do in their lives and in the future. It's one of the best parts of their friendship. Antonio has told Jennifer of his dream to be a writer. He'd really love to write material for inspirational magazines. Jennifer has a dream to host a bed-and-breakfast in the mountains of Colorado. She'd like to have one where she could regularly go for walks along mountain trails because she has always loved the outdoors and hiking in forests.

Jennifer and Antonio have talked about many things as they have walked through life together. If they decided to work toward making these dreams happen, they could move their talks from musings about dreams to plans for reaching goals. They may yet decide to do that. For now, these are dreams that could, but don't have to, come true. Antonio loves to write. He has been putting his thoughts down on paper (computer, these days) for years, becoming comfortable with words and how ideas can be expressed. He has not tried to get any of his work published because he has been so focused on raising their kids and running the store. For her part, Jennifer regularly reads books and magazines about bed-and-breakfasts, along with anything she can get her hands on about the mountains of Colorado.

Jennifer and Antonio find blessing in their ability to share. Sharing dreams in this manner has many benefits for them. First, each feels that the other can hear about and validate the deeper regions of who each is. Sharing in this way knits their hearts closer together.

Second, having this window into each other's dreams allows both to look out for interesting connections to the dreams. For example, if Antonio notices a commercial for a TV show coming up about mountains, he tells Jennifer about it. Simple things like that remind her that he loves her and cares about her interests. If Jennifer reads something that is written particularly well in a way that touches her, she can show it to him so that he can think about how the writer accomplished that.

Third, if they choose to move their dreams more into the category of goals, they have a sense through life of what could be in the future. They could end up selling their dry cleaning business, buy a bed-and-breakfast, and move to the mountains when they retire from the faster pace of their current lives. Both have noted that such a setting could provide wonderful peace and inspiration for writing. There are blessings for them in the present and the future that come from sharing their dreams.

What do you dream about? Have you and your mate shared such things? Knowing about the individual dreams of your mate makes it more likely you'll be able to develop dreams for your life together. What do you want the two of you to be doing together when you are sixty, seventy, or eighty years old? Do you see yourselves traveling places? Baking? Exercising? Making love in the afternoons? Praying together for your grandchildren? Working together in a ministry? Holding hands while swinging on a porch somewhere? Reading good books side by side and snuggling? You don't have to be clairvoyant to believe in a future. Having a sense of a future can bring many blessings to the present.

When I was in my late teens, I really admired a couple in my church. They had what seemed to me a big love for each other and for other people. They were engaged in the ministry of the church together, but not full-time. He worked for the government in a job that allowed for early retirement if they desired that. They were some years away from retirement, but I remember that both dreamed of getting to that place, taking advantage of the early retirement benefits, and moving into full-time ministry together. I have forgotten what ministry they had in mind, but I have not forgotten the wonderful sense of the future together that they shared.

One more word on sharing dreams. If you have tried to share your dreams but have been put down, don't give up. Keep doing what you can do to make your marriage safer for this kind of intimacy. For some of you, that means learning more about how to handle conflict well. That's why Howard Markman and I and other colleagues have so strongly focused on ways that couples can handle issues and differences well.[13]

PLANNING FUTURE FUN

This is not the deepest idea in this chapter, but planning for future fun can be motivational. I don't know about you, but I derive pleasure from anticipating fun things that we've planned in the future. For example, last summer, I was working very hard on several projects, all with serious deadlines in early August. Having something to look forward to in the not-too-distant future can keep me going. Of course, when I'm really working hard, the rest of the family is affected, so having something we're all looking forward to is a real plus.

We planned a vacation in our favorite part of the state (Durango and Silverton, Colorado, if you want to know). Nancy and I have special memories of this part of the state, and it's a delightful place to go. There are old restored towns, historical sites, wonderful vistas, trails, and a really awesome train ride with old steam engines. I looked forward to that trip all summer. It helped me get through the tougher parts of some projects, and we had a really enjoyable family time.

Anticipating something is almost as fun as getting there. Sometimes it's even more fun. These plans don't have to be grand or elaborate to produce this benefit, either. Planning for a special date a few months away or planning some events around an upcoming holiday can help a lot. I know many families who have built into the schedule pizza and movie night every Saturday as a way for the whole family to relax together. I don't know about you, but something as basic as that can see me through a tough Thursday.

What's fun for the two of you? Do you do these things very often? Do you have any plans to do the things both know are fun? Fun is amazingly powerful in helping a couple stay bonded together in marriage, and planning for it involves a vision.

FOLLOWING RITUALS AND TRADITIONS

Rituals get a bad rap. The term is associated with stilted, overly regulated behaviors that have lost whatever power and meaning they once had. This can be a downside to the practice of rituals. For example, the religious leaders of Jesus' day had a view of the Sabbath that was far from God's idea of a day of rest and reflection. They had turned the Sabbath into a day of anxiety, performance, and legalism. We should be cautious so that our rituals and traditions do not become separated from their original intention and blessing. However, let's not throw the concept out because it can be misused. Many marriages and families derive blessing from rituals and traditions that are repeated through the life together. Such traditions anchor us in the past while helping us look to the future. Therefore, they can enhance the overall vision for the marriage.

Here's a personal, family example. Our boys are fairly young at the time of this writing. Like so many other baby boomers, we waited until we were older to do the parent thing. One activity that is becoming a tradition in our home is the lighting of candles during Christmas week. Our boys love fire—anywhere, anytime, and probably anything! They love to see fire on a birthday cake; they'd likely be happy to see the entire birthday cake on fire. They love campfires. They love fires in fireplaces. If they grow up to be pyromaniacs, perhaps we'll regret some of our family experiences. But hey, that's the future, and it's not a vision we want to nurture! Having special candles on Christmas Eve is a nice tradition for us. It will become one of the things we'll look forward to each year as the holidays approach. If we're wise about it, we can work this interest into learning about Advent and use candles to teach about that ritual in the church. It's a family tradition that can grow in meaning as the boys grow in their ability to understand and appreciate spiritual things.

Another example is taking a yearly vacation to the same place. I know that's a boring idea for some people, but I also know that for many families it's a powerful tradition that undergirds the sense of being family. For instance, I know many people from the East Coast who went to the shore every summer with their families. In Ohio, we didn't have a shore to go to, so we went other places. But for those families, it was part of what summer with family meant. That could be going to the beach for the day or for the week, at the same spot year after year. The important part is the practice of the ritual as a couple and as a family together. It cements the sense that "we are a family," "we do things together," and "we have a perpetual future." Simple behaviors can exert a powerful effect.

These traditions are beneficial for families and also for marriages. They exist in the background of day-to-day life as part of your vision of what your life together is about. Their very power is often in the mutual experience of something meaningful. So traditions and rituals contribute to the vision of a life sharing things together. Here are a few examples:

- Walk together after dinner, talking about things friends talk about.
- Go to sporting events together and root for "the team."
- Give presents for the twelve days of Christmas.

- Plan a yearly weekend getaway to a romantic setting—just the two of you.
- Have a special meal on certain holidays. Prepare it together!
- Pray together about major goals on New Year's Day.

We are told in the book of Hebrews that God is the "rewarder of those who diligently seek Him" (11:6 NKJV). There are many ways to seek God, including through prayer, worship, praise, Scripture, and so forth. To reinforce your vision, you and your mate can seek God together. When you do this, you join together in the pursuit of the very One who gave you life and was the Creator of marriage.

For several reasons, too many couples are reluctant to do this. For example, in many marriages, there is a difference between mates in either beliefs about God or the degree of commitment and involvement accompanying the beliefs. Seeking God together is not likely to happen in marriages where there are major spiritual differences, or at least, it's going to be much more difficult under those circumstances.

Even in marriages where both partners share a common, strong faith in God, seeking God together seems to me to be a relatively rare thing. One reason is that so many things get in the way. Have you noticed how many times I have pointed out that many things get in the way of what is truly important in our lives? There is a reason for that and I hope it's obvious. We let too much interfere with what really matters in life. We tend to let the bustle of today crowd out our time with God.

Another reason that many couples do not seek God in any regular way together is that they have been given no model for how to do it. Having not seen it done, where does one begin? Many materials can help you develop a pattern of seeking God together in your marriage. The topic deserves far more attention than I can devote to it here. Trust me. If you go to a Christian bookstore, you'll find many resources to assist you. For example, there are various devotionals, some even just for couples, that you could get and read together. That can help you develop a focus in spiritual time together.

Seeking God together in a regular way is a powerful thing to do. Scripture makes it very clear that it's wise to seek the Lord and, therefore, wise to seek the Lord in and about your marriage. You may not realize that secular research also shows that marriages benefit when partners find ways to join together spiritually.[14] For example, couples have some advantage in life when they pray together and attend church together.

How do such basic spiritual activities relate to having a vision? I think that being more connected to God keeps you more connected to everything, especially the meaning of life, the importance of marriage, and the reality of eternity—in essence, the ultimate reasons for the long-term view. Therefore, engaging in spiritual activities and seeking God together support your overall sense of a future and a vision for it. You can enhance this immensely by deliberately thinking about, praying about, and seeking God about His will for you in the future together. Seeking to know it *together* reminds you of what matters most and who is most important in your life and future together.

Now, let's finish this chapter by identifying key themes about vision in the life of David.

DAVID, A MAN OF VISION

The ark of the covenant was the most tangible, physical reminder of the presence of God to the Israelites in ancient times. At one point, the ark had been captured by the Philistines. Then it was returned, but through a series of misadventures the ark had not made it back to a central place of worship for the Israelites. The day that David finally returned the ark to the City of David was a day of great rejoicing. On that day, David celebrated with a beautiful psalm. Notice the attention given to the *past acts of God, the present relationship with God, and the future blessing of God* in passages selected from this psalm:

> On that day David first delivered this psalm into the
> hand of Asaph and his brethren, to thank the LORD: . . .
> Sing to Him, sing psalms to Him;
> Talk of all His wondrous works! . . .
> Seek the LORD and His strength;
> Seek His face evermore!
> Remember His marvelous works which He has done,

His wonders, and the judgments of His mouth. . . .
Remember His covenant forever,
The word which He commanded, for a thousand
generations,
The covenant which He made with Abraham,
And His oath to Isaac. . . .
Oh, give thanks to the LORD, for He is good!
For His mercy endures forever.
And say, "Save us, O God of our salvation;
Gather us together, and deliver us from the Gentiles,
To give thanks to Your holy name,
To triumph in Your praise."
Blessed be the LORD God of Israel
From everlasting to everlasting!
And all the people said, "Amen!" and praised the
LORD. (1 Chron. 16:7–36 NKJV)

Here you can clearly see remembrance and thanks for the *past* blessings and works of the Lord. This theme appears throughout Scripture. Remembering the works of the Lord is a way of remaining conscious of Him and His purposes in the present. Here you see a reminder of the covenant relationship between God and His people—a commitment anchored in the past with the promise of blessing for the *future*. The *future* is also implied in the reminders that God's mercy endures forever and that He is to be blessed from everlasting to everlasting. In the *present*, David used the entire psalm to call the people to give thanks, make known His deeds, sing, *seek*, remember, give, worship, tremble, rejoice, be glad, give thanks (again), and triumph. That's a pretty active present, and a lot of it is about staying aware of God as the Lord of the past, present, and future.

Such a focus on the past, present, and future keeps us mindful of God's purposes beyond the immediate circumstance in life. It stretches our sense of time and of God. The phrase "practice the presence of God" has been popular for some time in Christianity. I think David was expressing the essence of that. He encouraged God's people to have an expansive vision for the purposes and person of God. And when things are not pleasant and life is harder, this expanded sense of what it's all about inspires us to greater acts of love and dedication.

Now, back to marriage. I don't see how you could have any fuller vision in your marriage than by turning together to the God who formed everything and created you. I am a social scientist. I can tell you of many studies that point out the value of marriage to society, but the studies can't tell you anything about the meaning of marriage. Research on commitment can tell you that thinking and behaving in certain ways will help a marriage to be happier, less prone to divorce, and more open for deeper sharing. However, research can't tell you why your marriage has meaning or why your marriage matters to God. To have a grander vision for your marriage and your future, you need to look to Him. *Where you are looking has a lot to do with where you are going to end up.*

INTO YOUR FUTURE

Do you want to be inspired about your marriage? You will not likely be inspired by your culture. That inspiration must come from another place. We are inspired by images, acts, and ideas that are bigger then ourselves. Belief in God and God's view of marriage puts you in touch with a bigger vision. Eugene Peterson is best known at this time for translating the contemporary language version of Scripture called *The Message.* I close this chapter with his introduction to the book of Philemon, where he writes words of power:

> Every movement we make in response to God has a ripple effect, touching family, neighbors, friends, community. Belief in God alters our language. Love of God affects daily relationships. Hope in God enters into our work. Also their opposites—unbelief, indifference, and despair. None of these movements and responses, beliefs and prayers, gestures and searches, can be confined to the soul. They spill out and make history. If they don't, they are under suspicion of being fantasies at best, hypocrisies at worst. [15]

Respond to God. Believe in Him. Let your life together be deeply affected by His love. And walk in hope together.

A Lasting Vision, A Vision to Last

Vision is crucial for a great marriage to come about. Your own vision as well as what you develop together matters.

- How are you affected by the messages about marriage from your culture? What negative messages play loudest in your head?
- What is your personal vision for your marriage? What do you think about what's in it? How much of what you hope for, dream about, or expect to come to pass would be something you've told your mate about?
- Sit down together and talk about your mutual vision for your marriage. This takes some time, and it can't happen unless you carve out that time. Talk about your dreams. Talk about where you'd like to be with your marriage in five, ten, forty years. Work through the list of other specific suggestions from this chapter, and see what you want to work on together.
- Together make a list of rituals that are important to each of you and that reinforce your sense of your future.
- How do you see God's role in the future of your marriage? Do you talk to Him about such things? Try it. Write out a prayer to God that reflects your vision.

Part 3

FOSTERING WE-NESS AND CONTAINING ME-NESS

*. . . in sickness and in health,
to love and to cherish; . . .*

In the two chapters of Part 3, we come to two concepts that have fallen out of favor in our world today: oneness or teamwork in marriage (remember, I'm not suggesting you and your mate become a blob together), and sacrifice in marriage. In the strongest and happiest marriages, there is a clear sense of "us" and "we." Further, there is an understanding—and actions to back it up—that sacrifice is a fundamental part of life together. Both oneness and sacrifice are notions that have fallen out of favor in part because they are misunderstood. Yet a discussion of true commitment in marriage would not be complete without discerning the deeper ways in which two people come together and move through life in marriage.

We are two vines curved to one another . . . twined into one stem—too like and near to discern the changes of our growing.

—Walter Benton

Chapter 8

ONENESS
AND TEAMWORK

So then, they are no longer two but one flesh.
—Matthew 19:6 NKJV

The essence of God's design for marriage has to do with two people somehow becoming one. As we saw in Chapter 1, the concepts of *choice, permanence,* and *oneness* go to the heart of what commitment is all about. When it comes to commitment, dedication really helps a marriage thrive. If you want to stick and not get stuck, you need to develop and keep oneness in your marriage. As we also saw, the healthy view of oneness is not that of a blob of goo, wherein one of you gives up your identity for the other. Instead, the identities of two mates are joined to form a new, third identity of "us," where "we" becomes a crucial element of life together.

In this chapter, I want to explore what oneness looks like and what you can do to keep it growing in your marriage. We'll also touch upon many common marital dynamics directly related to the basic theme of oneness.

Me or We?

I have been familiar with the biblical idea of oneness in marriage for many years. When I was beginning to study commitment in more depth, I found it interesting that secular marriage researchers and psychologists understood the healthy dynamic of oneness in marriage in much the same way that the concept is portrayed in Scripture. I've frequently heard the term *we-ness* used to describe a sense of having a team identity in marriage. Of course, we-ness is in contrast with *me-ness*. With me-ness, the focus is on self, not other and not us.

Various researchers and theorists have described the formation of commitment as a shift in thinking from what's best for self to what's best for the team.[1] I'm not talking about religious writers, mind you, but secular marital experts who have noted what happens in the development of strong marriages. I have called this sense of oneness *couple identity*. People who are the most comfortable thinking in terms of "we" tend to be the most dedicated and happy in their marriages.[2] That's not just an interesting finding; it flies in the face of the intense emphasis on individualism dominating our world today. Instead of two separate people out for themselves, a marriage that is really sticking tends to have two partners who think and act on what's best for the team.

When I was in elementary school, perhaps about ten years old, I remember meeting a friend of one of my friends. One day we went over to the boy's house to play. I don't remember much of anything about the boy since we never became good friends, but I do remember one thing very clearly. As I entered his garage, I noticed that each wall, left and right, of the garage was covered with a virtually identical set of garden tools. I'm talking a lot of tools. Those people were into gardening. It struck me that each parent must have had a complete set of garden tools. I can still visualize the startling picture of separateness. It was as if I could hear either of his parents saying, "Don't you touch my tools! Use your own!" I wondered then and am curious now about what that marriage was like. It could have been great. Perhaps they loved gardening so much that they needed all the tools, and keeping two separate sets allowed them to readily find what was needed.

I'm not saying that *everything* has to be shared in a good marriage. I have some of my favorite things, and so does Nancy. Some things are more personal, and I don't care to share them. For example, each of us has a favorite Bible that is not typically shared. It's not that we wouldn't, but that's a pretty personal item to many people, including us. The same goes for certain spaces in the house. Nancy has areas that are more hers, and I have areas that are more mine. However, there is a greater sense between us of our home being *our* home. I'm suggesting there are degrees of separateness and togetherness in terms of identity and possessions. What I saw in the garage of that boy's home was a strong depiction of two people who did not share together. The walls screamed, "Mine, mine, mine!" What do your walls say?

WE GOTTA BE ME!

There is nothing wrong with wanting to be an individual with a clear identity. Although I don't agree with all of the theories in my profession, I do agree with a commonly accepted view that many things go wrong when a person has no clearly developed sense of self. The problems that lead to disorders in one's sense of self happen so early in life that all of life is affected. People with some impairment in their sense of self are more likely to have trouble trusting others, are more likely to be insecure or arrogant, and are more likely to give others trouble. So as I focus on the problems of cultures that glorify self, realize that I am aware that some people really do need a greater sense of self. Without a clear sense of who you are, you'll be hampered in your ability to learn who you can be together as a couple. Exploring this psychological issue further is a topic for other books. Before I leave it, however, I want to suggest that the clearest sense of self comes from being connected to the One who is bigger than self. *If you really believe that God is there and that He made us, knowing who you are has everything to do with knowing Him and who He is.*

From the beginning of history, people have been fundamentally self-absorbed. Go back to Adam and Eve. They sinned, they covered up, and they hid from God. After being confronted by God, they blamed each other. Each was more concerned with self than with what had happened and how it affected the other. Look at Cain. He had his individual idea of a good sacrifice, but God didn't approve of what he offered. Cain was too proud to change his mind and offer the right thing. Cain killed his brother for having the gall to be more interested in what God wanted. If you keep reading through the Bible (or any history book), it doesn't seem to get any better. Most people focused on what pleased themselves and not others. There were exceptions, but perhaps not many.

The focus on self and not the team is far more prevalent in some cultures than others. The United States is a prime example of a nation where there tends to be an extreme focus on self. It has always been a nation with a strong orientation toward individualism. From what I understand, many Asian cultures are less this way. In the United States, self is king. This tendency was originally expressed positively, such as in the Bill of Rights to the U.S. Constitution. Aware of the tyranny among countries in Europe at the time, the Founding Fathers deemed freedom of the individual of paramount importance in the formation of this country.

Yet what started as respect for individual rights has steadily grown into worship of the individual. The cult of self proclaims that commitment to oneself is the highest form of commitment. You see it everywhere, and I think it has truly intensified over the past few decades.

At this point, if you are not committed to yourself above all else, you may be thought to be backward. People are getting in touch with themselves, finding themselves, and being themselves. People seem more concerned with knowing their rights than with accepting their responsibilities. As I noted in the last chapter, these attitudes infect everything around us. If we don't examine them, we absorb them.

These days, people want all the most enjoyable parts of relationships without all the hassles of commitment, dependency, and responsibility. That's harsh sounding, I know, but that's the way things seem to be. Why wouldn't someone want all the good bits without having to work? In the short run, committed relationships take work, lots of it. But that work is usually well worth it in the long run. Those who cling to excessive individualism are prone to ending up with little or nothing in terms of quality relationships.

Fyodor Dostoevsky wrote during a time when he could see greatly increasing attention to self and individualism in his homeland, Russia. In *The Brothers Karamazov* he put the following observations in the mouth of Fr. Zosima, a monk and a deep-thinking Christian:

For every one strives to keep his individuality as apart as possible, wishes to secure the greatest possible fulness of life for himself; but meantime all his efforts result not in attaining fulness of life but self-destruction, for instead of self-realisation he ends by arriving at complete solitude.[3]

Most people do not get married to have complete solitude, but too many live their married lives in ways that promote exactly that. Intense individualism doesn't make for a good marriage. Marriage is about commingled lives. Marriage is about sharing and learning to share more. Marriage is about teamwork. That's probably one of the most significant benefits of strong marriages for people and societies. With the greater connectedness in marriage comes someone to lift you up when you fall, encourage you when you are low, rejoice with you in the joys of life, and share day-to-day experiences. Furthermore, when people are more connected in strong family relationships, all of society is the better for it. There are much pain and misery in isolation, and isolation haunts too many Americans. Most people, deep down, want to be connected to others, but if they worship extreme individualism, they will not ever get there.

WHAT'S MINE IS MINE

Randy and June started their marriage of five years on a happy note. Both had seen a number of friends divorce young, so they searched carefully for the right person to marry. Finding each other in their early thirties was delightful. Both were rising stars in their field of electrical engineering. Both were very bright and very intense about their work. Both had waited until their thirties to marry because they were so intent on getting their careers going. There were some good points about their waiting to get serious in a relationship. Each worked a ton and likely would have made a mate miserable by marrying earlier.

Both Randy and June were Christians, but they didn't give much place to a relationship with God in their lives. Again, they were too busy. Neither took much time to develop a connection with a community of believers. They were individuals and proud of it. Each was a dedicated, hardworking, successful person. It took a few years for the excitement of all that to wear down a bit for each of them. Having a career zooming along can feel thrilling, but it doesn't satisfy the deeper desire for relationship.

Randy and June married after dating a little more than a year. They truly did love each other, and they had a lot in common. They enjoyed discussing work and projects, and they enjoyed working out together, walking, hiking, talking, and listening to all kinds of music. Life was good. As is true for many couples in which both partners have been out on their own for years, they decided to keep fairly strong separate identities in their lifestyle. Both kept their own bank accounts. They bought a house together, which represented a major departure from their individualized lives. Owning something together was a big step for both. Neither was interested in having children, with all the responsibilities involved. Given their priorities, that was a pretty responsible decision. They would not have been willing to give up what they were putting into their work to give children the necessary time and attention.

Oops. Two things happened in their fifth year of marriage that threw Randy and June for a loop. First, her company decided to move from Denver to Houston. That sparked fireworks. Whose career was more important? Randy made it clear to June that ending his work with his firm where he was a rising star was out of the question. "I never agreed to give up my career. That's like my whole life, what I've worked for all these years!" he protested. "But what about my career?" June pleaded. "My work is just as important as yours!" They had come head-to-head with a dilemma many dual-career couples will face at some point. Neither was sure that the commitment to the marriage could compete with the commitment to work. The argument grew more frequent and more intense. June knew she had to make a decision. She was convinced that Randy was not going to move to Houston, and she felt that the future of the marriage was up to her to decide.

Someone was going to win, and someone was going to lose on the issue. "This is not like working through problems at work," June noted. At work, they were used to functioning as a team. That's not typical for most companies, but it was for hers. It was part of why she didn't want to leave her company. The people in her work group understood teamwork. The realization grew in her mind that she and Randy were not really a team.

They were two individuals trying to get the most out of their lives. Would they be a team only when they were winning?

Sometimes just when you think you are in the middle of a very long, dark tunnel, a train comes to run over you. For June, the train came in the form of a growing queasiness in her tummy. *No way,* she thought. *It can't be. We're really careful!* She went out to buy a test kit. It said to wait until the morning. She did.

In the meantime, she debated about whether to take the test without telling Randy. She decided, *Enough of this me versus you business. If I'm pregnant, he's going to know about it from the start.* When she told Randy about the test planned for the next morning, his initial response was not exactly gallant. He exploded and said, "That's just great. That's all we need now!" June was devastated. Randy was, too, but he was not showing it in the most helpful way.

The next morning, the ten-dollar test kit worked its magic. The stick turned red. Red meant baby. June felt blue. Randy turned green. Randy, quite shaken, looked at June and said, "Well, there we are."

Both were silent for a very long time. Then Randy said, "What are our options?" June's eyes filled with tears as she choked out, "What do you mean, what are *our* options? You don't mean . . . you'd do that?" Well, Randy had thought of abortion. It wasn't so much that he wanted it, but life was becoming a bit too inconvenient with all these relationships and responsibilities and all this . . . this . . . married stuff. Although June wasn't exactly eager to have children, abortion was *not* a possibility. She believed that children were from God, and even if she hadn't been asking for such a gift, she couldn't see how she could reconcile abortion with what she believed about God.

As Randy saw June crumple on the floor in a flood of tears, he realized he had shredded her. Seeing the immense pain on her face, he felt ashamed that his first thoughts had been about keeping his life simple. He did love June. He made the first move toward her that he had made in weeks. As he hugged her, he said, "That was a stupid and selfish thing for me to say." Randy cried, too, and they sobbed and hugged on the floor for about an hour.

They hadn't been close like that since, well, they hadn't ever been close like that. The idea that they had not really been so close before startled

Randy. He realized that they had not faced anything tough before, and that they had not had to pull together as a team. Well, when flattened by a train, you sometimes end up more squished than you realized you could be. They were squished, but they were starting to be squished together. Squished, not squashed.

Both June and Randy had quite an emotional day. Each went to work late, but neither got much work done. June's day was full of anxiety about the future. *What's going to happen to me, to us, to this baby?* She felt waves of panic that came and went as she paced in her office. She also prayed. She hadn't prayed so much since the time her mother had a cancer scare a few years ago.

Randy's day was even more unpleasant. He didn't feel panic. He felt something that shook him to the depth of his sense of himself. For the first time ever, he felt unsure of who he was or who he wanted to be. Everything had always been about *his* needs, *his* dreams, *his* desire to get ahead. To his credit, he did something few people ever do. He asked himself what he was living for and where he wanted to be. The possibility of an answer not framed around self-interest grew in his mind.

He prayed. He prayed some more. Somehow, it seemed that thinking about God worked against thinking about self, and at the moment, he was a bit sick of what he saw when he thought about himself. He asked God for help. His thoughts crystallized around the question of whether he wanted to go through life alone—successful in his work, but very alone. He decided he did not, and that meant his ideas about marriage needed to change.

It doesn't always work this way. God does tend to bring us into circumstances that give us a chance to see reality more clearly and to grow closer to Him, but we can refuse to grow. We can hold tightly to our hearts of stone rather than allow Him to give us hearts of flesh. Randy chose to grow.

That evening, after dinner, Randy choked up a bit and said again to June that he was sorry for his first response of the morning. He explained that he felt that God had been speaking to him all day about his life and what he was living for. In what she thought was an amazingly humble and strong step forward, Randy said, "I've been thinking that I've really not taken being married very seriously. I've been looking at what that means to me, and I didn't like what I saw. I wanted all the best of what we could have together without really wanting to be together. I don't think being married is all about me or you; it needs to be about us. I don't know how to do 'us,' but I'm willing to start learning."

What he did next stunned June. Randy looked her in the eyes and said, "I don't think we've really been married. We had a ceremony, but I don't think I have fully given myself and my future to you. I think I wanted this marriage only as long as it was good for both of us. I don't believe that's commitment. I want commitment. I want you to know I'll be by your side, no matter what *we* decide to do. Will you *be married with me*? I mean, you and me together."

June was shredded for the second time of the day, but this time felt much better than the first. She felt something jump to life in her—the desire to join more deeply with Randy. After more tears and some deeply squishy hugs, they started to talk a bit about *their* future. June was not sure, but she suspected that their talking that night was more sprinkled with the words *we* and *our* than any other discussion of their married life.

After the baby arrived, both were amazed at how wonderful being parents turned out to be. The baby redefined for them what hard work meant, but they were working together. Their parenting would not have gone as well had they not been through a process together that changed their sense of themselves as individuals and as a couple. By the time that Melissa arrived, they were eager to be parents.

I won't tell you what they did about the career dilemma. I could, but either way I could tell that story would make some of you upset about how it was resolved—as if I were making a broader statement about marriage. I don't want to detract from the far more important point about the way they turned the corner to draw together as a team for the first time in their marriage.

Randy and June took what could have been the end of their marriage and turned it into the beginning of a new life together. I know for some of you this example brings up a level of pain that would be hard to put in words because you have come to some crisis points like these with your mate and you did not come out better. That happens, and I understand the immensity of the pain. Those of us who are married face this dilemma of "me versus us" almost daily, both in big and in very small decisions. It takes fortitude to keep asking yourself, "What does this mean for *us*? What's best for *us* in how I handle this?"

Many couples start off thinking and acting in ways more consistent with being one, or a team. Many do not. Those who do not get there are not as likely to have the deeply fulfilling marriages that they really want. You can't have hyperindividualism and also have a clear and strong "us." You can be an individual, but in a strong and happy marriage, you join your individuality to another to make "we."

A FEW THOUGHTS ON PRENUPTIAL AGREEMENTS

Given that I study and think a lot about commitment, I am often asked about what I think of prenuptial agreements. These legal contracts bring up many issues directly related to oneness, so I want to discuss them briefly. A prenuptial agreement is a legal contract that a couple enter into prior to marriage that specifies how assets will be divided up should the marriage end. Most commonly, fairly rich people have them because one or both partners may have a substantial fortune that they do not want to risk dividing up in a divorce. I have mixed feelings about these agreements. I think they are mostly a symptom of a divorce culture; therefore, I see them as something negative. On the other hand, I can understand why someone with a vast fortune would view such an agreement as prudent. I once read a lawyer's opinion that every couple should enter into such an agreement. After all, marriage may not be forever, but assets are, right?

Although I can see a certain pragmatism to the idea for some couples, the process of coming to a prenuptial agreement essentially calls for a couple to plan the ending of their marriage at its very start. From the couples I have seen in counseling, this puts horrendous stress on the relationship. Keep in mind that most of the couples who come to counseling are already having trouble, so people like me may never see couples who have no trouble at all with the prenuptial agreement process. However, if the couples who, on average, do best in marriage are those who develop the clearest sense of "us," imagine the implications of the prenuptial process. These agreements make couples clarify what's "mine" versus "yours" at the very time when most couples are working the hardest to develop the "us."

You may be familiar with the much-publicized marriages and divorces of Donald Trump. Donald Trump left his first wife, Ivana, for Marla

Maples. Ivana left their union $25 million richer, with frustration and the motto: "Don't get mad, get everything."[4] Donald and Marla married after he and Ivana broke up. They had a prenuptial agreement. It had an interesting clause specifying that Marla would receive a substantially greater portion of his wealth should their marriage go longer than five years. You can tell the rest of the story by the headline in *People* magazine: THE DONALD DUCKS OUT WITH HIS EYE ON THE BOTTOM LINE OF HIS PRENUPTIAL DEAL, DONALD TRUMP SAYS GOODBYE TO MARLA.[5]

Regardless of the legal wisdom of the process, prenuptial agreements are a reflection of our times. As a society, we here in the United States have a high divorce rate, a lot of material assets, and a very individualistic approach to life. Such agreements are strong reminders of the individualistic orientation of many people toward marriage. As I said earlier, a strong individual orientation generally does not a good marriage make. A marriage can be approached as just another business deal, but that's not really what marriage is about.

COMPETITION

We live in a very competitive world. Some forms of competition are good and some are bad. One kind that is very bad and that is fundamentally inconsistent with oneness is competition between two mates. There is nothing wrong with friendly competition, such as playing a game of rummy. What's bad for marriage is competition between the two of you about whose priorities are more important, who is more capable, who is going to get his or her way, or who controls key resources. When problems are approached as if there will be a winner and a loser rather than a team, trouble is brewing. It's hard to say whether this is more a cause or a symptom of low levels of dedication. It probably cuts both ways.

In a nationwide poll that I conducted along with my longtime colleague, Howard Markman, we found that people who were happiest and the most dedicated in their marriages were the least likely to say that there had to be a winner and a loser when they dealt with problems.[6] This finding was independent of financial status. Rich people, poor people, and all those in between showed the same pattern. Simply put, win-lose dynamics are a sign that you are not on the same team, and that contributes to increased conflict and a deep sense of loneliness over time.

How does your commitment to individualism compare with your commitment to teamwork in your marriage? For Randy and June, the turning point in their marriage came when they had to face the choice between a life of individualism or oneness. In a way, it's unfortunate that more couples do not have to deal with such a crucible that drives the point home. Randy and June did, and they came out of it stronger. It can go the other way too. When the conflict is over a major issue and neither will back down, that often spells the end of a marriage. It's far better to work together as a team to find a solution than to have either person be forced to back down and feel like a loser.

POWER

Win-lose dynamics are really about power, with each individual trying to have power over the other. When you are in competition, you are trying to win. Ponder this statement for a few minutes.

The one who has the least commitment has the most power.

The commitment indicated here is dedication. The one least interested in sticking has the most power because that person cares less about what happens to or in the marriage. If it's me versus you, and you are more committed to me than I am to you, then I have you over a barrel.

Think about another car-buying analogy. If you walk into the dealership to look at cars, and the salesperson can tell you are very interested—even committed—to leaving that day with a new car, you are dead meat. You'll pay the highest price, and the salesperson will win. Notice how good salespeople often ask, first thing, "If I can come up with a great price for you on this today, are you really interested in making a deal?" They want to know how much leverage they have with you. If you say, "Yes, sir, I really must have this new car today. I'm totally committed to driving away today with a new car. Let's make a deal," their eyes will light right up. On the other hand, if you walk in and convey a sense that you are merely looking, not sure, and certainly not going to act rashly, you have the upper hand. Okay, let's see how these dynamics can look in marriage.

Carol and Bill have had a stormy marriage of twenty-four years. They argue about most major decisions because they have different instincts on many issues. Their commitment has been severely tested on three occasions in their life together, and they barely survived each one. The first crisis was about where they would live. He wanted to move across country for a better job, and she wanted to stay close to her family. Ultimately, she won by refusing to move with him. He was not really sure if she meant it, but he decided not to test her resolve.

The second crisis was about whether they would send their kids to private or public school. He favored public; she, a private Christian school. They went to the mat on that one too. People can become passionate when they think their children's well-being is on the line. They could not get to a resolution until he threatened to leave her. She backed down. The kids went to public school.

The third crisis came in their twenty-second year of marriage when her widowed mother became too frail to live on her own. She had fallen a few times trying to get through her basic daily routine, and Carol decided that enough was enough. She convinced her mother to live with them. It was far harder to convince Bill. Guess how she won the argument? Yep, she threatened to leave Bill and move in with her mother if he didn't agree to have her live with them.

You notice the pattern here, right? On major decisions, the commitment in their marriage became a pawn to sacrifice in order to gain the upper hand. This strategy can work for resolving an impasse, but with it comes a terrible cost to the sense of commitment between two mates. The strategy gives one mate more power in the argument at hand, but it undermines trust and the sense of a future, which are crucial for a thriving marriage.

How often do you pull back on your commitment in order to gain the upper hand with your mate? Such a dynamic is the very essence of the me versus you, winner-loser dynamic. It's competition in marriage at its worst. The competition tells you it's not a relationship of commitment. In reality, couples do not fall into either-or categories on these things. Sometimes, the commitment is clearer, and the power and competition dynamics are not evident. At other times, you may not be doing so well together, and it gets more competitive and win-lose. Who said marriage was boring?

GENDER WARS AND TEAMWORK

If you've been living on some other planet, perhaps you would not have noticed that the topic of the roles of men and women in marriage has been hot for a few decades. Actually, it's been a fairly hot topic since the Garden of Eden. Have you ever wondered about the conversation between Adam and Eve after God pronounced the Curse and expelled them from the Garden? It's just a guess, but perhaps it went something like this:

ADAM: Well, you certainly screwed that up, didn't you?

EVE: What do you mean, I screwed it up? You're the one who blew it.

ADAM: Excuse me, but I'm not the one who prepared that meal. You were the one that the tempter worked over.

EVE: Oh, yeah? You knew what was up, and you didn't protect your marriage. Besides, you seemed just as interested in that fruit as I did. You just can't admit it, can you?

ADAM: Do I have to make all the decisions around here? You should have known better than to mess with that tree. I could have resisted temptation just fine all by myself.

EVE: Oh, like you're this big spiritual leader, right? Where did you lead us now, Buddy?

ADAM: The name's not Buddy. It's Adam. I'm the first man, remember that.

EVE: I'm in awe! You might just be the last man, too, if you don't show some respect.

ADAM: Sure, start throwing threats around. I didn't want to be one with you anyway.

Pretty, it was not. Throughout time, couples have struggled with who does what, who is who in the marriage, and who is in charge. I'll bet some of you were beginning to wonder if we were going to get all the way through this book without discussing controversies about male and female roles in marriage. Nope. Here we are. However, I don't intend to discuss the best way to interpret key passages in the Bible on this topic, nor do I want to highlight all the nuances of these gender dynamics in our society. The point I want to make is far simpler than that. Once I make it, I'd much rather leave it up to you two to struggle together and with God about who is called to do what in your marriage.

Some couples have what are called *egalitarian* marriages; others have more *hierarchical* marriages. *Egalitarian* generally refers to a certain level of equality in how life is approached and in how tasks are divided. *Hierarchical* usually refers to what has been a more traditional model of the husband as head of the home and the wife in a position ranking somehow under the leadership of the husband. It gets more complex, of course. The dimensions in which gender dynamics are played out can vary greatly from couple to couple. Some couples are more egalitarian, some more hierarchical, and for many, it switches in interesting ways depending on the issue. Gender role issues can be sparked by everything from dirty dishes to spirituality.

Here's what I have observed in dealing with couples in both counseling and research: *it's very hard to tell what the two people in a marriage believe as a matter of doctrine on these issues if they have a strong sense of oneness and teamwork.* If you took ten awesome marriages from all sorts of backgrounds—couples who are committed, thriving, happy, and good friends—and asked each of the ten men and ten women to write out what they believe doctrinally about gender roles, you'd get a wide range of statements on paper. But when you watched how all of the people behaved in their marriages, it would look more like teamwork than anything else, no matter what they wrote down on paper. In great marriages, couples walk like a team and talk like a team. Mutual deference, respect, and love characterize them. Sure, in certain areas, you'll see one or the other take the lead. But at the root, these relationships are not competitive; they are more about mutual love and support.

Studies suggest that happiness in marriage is more related to *working together* on how to divide up all the tasks than on how the tasks are actually divided up.[7] Don't get me wrong. Women are happier in marriage when their husbands do more of the household tasks. But even more important is that you work together to decide how things will get done and that you follow through on the agreements. That's what you'll see in many of the best marriages: teamwork, agreement, and follow-through.

You may be thinking that oneness as portrayed here sounds more like the egalitarian model. That's not what I am trying to say. It really depends on the couple. I have seen many couples who would write out the most traditional understanding of roles that you could imagine, but because they are living a healthy oneness, what comes through is teamwork. My point is that healthy, growing, and flowing oneness has the power to easily overwhelm conflicts over roles or individualism. Paul expressed this same point very directly when talking about the diversity of the members of the church: "There is neither Jew nor Greek, there is neither slave nor free, there is neither male nor female; for you are all one in Christ Jesus" (Gal. 3:28 NKJV).

You probably realize that this is the same Paul who wrote passages that sound far more hierarchical than this verse implies. You can't easily reconcile the differences until you see the power of oneness to obliterate conflicts about differences. Differences do matter, but the way you deal with them matters even more.[8] When things are going right in a marriage, the needs of the team will override the concerns of self. When things are good, when the couple are experiencing oneness, you'll see something wonderful. You'll see love working its way out.

C. S. Lewis captured the essence of this dynamic in his book *A Grief Observed.* He noted: "There is, hidden or flaunted, a sword between the sexes till an entire marriage reconciles them."[9]

The power of oneness reconciles a woman and a man in an entire marriage. A marriage of me versus you is half a marriage at best—really more a battleground for two individuals of the opposite sex than a field on which love is played out.

ELEMENTAL SELFISHNESS

A culture that glorifies self encourages selfishness. A focus on "me" naturally leads to a focus on what I want, what I can get, and what you're going to give to me. We need to take selfishness head-on, or this review of individualism will not be complete. While some people become too easily mired in self-recrimination when others raise this topic, I am convinced that it's pretty healthy for most of us to include our selfishness in our evaluation of the way we act in our marriages.

If you think about what I've written to this point in this chapter, you can see how selfishness weaves its way through all the negative dynamics. Do you have trouble sharing your life and goals? Is that from selfishness? Do you more often think about how you can win with your mate than give to your mate? Where's that coming from? Do you see ways that you try to coerce or gain power over your mate? What drives you?

Selfishness does not make for thriving relationships. Giving to each other does, and that's why I'll devote the next chapter to that. Scripture speaks directly and frequently to selfishness, since it drives so much that harms relationships. Here are two key passages to make the point: "Let no one seek his own, but each one the other's well-being" (1 Cor. 10:24 NKJV); and "Let each of you look out not only for his own interests, but also for the interests of others" (Phil. 2:4 NKJV).

Jesus could say it in the fewest words, expressed in what has become known as the golden rule: "Do to others as you would have them do to you" (Luke 6:31 NIV). That's not "me first." That's treating the other unselfishly, the way we want to be treated.

Why do many passages hammer away at selfishness? Because this tendency is so pervasive that we need to be reminded often to think of others and not become caught up in personal desires. When it comes to commitment, people who are more dedicated are going to be less prone toward selfishness, more inclined toward teamwork, and more willing to do what it takes to make the marriage work.

GIVE AND TAKE: YOU GIVE AND I'LL TAKE

One of the saddest situations in marriage occurs when one person who is interested in oneness and teamwork is married to another who is infected with selfishness and hyperindividualism. Laura and Lee are such a couple. They have been married fourteen years, most of them very painful for Laura. She realized about two years into their marriage that Lee's vision was different from hers. She imagined a marriage where they would be a team. He apparently never got that message. Or he got it and said, "No thanks." Perhaps you've seen couples like this. Or worse, you're in a marriage like this. Or you may think you are in a marriage like Laura's, but you're missing a ton of evidence that your mate is not like Lee. Remember that the biases in perception are very strong. With Laura and Lee, there is no biased perception; Laura wishes she were so lucky. The reality is that, at least at this point in life, her husband is a selfish and self-centered man, and it hurts.

Laura noticed many things in the early stages of the marriage—things that she had seen prior to marriage but that she had merely chalked up to Lee's bachelor ways. He did not do much of anything around the house. Occasionally, he ran the vacuum or put the dishes in the dishwasher. But when he did even those small tasks, he acted positively put out that he "had to." Generally, he expected her to pick up the house, clean, do all the laundry, and serve freshly prepared meals every day. He rarely gave her the courtesy of checking schedules when he wanted to go out. He'd often announce at dinner that he was going over to Bill's or Fred's house to watch a game, and that he'd be back by bedtime—and off he'd go.

When they had their first child, Diane, things got worse. Laura assumed all the responsibilities of taking care of the baby while Lee continued with his routine. Marriages where the firstborn child is a girl may actually be at greater risk because fathers are less likely to become involved in the rearing of daughters compared to sons.[10] I know there are very many exceptions to this pattern, but Lee was not one of the exceptions.

Sexually, well, you can imagine. Lee was not overly concerned with Laura's needs in the bedroom. Oh, he wanted her to respond all right, but he was fairly insensitive to whether she was responding in any pleasurable way to what was happening.

When Laura wanted to talk about something important, such as budgets or key child decisions, Lee couldn't quite tear himself away from the television. On the other hand, he didn't have affairs, and he was a decent provider. But that was about it for the positive list for Lee as a husband.

Laura had been dying by inches for many years. She wanted a full life in her marriage. She wanted the team thing. She wanted oneness; in fact, she ached for it. Occasionally, Lee seemed different and came through for her. Sometimes, he took her out to eat and talked with her, or he brought her a gift that truly showed thoughtfulness. If it weren't for those little gestures, she might have given up altogether. She hung in there. I'm not sure what she'll do in the future. What would you do?

Some of you are thinking, *Leave the bum.* Others are thinking, *What a drag! He's just bad enough to make Laura miserable but not bad enough to give her a moral excuse to leave.* Some of you are even thinking, *It'd sure help her out if God would just take Lee out of the ball game.* Laura does fantasize from time to time about Lee's dying in a car accident. These thoughts come to her when she is the most deeply pained about things that remind her that he is not Prince Charming.

Theirs is a good example precisely because it doesn't make it easy on you if you have a conservative view of marriage and divorce. Some of you will be upset with me if I don't say she *should* leave him. Others want me to say, "Hey, there are no biblical grounds for divorce here, so let's move on and deal with it, Laura!" I can relate to both sentiments. I've heard them all in my office over the years. I can argue the doctrines and passages with the best of them. But to Laura, this is her life and real pain related to key biblical teachings. As so many know, these matters can be very complicated, and even when not complicated, they are very hard to deal with wisely.

I'm going to duck giving you a nice ending to this story. You see, I think Laura is going to have to grapple with God about her situation. She needs to seek Him and cling to Him. When a person does that, there is no telling what can happen.

As far as trying to change things with Lee, she has two basic options if she wants to remain dedicated to Lee. She can pray and gently seek changes in him, in response to changes in her. That's certainly the strategy portrayed in parts of the New Testament (e.g., 1 Peter 3). In contrast, she could confront Lee boldly and strongly—really get in his face, so to speak. Some of you may think, *That's not very biblical.* Actually, it is consistent with what Christ taught about confronting others who have personally wronged us (Matt. 18:15–17). It's also what Moses' wife, Zipporah, did when God was about to kill him because he had not circumcised their son. Check it out; it's a very short story in Exodus 4. No commentary is provided, but she saved her husband's life by bold action and confrontation.

My point is that sometimes dedication is quiet and sometimes it raises

Cain—if you are able. And sometimes dedication grieves. If you find your-self, as a male or a female, in Laura's situation, you'll have to seek God and decide what you're called to do.

REPENTANCE

You may see more of Lee than of Laura in yourself. If you do, it's won-derful that you are reading this book, and it's time to turn some things around in your life. Change your mind and go the other direction. Ask God for help. This book is filled with suggestions about what you can do to head the other way after you decide that's what you want to do. Part 2, especially Chapters 6 and 7, is filled with specific suggestions for acting on dedication. People can change. You can change. God loves to help people do just that.

If you are a sibling to a Lee, you may have more of an opportunity to say something than Laura is going to have. Better yet, perhaps you are a male friend of a Lee (or a female friend of a female Lee). You may be in the strongest position to ask some loving, direct questions: "Hey, I notice that you go out a lot and leave Laura home with the kids. What's up?" Maybe you're not your brother's keeper, but perhaps you can help your brother keep her in his marriage. Of course, part of a hyperindividualized society is that too many of us don't feel that we should ask others such personal questions. That's a problem in itself.

In some ways, it's probably harder to repent—change your mind about marital selfishness—when you are a more garden variety selfish spouse. If someone like Lee begins to look at himself, he'll see that he has been falling so far short that he may be propelled to a painful choice. Unfortunately, a lot of people like Lee in the world probably have no intention of looking at themselves in any serious way. What about you, though? You would not be reading this book if you were not open to being a better spouse for your mate. As we all know, it's easy to read a book like this and note all the ways your loved one is falling short. It's harder for most of us to say, "What's this saying to me?" That's a better question. Remember, you have more control over changes in your attitudes and behavior than in your mate's.

This chapter raises the important and delicate matter of oneness and teamwork. Mostly, the applications here are questions for you to reflect on. You'll gain a sense of how you may foster more of the "us" in your marriage.

- Do you feel that you and your mate are a team?
- What do you think about the concept of oneness as described here?
- In general, how oriented are you to individualism versus teamwork in life? How selfish do you see yourself with your mate? How can you be less so?
- When do you most feel that the two of you are a team? At what times do you feel alone or even as enemies? Are there areas where you are very competitive with each other in unhealthy ways?
- What three specific things can you do this coming week (and thereafter) that would foster a greater sense of unity in your marriage? Do these things.

However it is debased or misinterpreted, love is a redemptive feature. To focus on one individual so that their desires become superior to yours is a very cleansing experience.

—Jeanette Winterson

The true measure of a man is not the number of servants he has, but the number of people he serves.

—Arnold Glasgow

Chapter 9

Sacrifice
and Service

Let each of you look out not only for his own interests,
but also for the interests of others.
—Philippians 2:4 NKJV

*H*ave you ever given so much that it hurt? Have you put your self-interest aside for the good of another? If you are a parent, I'll bet you have many times for the sake of your children. However, how about in marriage? Is sacrifice relevant there? I think so, but it has become more difficult to talk positively about sacrifice in our society.

Sacrifice is a concept that has fallen on hard times. Particularly in a world where "me" and "my rights" take center stage, the notion of giving up something for another is less popular. I have given talks in some groups where *sacrifice* was considered a dirty word. People were offended by my suggestion that good marriages involved sacrifice, and I've had this reaction in churches as well as in secular settings.

Is sacrifice an outmoded notion? I don't believe it is. I think sacrifice is a crucial component of commitment in a strong and healthy marriage. This point is very clear in Scripture, and I think it is quite clear in marital research. That's what this chapter is about—the meaning and effects of sacrificial giving in marriage. After making some foundational points about the meaning of sacrifice, I will discuss some legitimate concerns that you may have about sacrifice. Then, I'll end this chapter with several stories that poignantly display sacrifice in marriage. If you are skeptical about this topic, please hear me out before drawing further conclusions. Here we go.

FOUNDATIONS OF SACRIFICE

What is a sacrifice? Three definitions of the verb *sacrifice* are offered in the dictionary that I use most often:

1. To offer as a sacrifice to a deity.
2. To forfeit (one thing) for another thing considered to be of greater value.
3. To sell or give away at a loss.[1]

In marriage, we are not talking about sacrifice to a deity. If one partner thinks of himself in that manner (and some do act as if they think they are gods), it's a bad sign and not a cause for sacrifice. Definitions two and three are closer to the emphasis here. Three is very straightforward. It speaks of giving up something of value. That could be your time, your pride, your money, or just about anything else you value that you might give up for another.

Definition two is most interesting to me. Two speaks to the idea that a sacrifice is giving up something for a greater good. In marriage, one "greater good" is the needs of your mate. The other is the needs of your marriage. While your mate is not of any greater value in God's sight, the act of sacrifice treats those needs as more important. In that sense, sacrifice is an act of service. In a healthy marriage, one often also gives up something that might have been more personally desirable for the good of the team. That's why this chapter is in this part of the book on oneness.

Healthy sacrifice in marriage flows most readily from a clear sense of oneness. In that context, sacrifices may be less obviously viewed as sacrifices when everything is going well in a marriage. Giving to your mate may not feel all that much like giving anything up if you have brought your desires and vision for life alongside.

Sacrifice is a notion so contrary to the dominant worldview of our day that I find many Christians are unaware of the biblical call to live in this manner. Let's look at that for a bit, then come back to the messages of our world that are hostile to sacrifice. Consider the context of the quote given at the outset of this chapter:

> *Therefore if there is any consolation in Christ, if any comfort of love, if any fellowship of the Spirit, if any affection and mercy, fulfill my joy by being like-minded, having the same love, being of one accord, of one mind. Let nothing be done through selfish ambition or conceit, but in lowliness of mind let each esteem others better than himself. Let each of you look out not only for his own interests, but also for the interests of others. Let this mind be in you which was also in Christ Jesus, who, being in the form of God, did not consider it robbery to be equal with God, but made Himself of no reputation, taking the form of a bondservant, and coming in the likeness of men. And being found in appearance as a man, He humbled Himself and became obedient to the point of death, even the death of the cross. (Phil. 2:1–8 NKJV)*

Notice several points here. First, Paul said something pretty striking: "If there's anything real about this Christian stuff, act out your committed love to one another" (my paraphrase). Paul linked the concepts to being of "one accord." That's teamwork and oneness. Second, he covered the same point as the second secular definition of sacrifice given earlier. He declared that we should consider others more important than ourselves. This attitude of humility represents the most profound sacrifice one can make for another. It's far easier to consider our needs and concerns of greater importance, but that's not sacrificial humility. Third, Paul looked to Christ as our example of humility—that Jesus would lower Himself from the form of God to the form of man, a man of humble means at that. Christ's sacrifice for us on the cross springs from the profound humility that is at the core of His being. He is our example, a radical example.

Gary Smalley has become a dear friend to me over the past few years. His organization produces a magazine called *Homes of Honor*. There I came across a story from early in Gary's marriage.[2] He was in seminary, was engaged in ministry as a youth pastor, and was in his second year of marriage to Norma. At that time, it was dawning on him that marriage was perhaps not all he thought or hoped it would be. Disagreements and conflicts were increasing. Then he went to a seminar and heard a message that, as he told the story, changed his life. The point that hit home was this: if you are irritated by many things in a relationship, perhaps you are fundamentally self-centered and primarily looking out for your own interests. Ouch!

Do you know this feeling? It's the feeling that God just tapped you on the shoulder and whispered (or screamed) a message of special importance to you. An old friend of mine used to express this feeling of conviction in a way that sticks with me twenty years later. He'd ask, "Is God dancing on your face, Bud?" When God really gets your attention, and it's about your self-centeredness, it feels as if someone is working you over. Frankly, I hope you know the feeling because it's a crucial part of being alive to God. Well, God was dancing on Gary's face through the message of that seminar. It didn't feel good; conviction about motives and attitudes often does not. He had a revelation of sorts about how he had been treating Norma. He expected her to respond to his various needs on his timetable and in the way he wanted.

If you are familiar with Gary's work, you know he has a gift for expressing the needs of the soul in graphic word pictures.[3] Upon realizing the depths of his selfishness, he held a funeral service for himself. As he told the story, he got down on his knees—just God and Gary—and prayed, imagining his casket, funeral songs, and being laid to rest in a deep hole in the ground. Six feet under. From there, he felt led to systematically give up to God various things that he held dear. He began to see just how much he had expected everything to go *his* way in their marriage—from the car they drove to the apartment they lived in to the priority placed on his work to about what they ate for dinner. Gary said of himself following this event, "I wasn't the same any longer. Things were changing about me that I would never have imagined."

We briefly examined repentance in the last chapter. This is a vivid example of what it really means to change your mind and head the other way. Norma noticed the difference and after a few days asked Gary what was wrong. Gary replied with words that stunned even himself: "Whatever you need is what is important to me." Now that's a change. It came from a depth of sacrifice of self that allowed him to fully give to Norma.

I know that Gary and Norma would be the first to say that life has not been perfect since that day—it's just not perfect for anyone. But that was a turning point in Gary's life and marriage brought on by a deep commitment to put the needs of self behind the needs of others in his life. The story gives fresh meaning to the words of Christ: "Greater love has no one than this, than to lay down one's life for his friends" (John 15:13 NKJV).

Many people in this day and age may think these words come from the Disney movie *Jungle Book* and not from Jesus Christ. Jesus said it first. Jesus did it best. It's not likely that you will be called to lay down your physical life for your mate. But you are called by Christ to lay down self every day in order to show His kind of love to others. That's committed, dedicated love. It's the kind of love that makes a marriage safer for the fullest expressions of intimacy. It's the kind of love that makes it safe to draw closer (1 John 4:18). It's love that sticks.

As Christians, we are called to sacrifice for others. It's a radically different message from that of our "me first" world. It's quite a challenge. You may be nervous about the way this is sounding. I am sensitive to the fact that people have concerns about what healthy sacrifice is and what unhealthy sacrifices would be in marriage. There are important questions to be dealt with.

WHAT HEALTHY SACRIFICE IS NOT

The term *martyr* used to have a very specific meaning throughout history. In our modern-day world, its meaning has shifted. Whereas it used to be a term for someone who had literally given his life for a cause, it has come to be a derogatory term for someone who gives with the wrong motive. As we use the term today, a martyr gives to you to put you in debt, not to benefit you. Perhaps you've done that at some point to someone. You are likely more easily aware of someone doing this to you (remember, we're all easily biased toward seeing these things better in others than in ourselves). You've been given a gift, so you now owe the giver—at least in the giver's mind.

Martyrdom, in the derogatory sense we give the word these days, is not the same thing as healthy sacrifice. When you give sacrificially in marriage, some of the good you give is very likely to come back to you. However, your motive for giving is the delight in knowing you are helping your mate. To be fair, sometimes it's not so delightful. You give because you judge it the right thing to do, but you don't feel good about it beyond that.

Christ is the supreme example of healthy sacrifice. Any fair reading of the New Testament shows that He was not excited about His impending death on the cross. He understood giving and sacrifice completely. He chose to submit to God, but He was truly anguished over what lay before Him (e.g., Luke 22:42). Sometimes real sacrifice really hurts.

CODEPENDENCY OR COMMITMENT?

My colleagues and I have discussed the matter of codependency elsewhere, but the highlights bear repeating because of the way this movement has affected our culture.[4] The codependency movement arose within the ranks of those who treat people with substance abuse. The original concept was a potent one: that people who abuse substances such as alcohol frequently have spouses who seem to want to help but do things that make it more, not less, likely that abusers will stay dependent. Some people seem to be so motivated to remain in this "helper" role that they seem to be *co*dependent on the continuation of the substance abuse. This whole concept was very helpful for unraveling what was going on in some families.

Unless you have been living in a cabin somewhere in the far regions, you are probably aware that quite a movement has sprung up around this concept of codependency. There are books, tapes, programs, you name it, to help people with codependency. Although this movement started with a useful idea, it has not been blessed with a lot of clear conceptualization. In effect, the term *codependent* has been applied to nearly everything bad in relationships (and even some things that are good). The original useful meaning of the concept has been obliterated, and now an industry has grown "dependent" on the movement.

Negative fallout from the movement has been confusion about whether it is healthy or right to give to others. Certainly, the notion of sacrifice would be a hard one to swallow in a movement intensely focused on the evils of being too helpful to others. If it's true codependency, that's a proper concern. It's not wise to give to people when the giving does more to harm them than help them. On the other hand, people now question all sorts of healthy giving because of the sloppiness of the conceptualization in the codependency movement.

This point was really brought home to me one day while counseling a couple. Deborah and Brian had been married twenty-two years. They were a strong couple with much going for them. They had their problems, like many other couples, but they were generally doing well. They liked each other and had a basic respect that was wonderful to see.

Brian's older brother, Max, had recently died from pancreatic cancer. Brian was still dealing pretty intensely with the grief of that loss. As we were talking, he expressed some of the loss he felt, not only about Max, but also about how hard it had been for Deborah to draw close as he was dealing with the pain of the loss. She agreed that she had held back a bit and said, "I can't really help him with his loss. That would be codependent."

Frankly, I felt sad for both of them at that moment. They had been harmed by this sloppy notion that giving to your mate is automatically codependent. There is nothing codependent about drawing close to your mate at such a time of need and helping him or her through emotionally, unless your mate is a grief addict. That's not likely.

It's right and wise to be careful about whether our giving is really in the best interests of the one to whom we are giving the gift. It's not loving to cover up the problems of another if that keeps him from changing or growing. But who wants to be in a marriage where one cannot draw alongside the other during times of grief, pain, or frustration? No one, I'd bet.

Many people could do a far better job of nurturing their partners than they do, and there is nothing wrong with desiring and giving such gifts in marriage. Who else you gonna call? It's not Ghostbusters. It's most often your mate who is in the best position to help you in life. When there is a

Sacrifice and Service

shared perspective on sacrificial giving in marriage, two people freely give to each other in delightful ways that nurture everything else good in marriage.

SACRIFICIAL GIVING TO AN ABUSER

Before we go on, I want to clarify something. I'm not suggesting that anyone should sacrifice her life or put her life in danger by remaining with someone who is a spouse batterer. I suspect that many women have maintained a strong commitment to truly dangerous mates out of a sense of either dedication or constraint. Others stay in true battering situations out of a fear of being hunted down. However, some women stay out of commitment, pure and simple. I don't think a woman (or a man) is called by God to remain in a physically dangerous situation for the sake of commitment or sacrifice. Furthermore, many passages in Scripture speak directly to the wisdom of pulling away and confronting such outrageous behavior (e.g., Matt. 18:15–17; 1 Cor. 5). I realize that there are debates about the theology of divorce and remarriage in a variety of situations, and this is not the venue for getting into that. Nevertheless, I don't hear anyone arguing that someone should jeopardize her (or his) life by remaining in a dangerous situation.

There are some things that should not be tolerated in marriage, but for most couples there are great benefits to sacrificial acts of commitment. In fact, the best marriages will have two mates who both understand the depths of love expressed in sacrifice for each other.

MARITAL RESEARCH SHOWS
THE BENEFITS OF SACRIFICE

Most people are not particularly surprised that Scripture extols the virtue of sacrificial giving in relationships. People do tend to be surprised that marital research strongly portrays the benefits of sacrificial attitudes and actions in marriage. In my research on commitment, I have developed many questions to measure both constraint and dedication in marriage. Under the heading of dedication, I asked people if they get some pleasure out of giving to their mates. Here are some sample statements to which they were to respond:

- I get satisfaction out of doing things for my partner, even if it means I miss out on something I want for myself.
- It makes me feel good to sacrifice for my partner.
- It can be personally fulfilling to give up something for my partner.

Research indicates that people who were the most comfortable with the notion of sacrificing for their mates were also those who tended to be the happiest together, the most dedicated to each other, and the most self-disclosing in their marriages.[5] Not surprisingly, people who tended to rate themselves as being religious were also more inclined to say they were comfortable with the idea of sacrifice. In essence, those who were more likely to be sticking and not stuck were also more likely to be giving to their mates in this way. I am sure there are exceptions to this—as with all research findings—but that's pretty compelling evidence that giving to your mate in clear, healthy ways strengthens your marriage. Furthermore, it's a very tangible expression of commitment in marriage.

Other researchers have had much the same findings. Researchers Paul Van Lange, Caryl Rusbult, and Stephen Drigotas have conducted research on commitment and sacrifice.[6] Caryl Rusbult has often talked of the notion in her extensive research on commitment. These researchers found that people who were more committed (in the manner I term *dedicated*) reported that they would give up activities that were very important to themselves individually for the sake of their relationships. The study was on dating relationships, yet the implications are directly applicable in marriage. They also found that people who were most inclined to sacrifice were the happiest in their relationships and the most likely to continue in them. Therefore, sacrificial attitudes and actions were more likely to be found among the happy, committed, sticking people.

One more interesting point emerged from the research I have conducted on sacrifice.[7] While getting pleasure from giving in these ways was equally related to all other good things in marriage for both men and women, women were somewhat less likely to report getting pleasure from giving sacrificially to their husbands. So, both men and women who felt better about giving sacrificially were more likely to have great marriages, but women found it harder to derive pleasure from giving to their husbands than vice versa. As with anything else in this kind of research, this finding is "on average." Your marriage may work differently.

Here's what I conclude from this finding. In our culture (and most others) it's more expected that wives will sacrifice than husbands. Hence when women give, the actions receive less notice and less reinforcement than when men do. Since men sacrifice less on average, the actions get more attention when they do, and they reap more praise. I apologize to the males reading this who are great givers. Nevertheless, on average, we men need to work harder on personal sacrifice in our marriages.

Whether you are a husband or a wife, you need to take the time to note what your mate does to benefit both of you. It's really powerful to express appreciation to each other. If you are inclined to think your mate does not do much, you could be right. Before you reach that conclusion, however, take a hard look at what your mate does that you have begun to take for granted. You are probably missing some actions in your biased scorekeeping. Furthermore, it's easiest to miss the small things that really matter a great deal—making a meal, cleaning up the bathroom, fixing something broken around the house, moving one's schedule to take a child to the doctor, listening to the other's feelings about something worrisome at work, regularly praying for each other, and on and on. Many daily sacrifices make it possible for a marriage to move through the average week. These things may not be a big show, but they show a big commitment.

STORIES OF SACRIFICE AND SERVICE

Giving sacrificially to your mate is not a concept that's tough to describe. Many concepts I've covered in this book are more complex than sacrifice. Of course, none describe actions that are more potentially difficult or rewarding. If you look back now at all the previous chapters, you could recast most of what I've said in terms of kinds of sacrifices. Sacrifice is fundamental to great marriages. For example, when you reorient your priorities to better meet the needs of your mate, you are making a sacrifice. When you protect your marriage from the attraction you feel toward someone else, you are making a sacrifice of some desires. When you stick with a choice and grieve about something given up, you grieve because of a good sacrifice. When you invest of yourself in your marriage, you are making a sacrifice of a sort. It doesn't always feel good to give sacrificially, but it usually leads to good in a marriage. Even when it's not so clear how it does, such giving blesses the giver when you know you have done a right thing.

A heart of sacrifice beats in everything I've said about commitment. Sacrifice is the highest expression of dedicated, loving action because it asks you to show by your actions that you really mean it when you say you are committed. Now I want to present a few stories that powerfully display what sacrifice can look like in marriage.

FOR BETTER OR FOR WORSE, IN SICKNESS AND IN HEALTH

Perhaps you have read the story of Robertson and Muriel McQuilkin. It first appeared in *Christianity Today* in October 1990.[8] In the early 1980s, Robertson was at the height of his ministry, as president of Columbia Bible College and Seminary (now Columbia International University) in South Carolina. He was in his fifties. During those years, he began to notice Muriel's memory slipping in small ways. He didn't really appreciate the growing significance of the lapses at first. As her condition became more serious, he took her to doctors for tests and initially was skeptical when they would bring up the possibility of Alzheimer's disease. He finally accepted the diagnosis after he took her to Duke University Medical Center for tests that suggested the likelihood of what he feared.

Several years after Muriel's diagnosis was suggested to be Alzheimer's, Robertson made an amazing decision. He went to the board of trustees of the seminary and told them they needed to begin searching for his replacement. He was fifty-seven at the time and had hoped to hold on until sixty-five, but he didn't think he could last that long *and* take care of Muriel.

His key personal struggle was whether or not to give up his ministry to care for Muriel at home. Close friends, advisers, and acquaintances encouraged him to go on with his work and put Muriel in a place where she could receive care. In other words, the advice of many was to "get on with *your* life," but he wasn't thinking about getting on with *his* life. He was still living *their* life. His story is one of sacrifice and true belief in oneness. While I understand the wisdom of professional care in many such circumstances, Robertson didn't perceive that as the right course for Muriel and himself.

Sacrifice and Service

In a follow-up piece, Robertson noted that his wife's progression through the disease was unusually slow.[9] Over a period of many years, he had watched Muriel slowly lose just about every ability and faculty from her once sparkling repertoire of gifts and talents. Some of you don't have to imagine this, but for the rest of you, think about that for a moment. He stayed by her side and slowly watched her lose every ability as he took on more and more of the challenge of caring for her.

Love. The watershed moment, many years ago, was when he decided that she needed his full-time care and he could no longer carry on the duties as president of the seminary. He wrote:

> When the time came, the decision was firm. It took no great calculation. It was a matter of integrity. Had I not promised, 42 years before, "in sickness and in health . . . till death do us part"? This was no grim duty to which I was stoically resigned, however. It was only fair. She had, after all, cared for me for almost four decades with marvelous devotion; now it was my turn.[10]

He recalled his vows, and they were not empty words to him. There he was, in the prime of his life and profession, faced with the decision about whether or not he meant what he vowed on his wedding day. He decided to serve her and not himself. Again, there are circumstances where the more loving response may well be to find alternate care for a loved one facing the progression of such a disease. But that was not for this couple.

As I read the story, Robertson did not really consider it a sacrifice to give up his work and spend all of his time caring for Muriel. It was, though. His devotion and dedication to her were so strong that he was propelled forward by his love, not pushed from behind by guilt or shame. He once heard a professional who dealt with Alzheimer's sufferers say that the only people who cared full-time for loved ones with the disease were those who were too poor or felt too guilty to do otherwise. Robertson could not relate to those sentiments. He had the means to provide a quality level of institutional care for her, but he also had the means to devote himself to serving her in the last years of her life. That's what he chose to do.

It was a very painful grief for him to be so close to her and watch her lose all her abilities. He wrote about one loss that moved him deeply:

It's true. Recently, Muriel's right hand went limp—her first major decline since she lost the abilities to stand and to feed herself 18 months before. A little loss, you would think, but I shed a few tears. I wrote in my journal that night, "It's almost like part of me dies with each of her little deaths." That precious hand was so creative, so loving, so busy for me and everyone else. But it wasn't just the old memories. That right hand was the last way she had to communicate. She would reach out to hold hands, pat me on the back when I hugged her, push me away when she didn't like what I was doing. I miss her hand.[11]

This man understands how commitment and grief work together. If you stay committed, you are going to grieve. One way or another, you will know you have given up some things when you stick. From what I read of his journey, he actively grieved and faced the losses and the pain. He also continued to find meaning in his ministry to Muriel. More than that, he noted the contrasting messages of the world today with the choices of commitment he was making. He wrote,

I came across the common contemporary wisdom in this morning's newspaper in a letter to a national columnist: "I ended the relationship because it wasn't meeting my needs," the writer explained. The counselor's response was predictable: "What were your needs that didn't get met by him in the relationship? Do you still have these needs? Can he do it?" Needs for communication, understanding, affirmation, common interests, sexual fulfillment—the list goes on. . . . I once reflected on the eerie irrelevance of every one of those criteria for me.[12]

Which of Robertson's needs was Muriel able to meet as her disease progressed? Not many at all. If that was the definition of what marriage is about, why did he continue to devote so much to her? His commitment overrode the easier path he could have taken.

Robertson McQuilkin wrote about one other observation that I found stunning. These next few paragraphs are particularly directed to my male readers, though the points are important for men and women. Robertson

Sacrifice and Service

was once talking to an oncologist who had watched many people go through the process of dying from cancer. The doctor told Robertson that "almost all women stand by their men; very few men stand by their women."[13] To be sure, I am no male basher when it comes to problems in marriage. Quite the opposite, in fact. What men give to their mates is often overlooked these days. Further, both men and women bring many complexities, many problems, and much selfishness to their marriages. However, the doctor who regularly dealt with dying people was plainly saying that men are more likely to desert their wives when their wives are dying. That's partly why Robertson's story is so powerful, because it is about a man choosing to sacrifice dramatically for his wife.

Around the world, countless women sacrifice for their husbands every day, and it's not going to make a compelling public story. Why? Most people expect that of women. That's exactly why I said earlier that women have a bit more trouble getting pleasure out of giving sacrificially to their husbands. Too many of us take it for granted. Men, there is something wrong with that.

Men in particular need to challenge each other and encourage each other in being more devoted husbands and fathers. Personally, I am blessed with several male friends who are very encouraging and supportive of decisions that put the home responsibilities at the priority level they deserve. I can do better, and it helps to have friends who are not afraid to say to me, "How are you doing with your commitments at home?" And when we make the better choices, we praise one another. Real men act on commitments they have made. Real men honor their wives and children. Real men encourage other men to do likewise. Real women do all these things too. It's the stuff of being a great spouse.

Robertson made a hard, tough choice to give deeply to his wife, and he learned to truly love his ministry of service to her. I am not God and I do not know, but I would hardly be surprised if he heard "well done, good and faithful servant" all the clearer in relation to his latter ministry than his former. That's taking nothing away from what he had done in his public ministry, but Christ particularly honored attention to the small things in life, being faithful in little: "And he said to him, 'Well done, good servant; because you were faithful in a very little, have authority over ten cities'" (Luke 19:17 NKJV).

It's far easier to be faithful in the big things because they come with their own reward and glory. In effect, Jesus said that your character is more evident in how you handle the little stuff of commitment than the big, glorious opportunities. In marriage, you're called to "sweat the small stuff." You know by now that I am a fan of Fyodor Dostoevsky. He put these marvelous words about love and commitment into the mouth of Fr. Zosima in *The Brothers Karamazov:*

> Love in action is a harsh and dreadful thing compared with love in dreams. Love in dreams is greedy for immediate action, rapidly performed and in the sight of all. Men will even give their lives if only the ordeal does not last long but is soon over, with all looking on and applauding as though on stage. But active love is labour and fortitude, and for some people too, perhaps, a complete science.[14]

I don't know about love being a complete science, but I do know committed love often calls us to give in small ways that, in reality, are huge. When Robertson was changing diapers for Muriel, bathing her, holding her hand, speaking words of love to her, or doing any number of small acts that let her know she was not alone and that he cared for her body and soul, he was sticking, not stuck. He was acting on the deepest kind of committed love. It's often not grand theater—it's love and commitment acted out on the small stages of life.

One way Robertson hung on to his memories of Muriel in her earlier days was to recall various conversations with her. One of her quotes is priceless for this discussion: "If it's worth doing, it's worth doing well? Pshaw. Very few things in this life are worth doing well."[15]

Profound wisdom from Muriel. Indeed, very few things in life are worth doing well. Jesus taught that we're often focused on the things that are really not worth the level of commitment we give to them, and we neglect the very things—often the small things—that really matter most. Part of commitment is being wise about which is which. The messages that swirl in our culture aren't often reinforcing the right choices. To give up some greater personal glory or desire to show true, dedicated love to your spouse is a sacrifice that's not easy to make. Much of the time, you won't make the best choice. However, the committed life is about making the right choices about small things more often over time. That's called maturing.

DARING TO BECOME DIFFERENT

One of the greatest pleasures of my life has been to work extensively with chaplains of the various branches of the United States military. They are a hardworking, dedicated bunch of people who are on the front lines of helping marriages and families of service people. One U.S. Navy chaplain whom I have known for seven years told me this story of a turning point in his marriage. It illustrates a change fueled by sacrifice and commitment. I have changed their names for this book.

At the time this happened, Dave and Melissa had been married six years. Like many couples, they were struggling along with various problems, and often they failed to handle their conflicts very well. They would become upset, things would escalate, and he would often pull away. If it's not obvious to you, let me tell you that military life is very hard on families. They move frequently. The service person has to travel a lot, sometimes to places where there is imminent danger. Schedules are not accommodating to the needs of family. Basically, it can be high stress and low pay with a ton of duties to fulfill. It's easy for spouse and marriage to fall somewhere down the list of the priorities in terms of time and action.

Dave is not only in the military on active duty, but is also a chaplain. Therefore, he is a pastor in full-time ministry. If being in the military is not hard enough on a family, think about being in the ministry! Pastors are pulled and tugged in all sorts of directions, many of them taking pastors away from important matters at home. They also tend to be very responsible people who have a hard time letting others down. As I said earlier in the book, most of us have this tendency to presume upon the commitment of our mates, so it's easiest to let the needs of our mates slide when pulled in various directions from outside the home. That happened to Dave and Melissa. Both of them are talented people, and others naturally are interested in availing themselves of their talents.

Back to six years in—and I don't mean six years in the military. Dave and Melissa had just been through one of their intense arguments when she leveled him. Here's how the conversation went:

MELISSA: I hate you. I just don't know if I love you anymore. But I am committed to you.

DAVE: (*she had gotten his attention and he was stunned.*) Are you saying you want a divorce?

MELISSA: You didn't listen to me. I said, "I hate you. I just don't know if I love you anymore. But I am committed to you."

DAVE: (*still reeling inside and not tracking very well*) What are you saying? Are you going to leave me?

MELISSA: Try again. I said, "I hate you. I just don't know if I love you anymore. But I am committed to you."

That time, Dave really heard the last part, and he realized that was his avenue of hope—her commitment. She surely was not a happy camper, but she kept her commitment clear. Score big points for a sacrificial spirit because that's what it took for her to confront him and make it plain she was sticking. It might well have felt easier to her to leave Dave. Commitment called her to a tougher choice, to hang in there with him and attempt to change things.

Dave recalls all this now, and he sees that they had experienced years of erosion in the positive bond in their marriage. Nasty arguments, misplaced priorities, and lost opportunities were taking a very heavy toll. Melissa was tired of driving on the toll road and wanted to find another road, but one with Dave.

Her statement of pain and commitment led him to conclude this, which he shared with me: "I knew I had done a lot to damage the relationship by engaging in what I now know as destructive communication, which eroded the bond of friendship and any endearment (I guess you'd say low dedication). I knew that I had 'dug a deep hole' and that it would take some time to get out of it. However, since she said she was 'committed,' I knew I could trust in that and work from there. It took about five years to rebuild and restore. Yes, we did have some good times during that time, and with each passing month it was getting better. But you and I both know that without her level of commitment (not just constraint) to make the marriage work, I would be in a second marriage and life would be so different."

He had the courage to invest in changing things with Melissa because he knew he could trust her commitment to be there. Without a sense of permanence coming from a clear commitment, who is going to put massive effort into a marriage? Sacrifice is hard enough as it is, but when there is no sense of a future, it will seem purposeless and be all the harder to accomplish in marriage. You don't invest if you don't believe that what you are investing in matters or that your investment has any time to work to make a difference. Melissa voiced her unhappiness, but she didn't threaten the commitment. Dave was moved by that. And he acted in positive ways.

From there, Dave took a three-hour walk of soul-searching. He committed himself to two things following that walk. First, he decided to immerse himself in the book of Proverbs and to soak up the practical relationship wisdom. Second, he decided to take the risk to ask Melissa for detailed feedback about what he was or was not doing that was causing her so much distress. That takes guts. That's a sacrifice. That's courage matching the courage Melissa showed in confronting Dave.

A few nights later, he sat down with her to ask her what she was concerned about. He told her he would just listen and not interrupt or debate about her concerns. He expected she would raise a few specific concerns. She began listing them and continued for a time. He filled up an entire 8 ½-by-14-inch piece of paper with the list of the things he did that pushed her away. He was humbled by it. Such humility is the root of real change in relationships.

They made up new ground rules for dealing with issues. From that day forward, they worked on their marriage in a different way. They mapped out the more fragile and volatile issues. They committed themselves to change and teamwork. He is still in the military and still a chaplain. There are still pressures on both. They don't always get along well, but they are a team. They have experienced the blessings that stem from working through the tough spots of life and coming out closer together. Commitment kept them hanging in there, and commitment to really stick led to powerful changes.

Fostering We-ness and Containing Me-ness

You are very likely aware of Billy Graham's ministry to millions of people around the world, a ministry that spans nearly six decades. Billy's companion, lover, and wife over these many years has been and remains Ruth Bell Graham. Articles and books have emerged in recent years chronicling these two remarkable people.[16] Ruth Bell was the daughter of parents who were missionaries to China. When she was a young woman, being a missionary was her fondest and deepest ambition. Although she and Billy fell in love rapidly, it took three years for them to iron out what was God's will for their lives and to clarify that their paths would become one.

Ruth had key issues to resolve before she decided to marry Billy. First, she had to decide if God was really calling her to give up her desire to serve as a missionary. That was a sacrifice of sorts because it was no small aspiration within her. Her determination was so great on the issue that Billy wondered if God was using her to speak to him about the mission field.[17] As she told the story, God was changing her heart about the direction of her life. Second, she had to decide if Billy was the man she was to join with in the journey of life. It's also clear from what Ruth has said that she knew something large was happening in the life of Billy Graham. There was no doubt that she was drawn to his strengths of humility and fearlessness, but the direction things were heading was clearly not what she had been expecting up to that point in her life. Commitment in marriage often calls us to put aside our individual plans for those of the team.

Billy Graham and Ruth Bell married in August 1943. Over the years, they brought five children into the world. This is where Ruth's sacrificial love really shows. Billy has been a rather busy man over the past fifty years, traveling about six months a year. Therefore, much of the day-to-day tasks of rearing those five children fell to her. Ruth was a very busy woman. I am sure it has been a labor of love; their children have had all the needs anyone else's have had. Raising five children is a huge responsibility. Furthermore, being the wife of Billy Graham carries with it a level of sacrifices that many other wives are not called to make. Hers has to have been a tough life. But she has handled it with love and joy. She once said of Billy's travel demands, "I'd rather have a little of Bill than a lot of any other man."[18] She has made all the daily sacrifices of raising five children, and she has shared her husband with the rest of the world.

Sacrifice and Service

What propels someone forward through a life of giving to others, especially when there has been so much travel? As I read about the Grahams, I could see that they have had a strong love and a sense of oneness from start to finish. The connection they shared though all those years of raising children and traveling around the world is still there:

> Their commitment was apparent to everyone. "He would stand up whenever she came in the room," says Graham biographer William Martin, adding that a 69-year-old Graham told him, "You know, we're still lovers." Today their intimacy has been hindered by the complications of old age. He is fighting Parkinson's disease; she, a chronic lower-back problem. They spend their time at home, in twin armchairs, in front of a real fireplace. "They don't like to be separated by a lot of miles," says Gigi [Gigi is one of the Grahams' daughters]. "They just like knowing the other one's right there."[19]

That oneness has lasted for fifty, going on sixty years. That's love. Billy and Ruth Graham have both done incredible things with their lives. Both have sacrificed a great deal, but their love is stronger for it. A passage in Galatians, as paraphrased by Eugene Peterson in *The Message,* sums up my sense of the relationship between Ruth and Billy Graham:

> *But what happens when we live God's way? He brings gifts into our lives, much the same way that fruit appears in an orchard—things like affection for others, exuberance about life, serenity. We develop a willingness to stick with things, a sense of compassion in the heart, and a conviction that a basic holiness permeates things and people. We find ourselves involved in loyal commitments, not needing to force our way in life, able to marshal and direct our energies wisely. (Gal. 5:22–24, emphasis added)*

Exercise Your Heart

Sacrifice is to love what exercise is to muscles. Sacrificial giving to each other is the expression of love, and it makes love grow. When you don't use a muscle for a long time, it literally shrinks. When you use it a lot, it will probably hurt. However, the pain of exertion is followed by the muscle's repairing itself to a state of greater strength. If you exercise in a way to build greater strength, this is just what you are doing. You push your muscles a bit beyond the comfort zone in order to build more strength. Building strength over time involves discipline. You have to decide to push yourself a bit to reap the benefits of the work.

When you give sacrificially, you are pushing your commitment muscles, and the exercise of commitment in this way strengthens your ability to love. Are you exercising your commitment muscles? It's a well-tempered commitment that is strong enough to move the heavy loads of life. That's love in action. That's sticking with strength.

Point of Application

Here we have looked at the great concept of sacrificial giving. Here are some tasks to amplify the impact of these points in your life:

- Take fifteen minutes right now to meditate on how God has demonstrated sacrificial love to you. Doing this from time to time is an excellent way to ground yourself in the One who is the very source of love and life.
- Ponder the ways in which your mate sacrifices for you. There are likely many. Increasing your awareness of them can have a very tangible positive effect on your outlook and motivation in your marriage.
- Ask your mate to share one specific way that you can give to him or her. Do it. Ask God for guidance, wisdom, and strength to do such things well and with your whole heart.

MOVING FORWARD

Duty does not have to be dull. Love can make it beautiful and fill it with life.

—Anonymous

Chapter 10

*L*IVING ON *L*OVE

Love never fails.
—1 Corinthians 13:8 NKJV

*Y*ou've probably heard the expression "living on love" before. Whenever I've heard it, it has conveyed the suggestion that a couple are so much in love that they don't need food, water, sun, moon, money, shelter—they have love. "Living on love" usually refers to an intensity of passion that will overcome all obstacles. Passionate love is a pretty grand thing. People see it in movies, read about it in novels, and desire some of it in their lives.

In a marriage, you can't really live on the kind of love that makes you forget about food and shelter. Don't get me wrong; I'm not antipassion. But what we all need over the long term is a much more powerful kind of love, a love rooted in and expressed through commitment. This is the kind of love you'll read about in this chapter—the kind of love on which you truly can live.

What's Love Got to Do with It?

Perhaps the greatest passage ever written on love is found in the first letter of the apostle Paul to the Corinthians. These verses are quoted at weddings, stitched in needlepoint hangings on the walls of homes, and commonly memorized. The subject is love:

> *Love suffers long and is kind; love does not envy; love does not parade itself, is not puffed up; does not behave rudely, does not seek its own, is not provoked, thinks no evil; does not rejoice in iniquity, but rejoices in the truth; bears all things, believes all things, hopes all things, endures all things. Love never fails.* (1 Cor. 13:4–8 NKJV)

The Greek word for "love" that Paul used in writing these verses is *agape*. You may be familiar with the different Greek words used by ancient writers that we translate into "love" in the English language. *Agape* is one of these words, and it is exclusive to the New Testament. *Eros* is another Greek word for "love"; it typifies erotic arousal. Perhaps it's the closest to the understanding of "love" in our world today. In the New Testament, *phileo* is used to describe brotherly (or sisterly) love; it literally means "love for man." *Phileo* conveys the idea of kindness, friendship, and tender affection for another. There are other Greek words for "love" as well. Agape love is the highest form of love expressed in the New Testament. Here is how *Vine's Expository Dictionary of Old and New Testament Words* refers to agape love:

> Agape and agapao are used in the NT (a) to describe the attitude of God toward His Son, (John 17:26); the human race, generally, (John 3:16; Rom. 5:8), and to such as believe on the Lord Jesus Christ particularly (John 14:21); (b) to convey His will to His children concerning their attitude one toward another, (John 13:34), and toward all men, (1 Thes. 3:12; 1 Cor. 16:14; 2 Pet. 1:7); to express the essential nature of God, (1 John 4:8)[1]

Agape is love that acts. It's the kind of love God shows toward us, with the highest expression found in the work of Christ on the cross. Agape love casts out all fear (1 John 4:18). You could take 1 Corinthians 13 as the essential definition of it. As theologians have commented, *agape* is the central word of Christianity.

What I call dedication as a form of commitment in research is what the New Testament calls agape love.[2] The bulk of this book is about commitment in the form of dedication. I may not have mentioned the word *dedication* in every chapter, but the concepts and strategies of Chapters 2 through 9 point to living out dedication as the highest form of commitment. If you prefer, you could think of this book as a discussion of committed, agape, love. The passage quoted from 1 Corinthians 13 could just as well serve as the outline for this book.

I hope you'll let that sink in for a moment. The kind of love shown toward us by God through Christ is the kind of love that Paul was rousing us to live out. This kind of committed love underlies great marriages. By "great," I mean marriages that not only are satisfying and stable over time, but that also reflect the character of God. This kind of love powers everything else that's most wonderful in relationships.

Here's another look at how this kind of committed love acts, in the words of Eugene Peterson's *The Message.* I include it here because I want you to savor the full flavor of this commitment:

Love never gives up.
Love cares more for others than for self.
Love doesn't want what it doesn't have.
Love doesn't strut,
Doesn't have a swelled head,
Doesn't force itself on others,
Isn't always "me first,"
Doesn't fly off the handle,
Doesn't keep score of the sins of others,
Doesn't revel when others grovel,
Takes pleasure in the flowering of truth,
Puts up with anything,
Trusts God always,
Always looks for the best,
Never looks back,

But keeps going to the end.
Love never dies. (1 Cor. 13:4–9)

Either that's inspiring to you or convicting to you, or you're pretty dead inside. Personally, I find this passage challenging, which to me is being inspired and convicted at the same time. It's something to aim for. But what fuels this kind of love from one to another?

FUELING AGAPE COMMITMENT

In *Making Love Last Forever,* Gary Smalley has a chapter titled "Finding the Power to Keep Loving."[3] Good title for a great chapter. Gary makes the point that your spiritual relationship with God is the only reliable source for fueling your "battery pack." Too many people are drained and look to their mates to refuel them. Many times this works. In fact, that's one of the greatest blessings of being in a marriage where each cares for and supports the other. But where do you both go to keep your battery packs charged and ready? Through the kind of personal example that makes his writing so powerful, Gary says,

> Finally, and this is the hardest part, I tell God, "I honor you and your ways that are beyond my knowledge. Lord, I'm willing to wait until you 'charge my battery.' I know it may take awhile before I'm content with what you provide rather than secretly expecting my spouse or my house or my job to meet my needs. But I want you to be the source of my life, the source of my strength, my power to love others as I should."[4]

Your spouse can—and likely does—meet some of your needs, but the real fuel for the depths of the soul comes from God. He is the source of all life and all love. Some people believe this, and therefore act on it; others do not. Do you believe it? Do you act on it? More important, do you fully comprehend the depth of God's love for you? I am convinced that the more you understand God's love for you, the more you will be able to live out that love with others, including your mate. The apostle Paul clearly understood this principle of filling one's tank with the knowledge of God's love:

Moving Forward

For this reason I bow my knees to the Father of our Lord Jesus Christ, from whom the whole family in heaven and earth is named, that He would grant you, according to the riches of His glory, to be strengthened with might through His Spirit in the inner man, that Christ may dwell in your hearts through faith; that you, being rooted and grounded in love, may be able to comprehend with all the saints what is the width and length and depth and height—to know the love of Christ which passes knowledge; that you may be filled with all the fullness of God. (Eph. 3:14–19 NKJV)

Knowing the love of Christ is the way to be filled to the fullest. When you are filled to the brim, the love that fills you will overflow into the lives of others. Are you running on empty? Where do you go to recharge the deepest levels of your soul? How would you describe your relationship with God? Important questions that I leave for you to ponder.

You Don't Know My Mate

I think I have heard it all at this point (when it comes to marriage), but I don't know your situation or your mate. I know some people reading this book will be led to deeper levels of pain and grief about their marriages than they ever felt before. For some of you, the examples and the concepts that I have presented will remind you of elements you dearly wish you had in your marriage but do not have now. I want to encourage you if that's what you have been feeling as you read this. It's almost an inevitable reaction for some people since I am laying out a vision for a full and ideal commitment in marriage. That's just not where some of you are in life.

For example, some of you are married to someone who will not try in any way to build your marriage. Perhaps you've been unhappy for some time with your mate to the point of feeling stuck, and having something really change in a big way seems astronomically unlikely. I don't know, but you could be right. You could do everything we've talked about to try to make your marriage one that is really sticking and not just stuck, but your mate will not help you in any way with that task. Perhaps he or she doesn't care or doesn't believe anything more is possible than what exists at present in the marriage.

I cannot tell you what you should do in your marriage. I do believe that one person in a marriage can act on many suggestions in this book, and that in doing so, you give your marriage the best possible chance. Very often, good things are eventually, if not rapidly, reciprocated in a marriage. I don't know if that's true for you or not, but it's worth a valiant effort. You can try to be sticky even if your mate seems not to care at this time about being stuck. That will take a lot of effort on your part. You might feel as if you're trying to climb a tall tree that doesn't have any low branches. You might need a leg up. You might need to ask friends to encourage you.

I'd like to warn you about one thing in particular. I've heard my friend Howard Markman say this to couples in workshops for years. Even if you don't think that your mate is doing his or her part, that's no excuse for you to behave badly in your marriage. You may allow your judgments of your mate's failings to justify your poor conduct, but tit-for-tat negativity destroys marriages. It's a long way from working at sticking.

My main concern in writing about these tougher circumstances is acknowledging those of you who really do have it harder. I know you are out there, and I know some of you are reading this book. I know you are likely in pain, at least at times. If empathy helps, you have it from me and many others you will likely not meet. It's tough to try to stick when so much in your life says to just stop and quit. May God help you find wisdom for how you should walk. The Bible says He'll provide wisdom if you ask for it (James 1:5). Seek Him out.

SAILING TOGETHER

Let's take a little trip. Think of your marriage as a long voyage in a sailboat. Using that image, I can give you a view of what it really means to set a course and stick to it for the journey ahead. Let's push off.

CHRISTENING

Have you ever seen a ship being christened? I'll bet you have. Usually a dignitary smashes a bottle of champagne on the bow of the new ship as it slips into the sea for the first time. It's a dedication of the ship for the mission and the years ahead. A wedding is a lot like a christening. The ship is being set afloat for the first time. There are a celebration and much happiness.

Think back to Jeremy and Suzanne from the first chapter. They were getting married with the best of intentions and the brightest of ceremonies. They had a particularly clear sense of commitment as their ship entered the water. Off they went, sailing their way into their new future.

It is a time of excitement and hope for the new union of the two partners. No one knows for sure at the start what's to come, whether on the marital journey or the seafaring journey. The optimism of the wedding day can very soon give way to the reality of problems and hardships.

Several groups of researchers have found that certain premarital dynamics can put a couple at risk for divorce or marital distress in the future. Using only premarital variables, various researchers have been able to correctly classify which couples will do well and which will not, with up to 90 percent accuracy.[5] That means most couples who are going to divorce have the seeds of their divorce present within them and their relationship as they walk down the aisle to say, "I do." My basic point is that all the optimism in the world on the wedding day is not nearly as crucial as the commitment that's enacted in the ensuing years.

SETTING A HEADING

Since the most ancient of times, sailors used reference points to guide them in their journeys. Often, they relied on the stars to help them pinpoint their position relative to their destination. Nowadays, a compass and much fancier equipment help them fix their position on the globe. Of course, it really doesn't matter much if you know where you are if you don't know where you are headed. Knowing the intended destination is a critical part of your journey together. The best compass in the world can tell you which way you are heading, but it doesn't tell you if that's where you ought to be headed.

In marriage, your intended destination is a complex thing, made up of your dreams, your goals, your sense for the future, and your beliefs of what marriage is all about. You can't predict everything about your journey from the start, but you should have a pretty good sense of where you are headed. Jeremy and Suzanne were very clear about their heading, even if they were not sure what life had in store along the way. Setting sail for the continent of India, Columbus didn't know what he would find along the way, but he did know where he was trying to land in his travels. Of course, he landed somewhere else, but there was nothing wrong with where he was heading.

Do you know what heading you are on? Is it the direction you want to go? Too many couples know they want to travel through life together, but they have not thought through or talked about where they are trying to be by the end of the journey. Slicing along through the seas at steady speed is not really getting you anywhere if the direction you are headed isn't the right one. It may be fun for a time, but it's important to know where you are trying to end up. That's why what you read in Chapter 7 on vision is so crucial. Doing the work of that chapter can go a long way toward defining a steady heading for your journey together.

SMOOTH SAILING AND ROUGH SEAS

Most, but not all, couples have fairly smooth sailing for a few years. Most people don't leave port in the first place unless the weather looks favorable. This is a great time for couples. You sail together without the winds and the waves giving you much of a challenge. Of course, that's for a first marriage. Second marriages often start off in rougher waters, demanding that the couples quickly learn to run the ship together or suffer the risk of shipwreck. But for the first-time marrieds Jeremy and Suzanne, the sailing was smooth as silk for about five years. No gale force winds, no dead calms, and a strong and sleek ship to enjoy.

No sailor would be wise to expect perfect weather. In many respects, sailing must be like farming. You are at the mercy of some things over which you have no control. You can prepare. You can outfit your ship as well as can be. You can check the weather and try to steer clear of trouble. *But sometimes you'll encounter the roughest weather precisely because you are holding to your course.* If you've read much of the Bible at all, you are aware that you can be heading just where you should be headed, doing the things you need to do, and still hit rough storms.[6] That may not be comforting at times, but it's true. So you press on.

Expecting some storms and waves makes more sense than hoping they'll never come your way. No matter how well you learn to sail together, some storms will hit you. Water will pour down. Your ship will toss like a cork.

Perhaps a sail or two will tear. You'll take on some water and you'll have to bail. That's life. If you don't like variations in weather, stay in the port and don't go sailing. A person who never marries will never have troubles or trials in marriage. But is that a better life? Only for some.

The first storm came to Jeremy and Suzanne in the form of a premature baby. Two pounds. That's not smooth sailing. Ask someone who has gone through those waters. Even though everything went as well as possible, it was a big storm to take care of a premature infant. Stress, fatigue, and fear tested their sailing abilities. Some crews fall apart when a storm comes. They turn on each other instead of pulling together and working the boat. Many marriages have shipwrecked on the rocks of a child with serious medical needs. Jeremy and Suzanne worked the boat. Sure, they got tired. Sure, they wanted relief that seemed to come very slowly. But they were a team, a sailing team. Sticking when it counts most.

I don't know what rougher seas await you, but I do know you'll handle them best if you are a team. Storms can come in the form of financial problems, ill parents, difficulties with children, work layoffs, career moves, lack of agreement about household duties—just about anything can turn into a storm. If you run a tight ship as a team, you're as ready as you can be. To be ready for what comes your way, you can learn how to communicate and problem solve together about tough issues. Couples who handle issues poorly are unlikely to make it together through life. There are many books and other materials that can help you learn to handle problems as a team.[7] These resources can teach you specific skills that you can combine with your commitment to keep your marriage in tip-top shape.

Have you ever watched the America's Cup sailing events on television? The crews are much larger than two, but what's amazing is the coordination among the crew members. They work together to get the jobs done. They know when to pull this rope, when to turn (so no one is taken out by the boom), when to set another sail, and so forth. It's coordinated effort. It's beautiful to watch. It's beautiful to see in a marriage too. That comes with effort and practice.

ICEBERGS

Storms are bad enough. When you just want to sail pleasantly along, it's annoying at best and scary at worst to have a big storm overtake you.

However, even bad storms are manageable if you are working together to sail your boat well. Jeremy and Suzanne became better and better sailors over the years together. The seas were not always calm, but they managed. Better than managed, they grew wise in their abilities as sailors. They could read the weather and steer around some storms. They could keep the ship sailing smoothly through brisk seas, providing them with times of exhilaration. They even had fun when the winds were slow, learning how to appreciate the sunsets and sunrises together. But no couple can wisely pretend there are no icebergs.

You know it's coming, so here goes. The *Titanic*. It's not a sailing ship, but stretch a little. It's still a ship. It was a great ship actually. As you know, it was considered unsinkable. It had so many compartments that could be sealed off from others, even if one part of the ship was damaged severely, it was supposed to float and move through the water. The owners of the ship were so confident of its structural superiority that they equipped it with only half the number of lifeboats needed for the number of passengers it was designed to hold.

Even a wonderful ship can be handled poorly. You can have the greatest ship in the world when you leave the port, but if you are an unwise or arrogant sailor, you're going to go down. The *Titanic* left Southampton, England, for New York City on its maiden voyage in April 1912. At the time, it was the largest and most elegantly appointed ship in history. Big and beautiful and full of promise. The owners of the ship were eager for the *Titanic* to make the voyage in rapid time. They wanted to show off the new ship. However, the first major error was the course that was charted. The *Titanic* was "sailed" rapidly along a route far enough north that cold and ice were to be factors. The crew had been warned numerous times of icebergs in the area, but the ship sailed on at high speed. Nearby, at least one other ship had completely stopped because the captain had judged conditions too dangerous to proceed.

The *Titanic* struck an iceberg that ripped a very thin but very long gash across at least six of the compartments that could have been sealed off to prevent water leaking to other parts of the ship. The ship could have withstood a lot of damage, but not to six of the compartments at the same time. The rip was very thin, yet it was enough to let the ship take on water at a rapid rate. The passengers didn't know anything was amiss for a while,

Moving Forward

but the ship was already doomed—as are a number of marriages where the partners are poorly prepared. It went down in two hours and forty minutes, taking more than fifteen hundred people to the icy depths of the North Atlantic. Like most marriages that sink, the disaster was totally unnecessary.

I don't like to criticize dead people, but apparently, there is no better explanation for what happened to the *Titanic* than bad seamanship. The ship was pushed too hard, on a bad course, in the wrong conditions, and for no greater reason than the need for speed. Does that sound at all like your life? If so, think carefully about it. This is one of your warnings that ice is ahead. A marriage can usually take a fair amount of rough weather and keep moving forward. Some couples have an easier time handling stress and solving problems together. Perhaps those partners came from homes where they saw that done well. Many more people have not come from such homes, and they'll have to learn or risk the consequences.

No matter how good your ship, an iceberg can ruin your whole cruise. Icebergs are the devastating destroyers of marriages. However, you can steer completely clear of them by setting your course wisely. Even when you have to sail nearby, you can slow down and steer carefully around the dangerous ice. If you keep moving without caution on a bad course, you risk catastrophe. If you think you are somehow more capable than others to pull that off, you may be overconfident. I would think overconfidence has killed scores of seafarers over the ages. It has surely killed many marriages.

There are probably numerous kinds of icebergs for a marriage. Giving in to the temptations of an attractive alternative is certainly one way to flirt with the big ice. Affairs don't always sink a marital ship, but they do severe damage and cause you to take on tons of water. It's more work to pump the water out and fix the hull than to steer clear of the ice in the first place.

Another kind of big ice is chronic, nasty conflict. Though it may not seem that there is an iceberg around, regularly sailing in frigid water keeps you near the big ice. Is your marriage cold? If it's too often too cold, you are in danger of big things going wrong. Did you know that some experts have reasoned that the steel used in the *Titanic* was probably especially brittle because of how it was made and because of how cold the water was on that fateful night? A marriage that often sails in cold water may be in danger of hitting big ice and may be weakening the hull over time. Is your marriage getting stronger or weaker over the time you have been journeying together?

It's too easy to be arrogant and think that your marriage can survive anything. It can't. The *Titanic* was considered unsinkable. Sailing the wide oceans of life is challenging enough without adding the dangers that come from thinking *your* ship is unsinkable. It's not. We all do well to keep this in mind in a society in which nearly half the ships that are now putting out to sea (the young couples marrying for the first time) may eventually sink.[8]

BAILING

Bailing is a fact of sailing. No matter how nice a ship you have or how smooth the seas, you are going to take on water at some point. There may not be anything particularly wrong with your ship; it's just that water surrounds you. Taking on a bit is normal; taking on a lot is not. If you are taking on so much water that it seems you are bailing all the time, perhaps you need to pull into dry dock and fix some big leaks. Find some super sticky stuff and plug up those holes.

Otherwise, you need to keep regularly bailing. Bailing is not fun, but it is sometimes necessary. In marriage, you bail water when you work through a problem together or when you talk about something sensitive, but do it well. Bailing takes work. It's by far the best if you do it together and regularly. For example, in the other materials I've written with colleagues, we recommend that you have a regular meeting as a couple just for dealing with the problems and issues of life.[9] That's being proactive. That's keeping the water from building up in the bottom of your boat. Too many couples work on problems only when an event triggers an issue that has been neglected.[10] For example, a bill comes and you don't have enough money to pay it, and that triggers a big fight about money. Living that way keeps your boat riding low in the water. Regularly working on the issues in your marriage takes discipline and commitment, but doing so can make your ship run much better.

DEAD CALM

Imagine that you are out at sea, sailing along nicely, and then one day, you can't find the slightest breeze. Okay, you can stand that for a day. Next day, same thing. Next day, same thing. Next day, . . . you get the point. It keeps on that way for months, or so it seems. Marriage can be like that. You're sailing along just fine, and then it seems that you've stopped making progress. There is no wind at your back. At best, I would think this is a pretty boring time if you were out sailing. You aren't going anywhere, and there is not a lot you can do about it.

What can you do when there is no wind in your sails? For one thing, you can tend to the parts of the ship that have been neglected while you've been racing along through life. You can scrape barnacles so that your hull is smoother and ready to move when you do have wind. You can mend torn sails. You can polish the deck or clean out the areas below. Jeremy and Suzanne will hit some times like this. When things are moving slower, they could use that time to talk about goals. Clarifying their heading would be one of the best things they could do while waiting for a breeze. Perhaps they could use such times to plan ahead about a problem on the horizon. In many ways, they could nurture the vision for where they are headed.

My point is this: just because you are not moving through the water as easily as you thought you might, your marriage is not necessarily in trouble. The wind will come back. Use the times when you have to slow down to do some things that will allow you to sail more smoothly when the wind returns.

ROWING

Being very committed and learning to sail together do not mean you'll always have great wind. In the worst case, sailors in ages gone by sometimes had to get out the oars and put their backs into rowing. Rowing is not nearly as much fun as sailing. Same for marriage. When there is no breeze, you sometimes have to put your back into it and row. When you row, you move slowly. You apply more effort. You sweat. You ache. But you keep moving.

You didn't buy a sailboat because you like to row. Nevertheless, sometimes that's your only choice unless you want to stay dead in the water. In marriage, problems come up from time to time that take the wind out of your sails. Sometimes you lose the wind, and you have no idea why or when it's coming back. At these times, you may not even feel like sailing together. That's when the harder work of commitment comes in. To move your ship forward even when there is no wind will take all your strength. But unless you like to swim a very long way, rowing together is the best plan.

When you work together to get through a tough problem, you're rowing together. When you reach out together to seek advice from good friends about a struggle you are having, you're rowing. When you take the time to learn more effective communication or problem-solving skills, you're rowing. When you read a book on budgeting and work toward a budget that both can live with, you're rowing. When you pray together despite being displeased with each other, you're taking some big strokes of faith to get your ship moving again. All these actions take effort—effort that springs from dedication and, ironically, helps you build more dedication. That's sticking and not putting up with getting stuck.

When you have the wind with you, fill your sails, and let your ship roll on across the seas. Enjoy the view. At other times, when it's not so easy, row, and keep rowing. Either way, don't lose sight of where you're headed in the journey.

Getting Unstuck and Back to Sticking

Remember Lisa and Steven from the first chapter? Lisa was quite anxious on her wedding day, wondering if she and Steve had what it would take to make their marriage last. Let's fast-forward seventeen years. Lisa and Steve had two children, Kyle, age twelve, and Susan, age nine. Lisa was working in a department store as a buyer of women's clothes. The work was hard, but she liked it. Steven ran a little store that sold musical instruments. Music had always been something special for him, and his work allowed him to stay involved with musicians and music.

Lisa's initial fears about their marriage had grown into a reality over the years. They had a stable marriage. Neither thought seriously about divorce, but both had thought they would likely be happier with someone else. Neither wanted a divorce because there were too many constraints. He worried that if they divorced, he would not see his children often enough, and he didn't see how it would be workable financially. He just didn't make enough on his own. She had thought about divorce, but she was concerned about the kids and about what others would think. Both Lisa and Steve were committed to their Christian faith, and that played a role in their commitment in marriage. Most important to Lisa, she thought that divorce was usually morally wrong, and that there were only a very limited set of circumstances where divorce was acceptable, not circumstances she was living with. She couldn't see how God could approve of such a thing. So they plodded onward.

Lisa and Steve were not really sticking. They were stuck. Their marriage had once been a thing of real delight and beauty, like a newly cut Christmas tree with all the trimmings. However, like a Christmas tree that is not kept in water, it had become dry and brittle. In short, they had a high-constraint, low-dedication marriage. I don't know how many couples are in such lifeless marriages, but the number is probably large. Seventeen years earlier, Lisa had worried about whether or not they would make it. Her anxiety had revolved around divorce. Well, they weren't heading for divorce, but she thought that being stuck was not much better.

When mates reach this point, they have these choices: (1) they can remain stuck; (2) they can stop by getting a divorce; or (3) they can try to get back to sticking. I don't think that it is easy to redevelop dedication when it has been severely eroded, but I do think it can be done. I've seen it happen. In *A Lasting Promise*, my colleagues and I have described steps that can help you regain lost dedication, and we'll look at them here as well.[11] Furthermore, with God's help, amazing things are possible. Let me describe what it was like for Lisa and Steven.

A GOOD MESSAGE

Lisa and Steven were involved together in a fine church. Like anyone else, they had their spiritual ups and downs, but as each was feeling more and more concerned about the direction of their marriage, both began to pray more for something to happen. They didn't share these prayers with each other, but both were praying in the same direction. When people start praying, that's a serious start to changing the situation.

Both were looking for something, but neither had much of an idea about what exactly to do. Their pastor had been preaching a series of sermons through the book of Revelation. One Sunday, while they were not expecting anything in particular to happen, something powerful happened. Their pastor came to the section about the letters to the seven churches—and he discussed Ephesus.

If you have not ever read through or studied that section of Scripture, or if it has been a while since you have, take a moment to read this passage carefully:

> To the angel of the church of Ephesus write, "These things says He who holds the seven stars in His right hand, who walks in the midst of the seven golden lampstands: 'I know your works, your labor, your patience, and that you cannot bear those who are evil. And you have tested those who say they are apostles and are not, and have found them liars; and you have persevered and have patience, and have labored for My name's sake and have not become weary. Nevertheless I have this against you, that you have left your first love. Remember therefore from where you have fallen; repent and do the first works.'" (Rev. 2:1–5 NKJV, emphasis added)

REMEMBER, REPENT, AND DO

Have you ever had one of those times when you listened to a sermon or someone teaching and the message just hit a home run in your soul? Well, that was one of those times for both Lisa and Steve. The pastor's message dealt with devotion to Christ. In particular, the text focused the congregation on the point that a church can have everything just right in terms of outward appearances and programs, but have lost its core sense of devotion to the Lord. Jesus said the church at Ephesus had a great deal going for it (I'm paraphrasing a bit): a good youth program, support for missionaries, a wonderful ministry to the poor, and an awesome music program that brought tears to people's eyes. Small problem. They had left their "first love," Christ the Lord. Otherwise, they had perseverance, energy, and even zeal for good works.

So, their pastor pointed out how Ephesus was a great church where the central *love* for the Lord was seriously mislaid. Remember, what we're studying here as dedication is pretty much the same thing as the New Testament concept of agape love. Guess what Greek word is used for "love" in this passage from Revelation? *Agape.* Jesus was telling them that they had lost their agape love for Him. In other words, they had slipped from their *dedication* to Him.

The pastor preached,

> What Jesus says to the Ephesians following the diagnosis of the
> problem is one of the most powerfully simple calls to action in the
> Bible. Note that He doesn't spend time trying to explain to them
> how they had left their first love. I want you to focus on the rec-
> ommendation Jesus makes. He told the Ephesians to *remember,*
> *repent,* and *do.* This is not rocket science, folks. Three key words.
> Perfect for a simple sermon.
>
> Remember means to remember. Complicated, right? (*Laughter*)
> What happens when you remember the early days of a loving
> devotion now lost? I don't know about you, but to me, I start to
> feel things I felt back then. When I think of how I felt when I first
> really grasped all of what Christ meant to me, I can remember the
> feeling of excitement. Passion. Aliveness. Remembering reawak-
> ens your appetite for what has been lost.

Both Lisa and Steve felt something stirring deep inside. While neither
missed the more obvious points about the love of the Lord, both had reg-
istered the point as relevant to their marriage. They had lost their original love and dedication to each other. Their love and dedication had been
lacking somewhat toward the Lord as well. Both were attentive to what was
going on at various levels.

Each had already thought of a few special memories from early in their
relationship. Steve remembered a time they went hiking in the mountains
together, getting stuck out in a storm, then finding their way back to their
cabin—drenched and cold. They built a fire in more ways than one. Lisa
thought about all the times they used to go to a special pizza parlor, relax-
ing over their favorite pizza, listening to music, and talking about anything
and everything. Great times. Sometimes having memory is just as important as having vision.

The pastor kept preaching:

> The next thing Jesus recommends for the Ephesians to regain a lost
> love is to repent. There are many complicated ways to think about

what that means, but it's also not a complicated concept. It means to change your mind and head the other direction. One hundred and eighty degrees. You are going a direction that you don't want to keep going, and you turn around. Change your compass heading. What I like about what Jesus is teaching here is that it's simple. A plan can be simple but still be hard to do. It takes some humility to decide to change directions in your life, and that may be the hardest part about repentance.

For Lisa and Steve, the point about repentance also hit them. While they sat there, each being tugged at on the deepest levels, Steve reached over for Lisa's hand. It was a small outward gesture of a deeper turning. Lisa's hand met his with a strength he had not felt in years. That also reminded her of something from their past—how they used to hold hands whenever they were together. It felt good back then, and it felt good there in church on this Sunday.

The pastor was on a roll, and they were rolling along with him:

Now I love this last part of what Jesus says. It's the simplest thing in the whole plan. He says, "Do." Do what? Do the first things. Do the things you used to do. What kinds of things did you do when you first really were captured by a love for Christ? Did you pray in the various moments of life? Did you thank God for the good things in your life? Did you read Scripture and really think about what was being said? Did you go out of your way to help those less fortunate? Did you speak a kind word to a loved one at home? I don't know just what you might have done earlier in your love of Christ, but you do, and I'll bet you can still do it.

This reminds me of something very important here. Jesus is not only telling us how to regain our love of and devotion to Him. He is telling us how to regain both with others. For example, maybe you are sitting here today, and you've lost some love in your marriage. You've left it behind, just as Jesus said. This plan He is laying out for regaining love for Him is a pretty great plan in your marriage as well.

Bingo. Lisa and Steve were having a rare moment when two people in a marriage are being hit by the same message in the same way at the same time. God was dancing with them. They were feeling the beat.

GETTING IT DONE . . . TOGETHER

As the sermon concluded, the pastor came back to the three basic steps of *remembering, repenting,* and *doing.* Lisa and Steve could not have soaked up any more of the message. They got it about Jesus, and they got it about their marriage. The next thing they did was the hardest part, but it was also the real turning point about putting their marriage back on track. When they returned home, they talked about what they were thinking, and they did it without blaming each other. They talked and they talked. Then they talked some more. Both shared the sense of pain and distance they had been feeling. They even shared that they had been thinking that maybe their marriage could never be any more than what it had become. They shared that they were hungry to have a real relationship; they wanted to regain what they once had and go farther. They made a commitment together to do it.

Next, they made a plan of action. They planned time to talk about the past—not to talk about the hurts and failings, mind you, but to talk about what had been special. Steve talked about the fire. Lisa talked about the friendship. Both were encouraged to remember they had liked being close. Things could have become difficult for them if they had allowed their present pains and griefs to color their past. When some couples who are struggling remember the past, all they can think of are painful, hurtful, unpleasant times, as if that's all they once had together. That's usually rewriting history. Your mate may not be all you wish he or she could be, but a lot is probably there that you liked early on that can be resurrected and also grow if you nurture these things in each other together. Lisa and Steve were drawing closer together by what they remembered. Appetites that had become deadened were coming back to life.

People can decide they are going to repent in various ways at any time and make changes. In marriage, one person's decision that things are going to be different can often start many good things moving in the right direction. It's most powerful, though, when two people who are stuck decide together to get out of the ditch. That's what Lisa and Steve did. They prayed, they hugged, they talked, and they committed to each other to do what it takes to redevelop loving devotion—or dedication as we've been discussing it here. That's what repentance meant to them: to turn together and head the other way.

Lisa and Steve spent a couple of hours later in the week discussing all the things that they used to do together that they could do again. Taking walks together. Going for a ride to the forest with a picnic lunch. Going out to dinner and talking about whatever seemed interesting that day. Watching a funny movie together. Watching a romantic movie together. Sending the kids to Grandma's for a night or two and camping out in the bedroom. Basically, they thought of many fun things that drew them together but that they had quit doing years ago. "No wonder the life got sucked out of our marriage," Steve observed. "We weren't doing any of the things that used to really draw us together." "I know," replied Lisa, "we let a lot slip away, and we were paying a price."

Lisa and Steve also discussed other things that they had let slip in their marriage—things that are just as important for regaining and renewing dedication as those just mentioned. Early on they had been more polite, more willing to make time for each other, more concerned for what would please the other, more attentive to feelings in the other, and more open to talking problems out as a team. They rededicated themselves to being kinder and gentler with each other in the rush of life. That's a fundamental part of acceptance on the day-to-day level. It's the bits and pieces of a long-term love. A renewed spiritual connection between them, and between each and the Lord, fueled everything else that was happening. For the first time, they really saw their marriage as something that God was interested in and wanted to help them succeed in. They were no longer alone with their griefs, but had drawn together before God.

Is this a fairy tale? Nope. Lisa and Steve will have to keep at it to maintain a vibrant, committed marriage. The press and strains of life too easily encourage each of us to lose track of what matters most. Even the Ephesians, who had so much going right, had lost sight of the real beauty and power of their spiritual lives. There is an important message in that. You can have a whole lot going right in your life and not be living a life of love—both toward God and toward your closest loved ones. It's your choice whether things stay that way or not.

WHERE YOU GO FROM HERE

My friend Bill Coffin and his wife, Pat, experienced something that I think is increasingly rare and wonderful. In the same year, both sets of their parents celebrated their fiftieth wedding anniversaries. These were big events for the families. All the grandchildren were there. The milestones were celebrated. How many children ever see such a thing in this day and age? In a culture of high levels of divorce and many other marriages in distress, we sometimes get gloomy pictures of what marriage can be about. For far too many couples, marriage ends up being something more like a death march than a dance of devotion.

It doesn't have to be that way. Underlying all the advice and all the suggestions you could ever hear, *your* part in a great marriage comes down to what you do to act out your love through the channels of commitment. Committed love acts, preserves, and protects. Committed love fuels the dance. You *can* live on committed love.

ℐOTES

CHAPTER 1

1. U.S. Bureau of the Census, *Marriage, Divorce, and Remarriage in the 1990's,* Current Population Reports, report number P23-180 (Washington, DC: U.S. Government Printing Office, 1992).

2. David Blankenhorn, Nov. 1997, "I Do?" *First Things,* Nov. 1997, 14–15.

3. S. Stanley, D. Trathen, S. McCain, and M. Bryan, *A Lasting Promise* (San Francisco: Jossey Bass, 1998).

4. For example, Robert Wright, "Our Cheating Hearts—Devotion and Betrayal, Marriage and Divorce: How Evolution Shaped Human Love," *Time,* 15 Aug. 1994, 44.

5. M. P. Johnson, "Personal and Structural Commitment: Sources of Consistency in the Development of Relationships" (Paper presented at the Theory Construction and Research Methodology Workshop, National Council on Family Relations annual meetings, Philadelphia, 1978); Johnson, "The Social and Cognitive Features of the Dissolution of Commitment to Relationships," in *Personal Relationships: Dissolving Personal Relationships,* ed. S. Duck (New York: Academic Press, 1982).

6. Stanley, Trathen, McCain, and Bryan, *A Lasting Promise;* H. J. Markman, S. M. Stanley, and S. L. Blumberg, *Fighting for Your Marriage* (San Francisco: Jossey Bass, 1994).

7. Jeffrey M. Adams and Warren H. Jones, "The Conceptualization of Marital Commitment: An Integrative Analysis," *Journal of Personality*

and Social Psychology, 72 (1997), 1177–1196; M. P. Johnson, "Commitment: a Conceptual Structure and Empirical Application," *Sociological Quarterly,* 14 (1973), 395–406; M. P. Johnson, "The Social and Cognitive Features of the Dissolution of Commitment to Relationships," in *Personal Relationships: Dissolving Personal Relationships,* ed. S. Duck (New York: Academic Press, 1982); C. E. Rusbult and Bram P. Buunk, "Commitment Processes in Close Relationships: An Interdependence Analysis," *Journal of Social and Personal Relationships,* 10 (1993), 175–204; S. M. Stanley and H. J. Markman, "Assessing Commitment in Personal Relationships," *Journal of Marriage and the Family,* 54 (1992), 595–608.

CHAPTER 2

1. S. M. Stanley and H. J. Markman, "Assessing Commitment in Personal Relationships," *Journal of Marriage and the Family,* 54 (1992), 595–608.

2. Many books have been published with this title or subtitle, most notably, Helen Gurley Brown, *Having It All* (New York: Pocket Books, 1985).

3. Stanley and Markman, "Assessing Commitment in Personal Relationships."

4. Roger Fisher and William Ury, *Getting to Yes: Negotiating Agreement Without Giving In,* 2d. ed. (Boston: Houghton Mifflin, 1992).

CHAPTER 3

1. K. S. Cook and R. M. Emerson, "Power, Equity and Commitment in Exchange Networks," *American Sociological Review,* 43 (1978), 721–39; R. K. Leik and S. A. Leik, "Transition to Interpersonal Commitment," in *Behavioral Theory in Sociology,* ed. R. L. Hamblin and J. H. Kunkel (New Brunswick, NJ: Transaction Books, 1977); S. M. Stanley and H. J. Markman, "Assessing Commitment in Personal Relationships," *Journal of Marriage and the Family,* 54 (1992), 595–608.

2. S. Stanley, "Commitment and the Maintenance and Enhancement of Relationships" (Ph.D. diss., University of Denver, 1986); Stanley and Markman, "Assessing Commitment in Personal Relationships."

3. D. J. Johnson and C. E. Rusbult, "Resisting Temptation: Devaluation of Alternative Partners as a Means of Maintaining Commitment in Close Relationships," *Journal of Personality and Social Psychology,* 57 (1989), 967–80.

4. This error usually proceeds from the explanation that James 2:10 teaches that all sins are equal. James 2:10 actually teaches that all sins, and any sin, make you a sinner in need of redemption. The passage says nothing about all sins being equally bad. The Old Testament passages that call for different punishments for different sins as well as the teachings of Jesus recorded in the New Testament demonstrate that there are differences between various sins in God's sight (e.g., Matt. 11:20–22; 12:31; John 19:11; 1 John 5:16). So, one may commit adultery in the mind and still be in need of redemption by the Redeemer. But to commit adultery in the flesh would be far worse an act because it would directly involve many people in the breaking of the sanctity of marriage.

5. D. Arp and C. Arp, *Ten Great Dates to Revitalize Your Marriage: The Best Tips from the Marriage Alive Seminars* (Graand Rapids: Zondervan, 1997); H. J. Markman, S. M. Stanley, and S. L. Blumberg, *Fighting for Your Marriage* (San Francisco: Jossey Bass, 1994); L. Parrott and L. Parrott, *Saving Your Marriage Before It Starts: Seven Questions to Ask Before (and After) You Marry* (Grand Rapids: Zondervan, 1995); C. J. Sager, *Marital Contracts and Couple Therapy* (New York: Brunner/Mazel, 1976); Gary Smalley, *If Only He Knew* (Grand Rapids: Zondervan, 1982); S. Stanley, D. Trathen, S. McCain, and M. Bryan, *A Lasting Promise* (San Francisco: Jossey Bass, 1998).

CHAPTER 4

1. D. Arp and C. Arp, *Ten Great Dates to Revitalize Your Marriage: The Best Tips from the Marriage Alive Seminars* (Grand Rapids: Zondervan,

1997); H. J. Markman, S. M. Stanley, and S. L. Blumberg, *Fighting for Your Marriage* (San Francisco: Jossey Bass, 1994); L. Parrott and L. Parrott, *Saving Your Marriage Before It Starts: Seven Questions to Ask Before (and After) You Marry* (Grand Rapids: Zondervan, 1995); W. Roberts and N. Wright, *Before You Say "I Do"* (Eugene, OR: Harvest House, 1978); Gary Smalley, *If Only He Knew* (Grand Rapids: Zondervan, 1982); S. Stanley, D. Trathen, S. McCain, and M. Bryan, *A Lasting Promise* (San Francisco: Jossey Bass, 1998).

2. Markman, Stanley, and Blumberg, *Fighting for Your Marriage.*

3. Viktor Emil Frankl, *Man's Search for Meaning* (New York: Pocket Books, 1988).

CHAPTER 5

1. R. D. Storaasli and H. J. Markman, "Relationship Problems in the Early Stages of Marriage: A Test of Marriage: A Longitudinal Investigation," *Journal of Family Psychology,* 4 (1990), 80–98.

2. B. D. Whitehead, *The Divorce Culture* (New York: Knopf, 1997).

3. H. J. Markman, S. M. Stanley, and S. L. Blumberg, *Fighting for Your Marriage* (San Francisco: Jossey Bass, 1994).

4. L. A. Kurdek, "Predicting Marital Dissolution: A 5-year Prospective Longitudinal Study of Newlywed Couples," *Journal of Personality and Social Psychology,* 64 (1993), 221–42.

5. J. Gottman, *Why Marriages Succeed or Fail* (New York: Simon & Schuster, 1994); H. J. Markman, S. M. Stanley, and S. L. Blumberg, *Fighting for Your Marriage* (San Francisco: Jossey Bass, 1994); C. I. Notarius and H. J. Markman, *We Can Work It Out: Making Sense of Marital Conflict* (New York: Putnam, 1993); S. Stanley, D. Trathen, S. McCain, and M. Bryan, *A Lasting Promise* (San Francisco: Jossey Bass, 1998).

6. Markman, Stanley, and Blumberg, *Fighting for Your Marriage;* Notarius and Markman, *We Can Work It Out;* Stanley, Trathen, McCain, and Bryan, *A Lasting Promise.*

7. Glenn T. Stanton, *Why Marriage Matters* (Colorado Springs: Pinon Press, 1997).

8. Fyodor Dostoevsky, *The Brothers Karamazov* (New York: Barnes and Noble, 1995), 60.

CHAPTER 6

1. I got the idea for the term *relationship capital* after reading a discussion of *social capital* in Barbara Dafoe Whitehead's book, *The Divorce Culture* (New York: Knopf, 1997).

2. L. J. Waite, "Does Marriage Matter?" *Demography,* 32 (1995), 483–507; L. J. Waite, "Why Marriage Matters," *Threshold,* 57 (summer 1997), 4–8.

3. Glenn T. Stanton, *Why Marriage Matters* (Colorado Springs: Pinon Press, 1997); Waite, "Does Marriage Matter?" *Demography,* 32(4), 483–507.

4. Kristin Dunlap Godsey, "Winning Strategies for the Next Ten Years in the Financial World, 'Long Term' Can Mean Six Months from Now," *Fortune,* 12 Dec. 1995, 66ff.

5. John Gottman, "Lessons from the Love Lab," (plenary address to Smart Marriages, Happy Families Conference, Washington, D.C., May 1997).

6. Richard A. Swenson, *Margin: Restoring Emotional, Physical, Financial, and Time Reserves to Overloaded Lives* (Colorado Springs: NavPress, 1995).

7. C. I. Notarius and H. J. Markman, *We Can Work It Out: Making Sense of Marital Conflict* (New York: Putnam, 1993).

8. C. E. Rusbult, "A Longitudinal Test of the Investment Model: The Development (and Deterioration) of Satisfaction and Commitment in Heterosexual Involvements," *Journal of Personality and Social Psychology,* 45 (1983), 101–17; C. E. Rusbult and Bram P. Buunk, "Commitment Processes in Close Relationships: An Interdependence Analysis," *Journal of Social and Personal Relationships,* 10 (1993), 175–204.

9. Thomas J. Stanley and William D. Danko, *The Millionaire Next Door* (Marietta, GA: Longstreet Press, 1996).

10. D. Arp and C. Arp, *Love Life for Parents* (Grand Rapids: Zondervan, 1997); C. P. Cowan and P. A. Cowan, *When Partners Become Parents: The Big Life Change for Couples* (New York: Harper Collins, 1992).

11. S. Stanley, D. Trathen, S. McCain, and M. Bryan, *A Lasting Promise* (San Francisco: Jossey Bass, 1998).

12. D. Arp and C. Arp, *The Second Half of Marriage* (Grand Rapids: Zondervan, 1996); Michael E. McCullough, Steven J. Sandage, and Everett L. Worthington, *To Forgive Is Human: How to Put Your Past in the Past* (Downers Grove, IL: InterVarsity Press, 1997); Lewis B. Smedes, *The Art of Forgiving: When You Need to Forgive and Don't Know How* (New York: Ballantine Books, 1997); Stanley, Trathen, McCain, and Bryan, *A Lasting Promise.*

CHAPTER 7

1. George Seldes, *The Great Thoughts* (New York: Ballantine Books, 1985), 185–86.

2. Sir Winston Churchill, quoted in *Reader's Digest,* Dec. 1954.

3. Sir Winston Churchill, first wartime address, 4 Sept. 1914, Guildhall, London.

4. Sir Winston Churchill, speech, 18 June 1940, House of Commons.

5. Janice Levine, "The Couples Health Program Instructor Manual" (Lexington, MA: author, 1997).

6. Glenn T. Stanton, *Why Marriage Matters* (Colorado Springs: Pinon Press, 1997).

7. Robert T. Michael, John H. Gagnon, Edward O. Laumann, and Gina Kolata, *Sex in America: A Definitive Survey* (Boston: Little, Brown, 1994).

8. Sir Winston Churchill, *Time,* 12 Sept. 1960.

9. M. P. Johnson and S. Shuman, "Courtship as the Development of Commitment to a Relationship" (paper presented at the annual meeting of the National Council of Family Relations, St. Paul, 1983); S. M. Stanley and H. J. Markman, *Marriage in the 90s: A Nationwide Random Phone Survey* (Denver: PREP, Inc., 1997).

10. F. C. Dickson, "The Best Is Yet to Be: Research on Long-Lasting Relationships," in *Under-Studied Relationships: Off the Beaten Track,* ed. J. T. Wood and S. Duck (Beverly Hills, CA: Sage publications, 1995), 22–50.

11. S. M. Stanley, W. C. Lobitz, and F. Dickson, "Using What We Know: Commitment and Cognitions in Marital Therapy," in *Handbook of Interpersonal Commitment and Relationship Stability,* ed. W. Jones and J. Adams (New York: Plenum, in press); S. M. Stanley and H. J. Markman, "Assessing Commitment in Personal Relationships," *Journal of Marriage and the Family,* 54 (1992), 595–608.

12. Stanley and Markman, "Assessing Commitment in Personal Relationships."

13. H. J. Markman, S. M. Stanley, and S. L. Blumberg, *Fighting for Your Marriage* (San Francisco: Jossey Bass, 1994); C. I. Notarius and H. J. Markman, *We Can Work It Out: Making Sense of Marital Conflict* (New York: Putnam, 1993); S. Stanley, D. Trathen, S. McCain, and M. Bryan, *A Lasting Promise* (San Francisco: Jossey Bass, 1998).

14. Markman, Stanley, and Blumberg, *Fighting for Your Marriage;* M. L. Clements, S. M. Stanley, and H. J. Markman, "Prediction of Marital Distress and Divorce: A Discriminant Analysis," journal article submitted for publication; Tim B. Heaton and Edith L. Pratt, "The Effects of Religious Homogamy on Marital Satisfaction and Stability," *Journal of Family Issues,* 11 (1990), 191–207; Stanley and Markman, "Assessing Commitment in Personal Relationships"; Leroy Gruner, "The Correlation of Private, Religious Devotional Practices and Marital Adjustment," *Journal of Comparative Family Studies,* 16 (1985), 47–59; Richard A. Hunt and Morton B. King, "Religiosity and Marriage," *Journal for the Scientific Study of Religion,* 17 (1978), 399–406; V. R. A. Call and T. B. Heaton, "Religious Influence on Marital Stability," *Journal for the Scientific Study of Religion,* 36 (1997), 382–92.

15. Eugene H. Peterson, *The Message: New Testament with Psalms and Proverbs* (Colorado Springs: NavPress, 1996), 527.

CHAPTER 8

1. G. Levinger, "A Social Exchange View on the Dissolution of Pair Relationships," in *Social Exchange in Developing Relationships,* ed. R. L. Burgess and T. L. Huston (New York: Academic Press, 1979); S. M. Stanley and H. J. Markman, "Assessing Commitment in Personal Relationships," *Journal of Marriage and the Family,* 54 (1992), 595–608.

2. S. Stanley, "Commitment and the Maintenance and Enhancement of

Relationships" (Ph.D. diss., University of Denver, 1986); Stanley and Markman, "Assessing Commitment in Personal Relationships."

3. Fyodor Dostoevsky, *The Brothers Karamazov,* trans. by Constance Garnett (New York: Barnes and Noble, 1995), 281.

4. Karen S. Schneider, Don Sider, Mary Green, Elizabeth McNeil, and Krista Reese, "The Donald Ducks Out with His Eye on the Bottom Line of His Prenuptial Deal, Donald Trump Says Goodbye to Marla," *People,* 19 May 1997, 222ff.

5. Ibid.

6. S. M. Stanley and H. J. Markman, *Marriage in the 90s: A Nationwide Random Phone Survey* (Denver: PREP, Inc., 1997).

7. C. P. Cowan and P. A. Cowan, "Who Does What When Partners Become Parents: Implications for Men, Women, and Marriage," *Marriage and Family Review,* 13 (1988), 105–32.

8. H. J. Markman, S. M. Stanley, and S. L. Blumberg, *Fighting for Your Marriage* (San Francisco: Jossey Bass, 1994).

9. Clive Staples Lewis, *A Grief Observed* (Harper San Francisco, 1994).

10. M. J. Cox, B. Paley, M. Burchinal, and C. C. Payne, "Marital Perceptions and Interactions Across the Transition to Parenthood," journal article submitted for publication.

CHAPTER 9

1. *Microsoft Bookshelf Dictionary* (Redmond, WA: Microsoft, 1995).

2. Gary Smalley, "For Me, It Was a 'Living-Death' Certificate," *Homes of Honor,* fall 1997, pp. 1–2.

3. Smalley, *The Two Sides of Love: Twenty Specific Ways to Build*

Unbreakable Bonds with Your Family and Friends (New York: Pocket Books, 1993).

4. S. Stanley, D. Trathen, S. McCain, and M. Bryan, *A Lasting Promise* (San Francisco: Jossey Bass, 1998).

5. S. M. Stanley and H. J. Markman, "Assessing Commitment in Personal Relationships," *Journal of Marriage and the Family,* 54 (1992), 595–608.

6. Paul Van Lange, C. E. Rusbult, and Stephen M. Drigotas, "Willingness to Sacrifice in Close Relationships," journal article submitted for publication.

7. S. Stanley, "Commitment and the Maintenance and Enhancement of Relationships" (Ph.D. diss., University of Denver, 1986).

8. Robertson McQuilkin, "Living by Vows," *Christianity Today,* 8 Oct. 1990.

9. Robertson McQuilkin, "Muriel's Blessing," *Christianity Today,* 5 Feb. 1996.

10. McQuilkin, "Living by Vows," 40.

11. McQuilkin, "Muriel's Blessing," 34.

12. McQuilkin, "Living by Vows," 40.

13. Ibid., 40.

14. Fyodor Dostoevsky, *The Brothers Karamazov* (New York: Barnes and Noble, 1995), 50.

15. McQuilkin, "Muriel's Blessing," 34.

16. For example, Patricia Cornwell, *Ruth—A Portrait* (New York: Doubleday, 1997); William Martin, *A Prophet with Honor: The Billy Graham Story* (New York: Morrow, 1991).

17. Cornwell, *Ruth—A Portrait.*

18. "The Greatest Love Stories of the Century: Reverend Billy Graham and Ruth Bell Uplifted by Faith, They Tended Their Union Through Hardship and Separation," *People*, 12 Feb. 1996, 155.

19. Ibid.

CHAPTER 10

1. W. E. Vine, *Vine's Expository Dictionary of Old and New Testament Words* (Nashville: Thomas Nelson, 1997).

2. S. M. Stanley and D. Trathen, "Christian PREP: An Empirically Based Model for Marital and Premarital Intervention," *Journal of Psychology and Christianity*, 13 (1994), 158–65.

3. Gary Smalley, *Making Love Last Forever* (Dallas: Word, 1996), 103.

4. Ibid., 117.

5. M. L. Clements, S. M. Stanley, and H. J. Markman, "Prediction of Marital Distress and Divorce: A Discriminant Analysis," journal article submitted for publication; J. Gottman, *Why Marriages Succeed or Fail* (New York: Simon & Schuster, 1994); H. J. Markman, S. M. Stanley, and S. L. Blumberg, *Fighting for Your Marriage* (San Francisco: Jossey Bass, 1994).

6. J. C. Dobson, *When God Doesn't Make Sense* (Wheaton: Tyndale, 1995); P. Yancey, *Where Is God When It Hurts?* (Grand Rapids: Zondervan, 1990).

7. Markman, Stanley, and Blumberg, *Fighting for Your Marriage*; C. I.

Notarius and H. J. Markman, *We Can Work It Out: Making Sense of Marital Conflict* (New York: Putnam, 1993); Stanley, Trathen, McCain, and Bryan, *A Lasting Promise.*

8. U.S. Bureau of the Census, *Marriage, Divorce, and Remarriage in the 1990's,* Current Population Reports, report number P23-180 (Washington, DC: U.S. Government Printing Office, 1992).

9. Stanley, Trathen, McCain, and Bryan, *A Lasting Promise.*

10. Markman, Stanley, and Blumberg, *Fighting for Your Marriage.*

11. Stanley, Trathen, McCain, and Bryan, *A Lasting Promise.*

ABOUT THE AUTHOR

Scott Stanley, Ph.D., is a clinical psychologist specializing in research on marital success and failure. He is codirector of the Center for Marital and Family Studies at the University of Denver and coauthor of the bestseller *Fighting for Your Marriage* and *A Lasting Promise*. He has regularly appeared in the media as an expert on marriage, including *Focus on the Family*, *20/20*, *The Atlantic Monthly*, *USA Today*, and many others, and he is regularly sought after as speaker on marriage. He lives in Denver with his wife and two sons.